MANIC POWER

ALSO BY JEFFREY MEYERS

Fiction and the Colonial Experience
The Wounded Spirit: A Study of "Seven Pillars of Wisdom"
A Reader's Guide to George Orwell
George Orwell: The Critical Heritage
Painting and the Novel
A Fever at the Core: The Idealist in Politics
Homosexuality and Literature: 1890–1930
Married to Genius
Katherine Mansfield: A Biography
The Enemy: A Biography of Wyndham Lewis
Wyndham Lewis: A Revaluation
Ernest Hemingway: The Critical Heritage
D. H. Lawrence and the Experience of Italy
Disease and the Novel: 1860–1960
The Craft of Literary Biography
D. H. Lawrence and Tradition
Hemingway: A Biography
The Legacy of D. H. Lawrence
The Biographer's Art

MANIC POWER

Robert Lowell and his Circle

Jeffrey Meyers

ARBOR HOUSE

NEW YORK

Manufactured in the United States of America

10 9 8 7 6 5 4 3 2 1

Library of Congress Cataloging-in-Publication Data

Meyers, Jeffrey.
Manic power.

Bibliography: p.
Includes index.
1. Lowell, Robert, 1917–1977—Friends and associates.
2. Jarrell, Randall, 1914–1965. 3. Berryman, John,
1914–1972. 4. Roethke, Theodore, 1908–1963. 5. Poets,
American—20th century—Biography. 6. Poets—Psychology.
7. American poetry—20th century—History and criticism.
I. Title.
PS3523.089Z787   1987   811'.52   [B]   87-11387
ISBN 0-87795-920-X

For Arthur Miller and Inge Morath

Contents

Acknowledgments

In "Last Night," Robert Lowell spoke of the swift disappearance of his older poet-friends, the madness, suicide and death of Roethke, Jarrell, Berryman—and himself. And he once wrote of poetry to Theodore Roethke: "There must be a kind of glory to it all that people coming later will wonder at. I can see us all being written up in some huge book of the age. But under what title?" I am grateful to the University of Colorado for a Faculty Fellowship, which enabled me to fulfill his prophecy with a smaller book, *Manic Power*. In this group biography I have employed a musical structure, with an overture, theme and variations, and coda.

For personal interviews I would like to thank: Lady Caroline Blackwood Lowell, Gertrude Buckman, Jack Cutler, James Dickey, Paul Engle, the late Robert Fitzgerald, Anthony Hecht, Stanley Kunitz, Beatrice Roethke Lushington, Robie Macauley, Arthur Miller, Howard Nemerov, J. F. Powers and Karl Shapiro.

For letters about the poets I am grateful to: Al Alvarez, Stephen Axelrod, Dr. Sheldon Cooperman, Lord Gowrie, Helen Hagenbüchle, Elizabeth Hardwick, Seamus Heaney, Robert Heilman, Mackie Jarrell, Mary Jarrell, Mary McCarthy, Ralph Mills, Jr., Eileen Berryman Simpson, W. D. Snodgrass, Christina Stead and Robert Penn Warren.

I would also like to thank the following libraries, archives and friends for granting me access to unpublished papers:

University of Colorado (Jean Stafford), Houghton Library,
Harvard University (Robert Lowell), University of Minnesota
(John Berryman), Berg Collection, New York Public Library
(Randall Jarrell), University of North Carolina at Greensboro
(Randall Jarrell), *Partisan Review* (Randall Jarrell), Professor
J. F. Powers (Robert Lowell), Smith College (Sylvia Plath),
University of Washington (Theodore Roethke).

There is something I am convinced in the poetical temperament that precludes happiness, not only to the person who has it, but to those connected with him.

Byron to Lady Blessington

1

The Dynamics of Destruction

I

Manic Power: Robert Lowell and His Circle is both a group biography and a cultural history. It examines the nourishing effects as well as the destructive dynamics in the interrelated lives of four American poets, and explores ways in which their art reflected contemporary society. Robert Lowell, Randall Jarrell, John Berryman and Theodore Roethke, who followed the emotionally stable and long-lived generation of Frost, Stevens, Williams and Eliot, produced the greatest poetry since the Second World War. These poets were closely connected and knew each other well. They corresponded, visited, dined, drank, taught, wrote and lived together. They encouraged and criticized each other in interviews, letters, reviews, essays, eulogies and elegies; even rewrote, adapted and imitated each other's lines. They competed for lectures, jobs, grants, advances, loans, patrons and awards, for readers, recognition and praise, for success and security.

Each of these poets had an unhappy childhood. They suffered from unmanly or absent fathers and from strong, seductive mothers, and were haunted by nightmares of their parents' quarrels. Jarrell and Lowell idealized their grandparents, who seemed to possess the qualities notably absent in their immediate family. Owen Jarrell divorced his wife and disappeared when Randall was eleven; Berryman's father

1

killed himself when John was twelve; Otto Roethke died of
cancer when Ted was fifteen. When Lowell's father was forced
to live apart from his family, his mother (hysterical even in her
calm) rushed into her son's bedroom and exclaimed: "'Oh
Bobby, it's such a comfort to have a man in the house.' 'I am
not a man,' [Lowell] said, 'I am a boy.'"[1]

Both Helen Roethke and Anna Jarrell were humble
women who held the family together after the early death or
disappearance of their husbands. Jarrell was partly brought
up by his paternal grandparents and great-grandmother, and
celebrated their homespun virtues in his evocation of childhood, *The Lost World*. But Martha Berryman and Charlotte
Lowell were monster mothers. They drove their despised
husbands to an early death. And they devoured their sons,
unwilling sexual substitutes for their fathers, with an overwhelming passion. Gertrude Buckman, who knew both
women, confirmed that they *were* oppressive and unpleasant,
but felt that Martha (whose name Berryman gave to his eldest
daughter) was shrewder and more successful.[2]

At the beginning of the modern period, it was considered
quite shocking to condemn one's parents publicly. Orwell
once "startled a contemporary at Eton by cynically criticizing
his parents: 'He'd been the first person I ever heard running
down his own father and mother.'" And Hemingway—"the
only man I ever knew who really hated his mother"[3]—used to
startle Dos Passos in the same way. But Lowell and Berryman
found it quite natural to attack their parents in their poems.

In "Commander Lowell," "Terminal Days at Beverly
Farms," "Father's Bedroom" and "For Sale," and especially
in the fragmentary prose autobiography "91 Revere Street"
(all in *Life Studies*), Lowell portrays his father as a ludicrous
and pathetic failure, and records his decline and death. In
"Unwanted," Lowell laments the fact that he was an
unwanted child and reveals that Merrill Moore, the psychiatrist who told him about this pre-natal rejection, was his
mother's lover. When reading Berryman's death notice,
Lowell identified with his friend, recognized the emotional

failure of Charlotte in the description of Martha—who consumed her son with love but lacked a truly affectionate nature—and realized he had suffered in the same way. In "Grandparents," Lowell openly cried out for the affection that his mother had failed to provide and parodied the marriage service, begging his grandpa to have, hold and cherish him.

In his elegy on Hemingway, another suicidal son of a suicidal father, Berryman identified with the novelist and took him as the model of the self-destructive artist. Berryman damned his father for leaving his son the fatal legacy of a disastrous youth and tragic death. He pleaded with his father not to pull the trigger of his gun, which would kill his love as well as himself and condemn his son to lifelong suffering.[5]

The poets' serious problems with their parents led to tempestuous marriages, which were characterized by infidelity, alcoholism, violence and mental breakdowns. Roethke and Jarrell had no children. Jarrell was divorced once, Lowell and Berryman twice. They seem to display a similar pattern of behavior. They felt women were important as a support system but did not respect them, and were more interested in friendships with men who devoted their lives to poetry. They depended on women to care for them, to provide a stable world and to make their existence possible. But they behaved atrociously, then felt remorseful and finally wrote poems to exorcise their guilt. The poets saw love as a struggle of clashing wills in which man either maintains a precarious dominance or is overcome by humiliating defeat. The lack of a father and presence of an oppressive mother not only contributed to their emotional instability, but led them to mistreat their wives in order to vindicate their fathers and punish their mothers.

All four poets were eligible for the draft. But only Jarrell, an instructor in celestial navigation on army bases in America, actually served in the Second World War. Jarrell trained pilots to bomb German cities; Lowell, a conscientious objector, protested against their destruction. Roethke and Berryman had mental breakdowns before the war and were rejected for service.

Stevens had been an insurance executive, Williams a doctor, Eliot a publisher and Pound an independent man of letters. But the next generation of poets supported themselves by teaching. Despite their extraordinary talent, intellect and reputation, these unstable men had precarious careers in the postwar academic world. After tasting temporary glory at Harvard and Princeton, they spent a great deal of emotional energy searching for jobs, fearing (with good reason) the loss of employment, accepting temporary slots in undistinguished places and then, relatively late in life, securing permanent positions which were considerably less than they deserved.

Roethke taught at Lafayette College, Penn State, Michigan State and Bennington before landing a professorship at Washington at the age of 39. Berryman taught at Wayne State, Harvard, Princeton and Iowa before becoming a professor at Minnesota at the age of forty. Jarrell—like Roethke and Berryman, a lively and enthusiastic teacher— was for brief periods on the faculty of Kenyon, Texas, Sarah Lawrence, Princeton, Indiana and Illinois. But he was too intelligent and outspoken to get a permanent position at a first-rate university. From 1937, when he was 33, he taught at the Women's College in Greensboro, North Carolina, where the average girl talked "as if she were an imbecile with an ambition to be an idiot."[6] Only Lowell, who did occasional stints at Harvard and Boston University toward the end of his life, had a private income and substantial royalties, and did not have to teach.

All the poets enhanced their income, contacts, audience, reputation and sexual life by giving the disorienting and exhausting poetry readings that Auden wittily described in "On the Circuit":

An airborne instrument I sit. . . .
I bring my gospel of the Muse
To fundamentalists, to nuns,
To Gentiles and to Jews,
And daily, seven days a week,

> Before a local sense has jelled,
> From talking-site to talking-site
> Am jet-or-prop-propelled.[7]

These gratifying but frightening readings put the poets in touch with their readers and confirmed their literary status, but they also turned the solitary artists into public celebrities and encouraged bizarre behavior on the podium and at parties.

II

Lowell, Jarrell, Berryman and Roethke had two contradictory yet complementary models of personal behavior and poetic theory: Allen Tate and Dylan Thomas. Tate's tradition derived from Shelley's assertion that "poets are the unacknowledged legislators of the world" and from Eliot's belief that the poet should be learned, cultivate classical forms, work within the European tradition, act in a patrician and dignified fashion, express himself in an intellectual artifact, write in an impersonal and symbolic style, practice the New Criticism, and embrace conservative social and political ideas. Tate—who said: "*I looked up to [Eliot], and in doing so I could not feel myself in any sense diminished*"[8]—was an essential intermediary between Eliot and the younger generation of poets.

Dylan Thomas' tradition derived from Plato's assertion that the poet, by nature subversive and dangerous, should be excluded from the Republic "because he stimulates and strengthens an element which threatens to undermine the reason"[9] and from the Romantic lineage of the self-destructive poet exemplified by Eliot's teacher, friend and opposite: Ezra Pound. Both Pound and Thomas were lyrical, emotional, outrageous, self-indulgent and mad. In attempting to create a new American poetry, Lowell and his friends swung—in their lives as well as in their verse forms—from the controlled and conventional tradition of Eliot and Tate to the violent and iconoclastic examples of Pound and Thomas.

The unstable academic career of Allen Tate—author, teacher, editor and friend—was a paradigm of their own. Tate explained why in 1950 he finally accepted, *faute de mieux*, a job at Minnesota: "I was three years at Princeton, two years at NYU [New York University], at the University of Chicago, and at UNC [University of North Carolina] at Greensboro, but no university had ever given me tenure. And I was 51 and I began to feel I'd like that magic thing called security."[10]

Roethke had met Tate at Olivet College in Michigan in July 1937 and in London in July 1953, had corresponded with and been published by him. But he was always something of a Midwestern outsider in this circle of highbrow Southern and Eastern poets. He expressed scorn for the elite group that seemed to exclude him from the center of power and wrote to his future biographer, after attending the Modern Language Association conference in December 1940: "The aesthetics section was a howl: the Allen Tate protégées [*sic*] were going cross-eyed counting the pimples on each other's ass. God, what an I-love-me bunch!"[11]

In April 1937 the grubby young Lowell, his suitcase stuffed with bad poetry, drove up to (and almost into) Tate's "stately yet bohemian, leisurely yet dedicated" house in Tennessee. Lowell's most witty and self-mocking essay, "Visiting the Tates," describes how the Northern barbarian crashed the civilization of the South. They wrote and discussed poems, which Tate considered "a piece of [rational] craftsmanship, an intelligible or *cognitive* object." When Lowell returned in the summer to see Ford Madox Ford, Tate tactfully said there was no room for Lowell unless he pitched a tent on the lawn. A few days later the literal-minded youngster reappeared with a Sears Roebuck tent. He was taken in ("like a torn cat") and, in some ways, never left the protective custody of his early mentor. Lowell accompanied Tate to the writers' conference at Olivet that summer. He and his first wife, Jean Stafford, spent the winter of 1942 writing with the Tates at Monteagle; and Tate contributed an introduction to Lowell's first book, *Land of Unlikeness* (1944).

Lowell preceded Tate into the Catholic Church; and Tate was sympathetic and tolerant during Lowell's manic episodes. But he was furious when Lowell invaded his privacy and dramatized his grief by publishing a tactless elegy on Tate's eleven-month-old twin son, Michael, who gagged "on your plastic telephone, / while the raw sitter drew water for your bath, / unable to hear your groans."[12]

Jarrell met Tate, who thought him arrogant, during his freshman year at Vanderbilt in 1931. Tate praised his early poems and in May 1934 brought out five of them—Jarrell's first professional publication—in the short-lived *American Review*. Jarrell inflated Tate's reputation when reviewing *Reason in Madness* in the *Nation* in 1941: "As a critic of poetry he has the initial advantage of being one of the four or five greatest living poets; his judgments are occasionally perverse, always acute, and usually simply right." Tate advised Jarrell about selecting the poems for his first book, *Blood for a Stranger* (1942), and helped him place it with Harcourt Brace. Though Jarrell dedicated the volume to Tate, they were estranged for the next two and a half years, for Jarrell rejected Tate's advice and wrote a letter which made Tate seem a bit obtuse. Tate published Jarrell's work in *Sewanee* in 1945, but relations were still strained in September of that year. Jarrell, always a perceptive though severe judge, told Lowell: "Allen's greatest fault is a defect of sympathy in the strict sense of the word, a lack of ability to identify himself with anything that is fundamentally non-Allen."[13] Jarrell came to dislike Tate's poems and refused to review them for the *Nation* in February 1949. After Jarrell's death, Tate explained that Jarrell was jealous of Tate's admiration of Lowell and turned against his teacher.

Berryman was Tate's student at Columbia summer school in 1936 and visited the Tates in Connecticut after he had returned from graduate work at Cambridge University in the summer of 1939. Tate, always a generous friend, offered Berryman the editorship of *Sewanee* in 1946; and the two poets circulated a pro-Pound letter when he was awarded the

controversial Bollingen prize for the *Pisan Cantos* in 1948. Tate
later lent Berryman money and was instrumental in getting
him a permanent position at the University of Minnesota in
1954, after Berryman had been dismissed from Iowa. Tate
remained Berryman's close friend and protector at Minnesota;
and they collaborated on an anthology with commentaries,
The Arts of Reading (1960).

As Berryman's mental condition deteriorated and his
behavior became more bizarre, Tate lost patience though not
respect for him. Tate praised *The Dream Songs*, but criticized
the much weaker *Love & Fame* in a "venomous" letter that
provoked a bitter counter-attack. In January 1971 Berryman
told his former wife, Eileen, that Tate's poetry was overrated,
that his attack was motivated by jealousy and that his
character was corrupt: "Poor Allen, retired, neglected,
grandiose in Tennessee, with half a dozen lyrics to his credit
(not I'm afraid the famous Ode [to the Confederate Dead],
which suffers from characteristic inflation, also what Randall
hit in Washington as 'the lack of charm, feeling, tone of
forbidding authority')—sweating with unacknowledged
jealousy. . . . Tate used his hatred of *Love & Fame* as a
springboard for reading me out of not only the pantheon of art
but the Book of Life, accused me of every known immaturity.
. . . Allen is a very generous and corrupt man, open-hearted,
wily, spiteful." In a late interview, Tate (who knew his
criticism would have a devastating effect on the unstable
Berryman and must have wanted to sever relations with
him) clarified their conflict and defined the limitations of
Berryman's poetry: "I don't think he was great. He was an
original poet and a very interesting one, but he wasn't a great
poet. That last book *Love & Fame* was a calamity. I think his
publisher should have saved him from it, he shouldn't have
published it. I wrote Berryman it wasn't about love and fame;
it was about adolescent lust and notoriety. He never grew
up—that was his whole trouble. And *Dream Songs* are simply
paranoid projections of childhood manias and obsessions."[14]
None of the four poets could accept Tate's forbidding parental

authority or sustain their friendship when he criticized their intensely revealing poetry. Once Tate had recognized their talent and they had surpassed his achievement, they became more aware of his faults and felt compelled to break with that generous and loyal, critical and acerbic father figure.

III

Dylan Thomas was—for Berryman, Roethke and Lowell— both a modern and menacing example of the Dionysian poet, of the artist as public spectacle and destructive madman. He came from a Celtic background and from a powerful bardic tradition, and (like Malcolm Lowry and Brendan Behan) behaved more like an American than a British writer. Thomas talked, dressed and lived like a poet; and had all the qualities of the doomed and damned Romantic hero. He was— especially on his reading tours—intense, instinctive, idealistic; tormented, rebellious, escapist. As a public personality and phenomenon, Thomas gave charismatic performances that transfixed his audience. But he led a chaotic private life and depended on others to care for him. He was rude and drunken, irresponsible and embarrassing, and swung between euphoria and depression. Thomas himself confessed: "I hold a beast, an angel, and a madman in me."[15]

Karl Shapiro emphasized Thomas' personal and poetic anguish: "Thomas was the first modern Romantic . . . the first whose journeys and itineraries became part of his own mythology, the first who offered himself up as a public, not a private, sacrifice. . . . His audience wanted the poetry; they wanted the agony of the process. . . . Through the obscurity of the poetry everyone could feel the scream of desperation." Elizabeth Hardwick expressed her own anguish in an essay on Thomas and wrote about him, with adjectival insistence, as if he were Robert Lowell: "Here in America the approbation was extreme, the notice sometimes hysterical, the pace killing. . . . His last months, his final agonies, his utterly woeful

end were a sordid and spectacular drama of broken hearts,
angry wives, irritable doctors, frantic bystanders, rumors
and misunderstandings, neglect and murderous permiss-
iveness. . . . [He was] undeniably suffering and living in the
extremist reaches of experience. . . . Behind his drinking, his
bad behavior, his infidelities, his outrageousness, there was
always his real doom. . . . He had delirium tremens, horrors,
agonies, desire for death, and nearly every physical and
mental pain one can imagine."[16]

Lowell, Jarrell and Berryman all reviewed Thomas' *The
World I Breathe* in 1940 and, before he had achieved mythical
status, were rather condescending. Berryman and Roethke
later wrote self-reflective obituaries and elegies about him. In
the Kenyon College magazine *Hika*, the undergraduate Lowell,
still in Tate's critical camp, dismissed Thomas' thought as an
impediment and offered a pedestrian examination of his meter
and diction. He admired Thomas' energy and force, but said
"the struggle for simplicity produces only uninteresting
bombast." Jarrell's more confident and sophisticated judgment in *Partisan Review* was that Thomas' poems "are more
original, show a more extraordinary feeling for language and
rhythm, and are better organized [than Hart Crane's]. . . . If
poetry were nothing but texture, Thomas would be as good as
any poet alive." But Berryman, also established as a critic and
writing in the *Kenyon Review*, was as critical as Lowell:
"Thomas' verse does not show the major signs, such as a
powerful dramatic sense, wide interests, a flexible appropriate
diction, skill over a broad range of subjects that are clear in
the work" of Berryman's friend, Delmore Schwartz, who had
not yet begun his tragic decline. But Berryman acknowledged
that "Thomas has extended the language and to a lesser
degree the methods of lyric poetry."[17]

Berryman had met and drunk with Thomas in Cambridge,
England, in 1937. He claimed that Thomas made much of the
fact that he was exactly one day older than Berryman—
though Thomas was, in fact, two days younger (Thomas was
born on October 27, Berryman on October 25, 1914). Lowell

had met Thomas during a reading at Iowa in March 1950. Jarrell, who heard him in Princeton two years later, found him chaotically impressive: "Heard Dylan Thomas read to a large audience supposed to be at 5, but he arrived late on the wrong train. He began with a long, mannered, wordy, poetic, funny in spots, vain and self-obsessed performance in prose. . . . He has a wonderful voice and a fine sense of rhythm, but he reads most things just alike." All three poets wrote more favorable judgments of Thomas' later work.[18]

Roethke, also inspired by "the force that through the green fuse drives the flower," was closest to Thomas as a poet. Thomas asked to meet Roethke when he first arrived in New York, and in May 1950 they got on splendidly during a week's romp in the city. In his essay, Roethke self-reflectively stressed the exasperating charm and self-devouring brilliance of Thomas, who had to destroy himself to discover what he needed for his poetry. He was "someone to be proud of, to rejoice in, to be irritated with, or even jealous of . . . a fabulous aging cherub, capable of all things. . . . He was one of the great ones, there can be no doubt of that. And he drank his own blood, ate of his own marrow to get at some of that material." And in his elegy on Thomas, Roethke identifies with the poet's sacrificial death wish. He is convinced that each man wills his own death. Thomas' loneliness determined his fate and Roethke himself bears a Christ-like "weight of woe."[19]

Berryman, who also saw his tragic fate mirrored in Thomas, was outside the hospital room when Thomas died of an "insult to the brain" at the age of 39. In a late interview Berryman said: "I was very fond of him. I loved him, and I thought he was a master. . . . He was doomed already when I first knew him. Everybody warned him for many years." And in "In Memoriam (1914–1953)," which appeared posthumously in *Delusions*, Berryman described the panicky deathbed scene. He took his "last" leave of Thomas five different times and was alone in the corridor, only fifteen feet from his bed, when Thomas died. Berryman immediately called the nurse

and doctor, but it was already too late. He recalls that
Thomas, the prodigy of the age, liked to emphasize that he
was born one day before Berryman by demanding a little
more *respect*.[20]

IV

In his review of Mark Schorer's *Sinclair Lewis*, Winfield Scott
remarked: "Our saddest stories are biographies of 20th
Century American writers, Thomas Wolfe, Hart Crane.
Vachel Lindsay, Scott Fitzgerald, Edna Millay, Eugene
O'Neill, probably Hemingway when we know it. . . . It would
require . . . a combination of psychologist, sociologist, literary
historian and critic, as well as an expert in alcoholism, to try
to explain why." And Richard Blackmur (who knew all four
poets), after reading this review, "asked himself why so many
'eager young talents' had turned 'abortive and sterile,' or why,
if they 'succeeded in keeping their talent alive into middle age,
[they] either reduced their standards, fell silent, became
eccentric, or went abroad.' Perhaps the writer carried within
him the seeds of his own destruction." When Hemingway was
asked to name the concrete things that could harm American
writers, he said that they were condemned by both personal
and social factors, by commitment and withdrawal, and
fatalistically responded: "Politics, women, drink, money,
ambition. And the lack of politics, women, drink, money and
ambition."[21]

Lowell, Jarrell, Berryman and Roethke seemed trapped by
the same tragic pattern. They rivalled the previous generation
of novelists and poets in depth of genius and artistic
achievement, and surpassed them in the extremity of pain and
authority of suffering. Lowell, Berryman and Roethke were
eccentric, unpredictable, unfaithful; alcoholic, violent and
insane. Roethke had his first breakdown in 1935 at the age of
27; Berryman in 1939 at the age of 25; Lowell in 1949 at the
age of 32. Their intimacy was intensified in times of manic

crisis by the consciousness of a shared personal and poetic experience. The poets competed with each other in madness as an art, and flaunted their illness as a leper shows his sores. All feared the breakdowns of their friends either followed or foreshadowed their own.

Lowell, Berryman and Jarrell made pilgrimages to Pound when he presided in St. Elizabeth's hospital for the criminally insane. They shared a tender and terrifying kinship, believed there was a curse on the poets of their generation and saw themselves as victim–heroes of the age. Lowell noted that "John B. in his mad way keeps talking about something evil stalking us poets. That's a bad way to talk, but there's truth to it." In "For John Berryman" Lowell wrote that his generation of poets shared the same tragic life.[22] Berryman condemned the deity who devoured genius, wrecked the generation of Roethke, Blackmur, Jarrell and Schwartz, and also gorged on Sylvia Plath. But he also felt that anguish was the true path to art and declared that all the poets, though mentally ill, had to confront their deepest fears in order to survive and to write.[23]

Personal madness seemed to the poets an appropriate response to what Eliot called "the immense panorama of futility and anarchy which is contemporary history." Only disaster could offer a new experience. When asked about the personal wreckage of his friends, Berryman blamed the radical dishonesty of American society, which had alienated the poets and forced them to oppose the prevailing cant: "You ask me why my generation seems so screwed up? . . . It seems they have every right to be disturbed. The current American society would drive anybody out of his skull, anybody who is at all responsive; it is almost unbearable. It doesn't treat poets very well."[24]

The poets' careers began in the 1940s and coincided with the emergence of the United States as the most powerful country in the world. They believed they were truthtellers, bearers of culture, sacrificial victims driven mad by a need to escape from an increasingly crass and ugly society. As their audience diminished and their significance decreased, the poets felt they must transcend this hostile society through a finer and more intense conception of reality. Lowell first converted to Catholicism in the 1940s and then (fond of conflict) became politically engaged in the 1960s. His previous refusal to fight in the Second World War increased his moral stature during his public protest against the war in Vietnam. Berryman justified madness as a logical reaction to the collective insanity of the twentieth century and struggled to impose his idiosyncratic vision on the world. Jarrell cultivated the role of sensitive child in his poetry and of finely discriminating critic in his prose—though he could not always apply his severe standards to his own work. Roethke (like Yeats) sought mysticism as an alternative to commonplace reality and believed madness was a "purer" state than the so-called "sanity" of modern life.

All the poets felt they should seek suffering rather than happiness and all had a positive genius for disaster. All waited eagerly for the recognition and fame that would confirm their poetic stature, but rightly feared that what had come early and easily would vanish in the same way. All, as Saul Bellow observed, drew their writing "out of [their] vital organs, out of [their] very skin,"[25] and then had nothing left to draw on. All wrote obsessively and feared sterility, consoled themselves with alcohol and sex, reeled between hallucinations and breakdowns, mania and depression, and gradually destroyed their marriages, their health and their minds.

In his *Journals*, Kierkegaard perceived the ironic disparity between the ideal of the poet's art and the grim reality of his chaotic life: "What does being a poet mean? It means having one's own personal life, one's reality, in quite different categories from those of one's poetic work, it means being related to the ideal in imagination only, so that one's own personal life is more or less a satire on poetry and on oneself." As Berryman explained, using the exemplary career of Robert Frost, who had a vicious character and a disastrous personal life: "The problem with [understanding] Frost is how work of great moral depth and passion, beauty, came out of a life so inappropriate."[26] Yet Berryman and the others were not disturbed by the disparity between their own life and art. They not only used their art to justify their mania, but also used their mania as raw material for their art.

The poets who followed Thomas' way of life found they could transform negative into positive experience by using misery and maladjustment to create their poetry and intensify their public performances. The acceptance of Freudian ideas, the fascination with extreme mental states and the drug culture's desire for irrational experience allowed the poets to become privileged beings: free to express rather than hide their illness and encouraged to use madness to exalt the authenticity of their work.

These poets heroically continued to create despite terrifying obstacles. They drank both to stimulate their creative powers and to obliterate their pain and guilt. Like Coleridge, "when youthful blood no longer sustained the riot of his animal spirits, [the poets] endeavoured to excite them by artificial stimulants." In a late interview, Berryman again emphasized that the American poet, enduring the strain of creativity and the materialistic society's indifference to serious art, expresses the outrage of a sensitive victim, driven to alcoholism and suicide: "Our society, with all its vice and weaknesses . . . is really very unfavorable to higher talent. Somebody pointed out recently that out of our Nobel Prize-winners in literature —six,—four [Lewis, O'Neill, Faulkner and Hemingway] were alcoholics, and a fifth, Steinbeck, a very heavy drinker. And then you think of people like Poe and Fitzgerald. Vachel Lindsay killed himself. Hart Crane killed himself. . . . My friends have wiped themselves out in large numbers. Thomas died in an alcoholic shock. Ted and Delmore died of heart attacks, but they were both alcoholics."[27] Unable to reconcile his individual gift with the prevailing hostility to culture and unwilling to acknowledge that he may have incited his manic episodes to punish himself and relieve his guilt by alcohol and drugs, Berryman blamed society for his personal problems instead of accepting responsibility for them himself.

Jarrell, who did not drink, seemed stable and even invulnerable to disaster. But he too broke down and attempted suicide in 1964, at the age of 50, and killed himself the following year. Jarrell's unexpected death profoundly shocked Lowell and Berryman (Roethke had died of a sudden heart attack in 1963), and seemed to loosen their tenuous hold on life. They wrote elegies not only on Roethke and Jarrell, but also on themselves. Berryman placed fourteen "Opus posthumous" poems in *The Dream Songs*; Lowell included "My Death" and "Obit" in *Notebook*. Berryman committed suicide (like his father) in 1972. When Lowell died of a heart attack in 1977, his third wife, Caroline Blackwood, "called his death a 'suicide wish'; she felt he wanted to die, had given up."[28]

Yet mental illness *seemed* to stimulate their creative genius, for the constant anxiety, terror and sense of doom intensified isolation and introspection, heightened the intellectual defiance of the social outcast who questions and challenges conventional ideas about morality, and encouraged the poet to control the potentially dangerous element in his character through the order and form of art. As Nietzsche exclaimed of the *poète maudit*: "one must still have chaos in oneself to be able to give birth to a dancing star."[29]

The idea that madness and art were connected originated in ancient Greece and has persisted in our culture, with many variations, until the present time. The Greek concept of *furor divinus* was revived by Neoplatonic thought in the Renaissance, reappeared in the Romantic period, was extolled by Dostoyevsky and Nietzsche, and exerted a powerful influence on modern literature. Lowell and his circle followed the tradition that derived from the ancient Greeks. They too believed that madness—a gift as well as a punishment—could inspire great poetry, that pain and suffering were intrinsic to art, and that the artist sacrificed himself to achieve his vision.

In "In a Dark Time," Roethke equated insanity with moral superiority and heightened spirituality, and suggested that the crucified artist experienced a kind of virtuous sorrow. He defined madness as nobility of soul at odds with circumstance. He has experienced the "purity" of deep despair and compares himself to a shadow pinned, like a butterfly, against a wall.[30] And Berryman's discussion of "Skunk Hour," in which Lowell confessed, "My mind's not right," quite consciously placed himself and his friend directly in the English, Russian and American tradition of exalted, deranged and suicidal poets. Berryman then used this tradition to explain and to justify their own manic behavior. In "A Winter-Piece to a Friend Away" (in an asylum), Berryman portrayed the massive sorrow of a mental hospital and evoked the dismal shade of the mad Friedrich Hölderlin. The imagery of *The Waste Land*—dry fruit, tireless wind, rocky landscape—evokes the demented German poet and all insane and dead artists. When asked about the mental illness of his generation of poets, he again rationalized his illness and recalled his sacrificial predecessors: "To find anything resembling it, you have to look at two generations, at least that I think of offhand: the English poets of the nineteenth century —Beddoes, [George] Darley and so on—and the Soviet poets just after the Revolution. . . . And now! Well, I don't know. I don't know. Some people certainly feel it's the price you pay for an overdeveloped sensibility."[31]

The Greek idea of the deranged artist found expression in *Ion*, where Plato equated poetic power with a state of divinely inspired insanity: "the authors of those great poems which we admire, do not attain to excellence through the rules of any art, but they utter their beautiful melodies of verse in a state of inspiration, and, as it were, *possessed* by a spirit not their own. Thus the composers of lyrical poetry create those admired songs of theirs in a state of divine insanity. . . . For a Poet is indeed a thing ethereally light, winged, and sacred, nor can he compose anything worth calling poetry until he becomes inspired, and, as it were, mad, or whilst any reason remains in him." And in *Phaedrus* Plato declared that "madness, provided it comes as a gift of heaven, is a channel by which we receive the greatest blessings." According to E. R. Dodds, Plato believed that "divine madness" or "possession by the Muses" was "indispensable to the production of the best poetry."[32]

Artists have been treated like madmen since the Renaissance, when Neoplatonic doctrine extended the prerogative of the saint and the prophet to the poet and artist, and accounted for the superhuman achievement of the secular genius by a godlike inspiration. This dangerous gift placed the creative mind on a lonely height and threatened to topple him into the abyss of insanity. The artist saw the normal ways of established society as sick, while mental illness appeared to him as spiritual health.

The Romantic attitude toward the suffering artist was brilliantly expressed in a poetic apologue by Kierkegaard, who also believed that pain and suffering were intrinsic to art. He compared the torments of the artist to the prisoners roasted by Phalaris within the brazen bull. When reeds were placed in the nostrils of that taurine oven, the agonizing shrieks of the roasted victims were transmuted into music: "What is a poet? An unhappy man who in his heart harbors a deep anguish. . . . His fate is like that of the unfortunate victims whom the tyrant Phalaris imprisoned in a brazen bull, and slowly tortured over a steady fire; their cries could not reach the tyrant's ears so as to strike terror into his heart; when they reached his ears they sounded like sweet music."[33]

In *Notes from Underground*, Dostoyevsky insisted that "too great a lucidity is a disease, a true, full-fledged disease," because this heightened consciousness forced the hyper-sensitive artist to see unbearable truths about the tragic nature of human existence. Lowell expressed the same idea in "Home," when he exclaimed that the thin-skinned poet, who sees too much and feels too deeply, can never be contented.[34]

In a similar fashion, Rimbaud followed the Greek tradition and called for an artificially induced, self-destructive, deliberate derangement of all the senses that would enable the tormented, sacrificial, even insane artist to become "the great invalid, the great criminal, the great accursed" and to plunge into unknown, "unheard of, unnameable" spiritual visions. Contemporary writers from Updike to Sartre have emphasized and even glorified the tradition of deranged poets. "At least since Rimbaud's announced determination to become a visionary through the 'disordering of all the senses,'" Updike observed, "self-destructive excess has been a licensed force in the lives of many writers. [Malcolm] Lowry wrote, 'You cannot trust the ones who are too careful. As writers or drinkers. Old Goethe cannot have been so good a man as Keats or Chatterton. Or Rimbaud. The ones that burn.'" Sartre also believed that a writer's talent was closely connected to his capacity for self-ruin: "In relation to Gauguin, Van Gogh and Rimbaud, I have a distinct inferiority complex because they managed to destroy themselves. . . . I am more and more convinced that, in order to achieve authenticity, something has to snap."[35]

Roethke actually induced his own mania—which erupted in 1935, 1945, 1953 and 1957—and also rationalized his breakdowns. In 1946 he claimed that like Rimbaud he had deliberately *willed* his "derangement of the senses" and exploited the exciting, quasi-religious ecstasy for poetic purposes: "When [Henry] Vaughan says, 'When felt through all my fleshy dress, / Ripe shoots of everlastingness,' well, *that's* the feeling. You feel one way that you are eternal and immortal." Roethke (like Dylan Thomas) knew that he took foolish and dangerous risks to achieve the state that enabled him to create and certify his poetry—"My God, do you know what poems like that *cost*? They're not written vicariously: they come out of actual suffering; real madness"—but felt the poems were worth the risks. Like Rimbaud, Sartre and Roethke, Berryman believed that great art could be achieved only through great suffering: "Mostly you need ordeal. My idea is this: The artist is extremely lucky who is presented with the worst possible ordeal which will not actually kill him. . . . I hope to be nearly crucified."[36] Through this rationalization, the curse of madness could be tolerated and even thought of as an indispensable blessing. Seen in this light, suicide was not merely disabling derangement, but the ultimate sacrifice for art.

Nietzsche—who confessed that Dostoyevsky was "the only psychologist, incidentally, from whom I had something to learn"—associated the exuberant creative spirit with extreme pain and mental anguish. Nietzsche also felt that artistic greatness could be earned only by intense suffering: "To make oneself sick, mad, to provoke the symptoms of derangement and ruin—that was [equated with] becoming stronger, more superhuman, more terrible, wiser."[37] And he believed the artist's derangement gave him the power to see and tell the truth. Kierkegaard, Dostoyevsky, Rimbaud and Nietzsche all described the pathology of modern culture; they all thought that the illness of the artist, who represents his epoch, was a product of the sickness of society.

Jarrell, Berryman and Lowell had mental breakdowns and extensive therapy, and used their psychological insight to write poems about Freud. All accepted the value of his teaching—which illuminated the connection between the conscious and unconscious mind, and helped to explain the origins of creativity—and employed him for their own poetic, personal or political ends. Though Freud was not mentioned in "Deutsch Durch Freud," Jarrell used him to justify his refusal to learn German. For he believed with Freud that the sympathetic imagination acts more powerfully in the unconscious than in the conscious mind, that he could translate more effectively with intuition than with intellect:

> A feeling in the Dark
> Brings worlds, brings words, that hard-eyed Industry
> And all the schools' dark learning never knew.

In Dream Song 327 Berryman disputed the meaning of *The Interpretation of Dreams*, written by that all-wise Jewish ruler, guardian of the past and severe pedagogue of truth. And he respectfully told Freud that he had both enlightened and misled his followers. A dream, according to Berryman, is the representation of the entire mental life—rather than the hidden or overt content of a single subconscious vision. Lowell's "Freud" concerned his exile to England—where he wrote *Moses and Monotheism* and suffered the final torments of cancer of the jaw—after the Nazi *Anschluss* of Austria in March 1938. Lowell's theme was society's indifference or brutality to "the great man of culture."[38] Even when victimized and uprooted in old age, Freud remained a noble example of intellectual daring and moral courage.

The poets—who could admire but not imitate Freud's stoic example—were intensely anxious about their artistic role. They all wanted recognition and rewards for a highly specialized and perhaps superfluous activity that very few people considered significant. Jarrell saw madness as an escape from poetic sterility and artistic failure. Lowell saw it in dynastic terms, as if he were fated by genes and chemistry to fulfill his family's doom. Berryman saw it in terms of the poet's opposition to brutal society. Roethke saw it as religious ecstasy. All four poets obsessively pursued their private myths, and persuaded each other and the public to believe them. If the best contemporary poetry was the record of the most intense suffering, then their lives must inevitably lead to mania and suicide.

V

The literary manifestation of the mental illness of Lowell, Berryman and Roethke came to be known as confessional poetry. Jarrell was more covert in the expression of his psychological depression. But the careful reader could recognize it in his animal fables, *The Bat-Poet* and *Fly By Night*, and in his last volume of poems, *The Lost World*, which is filled with images of illness, pain, mutilation, terror, derangement, despair and death. The revelations of their personal horrors— conflict with parents, marital problems, sexual infidelity, alcoholism, depression, stimulants and tranquilizers, manic

episodes, nervous breakdowns and incarceration in lunatic
asylums (from which they were sometimes released to teach
their classes)—were not entirely original. For a literary
precedent existed in the oblique but astonishing confessions of
the greatest writers of the century: Proust's flagellations,
Forster's homosexuality, Woolf's insanity, Joyce's scatology,
D. H. Lawrence's impotence and T. E. Lawrence's perversity.

The Lowell generation reacted against the prevailing
dogma handed down by the literary pontiff, T. S. Eliot, and
helped shift modern poetry from self-consciousness to self-
exposure. In his most influential essay, "Tradition and the
Individual Talent" (1919), Eliot—who would compose the
intensely personal *Waste Land* after a nervous breakdown in
1921—insisted that private life and personal emotions must be
rigorously excised from poetry: "The progress of an artist is a
continual self-sacrifice, a continual extinction of personality.
. . . Impressions and experiences which are important for the
man may take no place in the poetry, and those which become
important in the poetry may play quite a negligible part in the
man, the personality. . . . Poetry is not a turning loose of
emotion, but an escape from emotion; it is not the expression
of personality, but an escape from personality."

Eliot not only defended self-repression but also emphasized
the poet's obligation to continue the Great European tradition:
"Not only the best, but the most individual parts of his work
may be those in which the dead poets, his ancestors, assert
their immortality most vigorously."[39] Lowell, in his use of
religious themes and imagery, had a cunning way of both
following and repudiating Eliot's precepts. In his poetry,
Lowell justified self-expression, substituted personal for poetic
ancestors and transfused his private problems into the poetic
tradition. In his life Lowell, like Eliot, combined the New
England and Southern traditions, converted to Catholicism
and moved to England. And he surpassed Eliot by marrying
an aristocratic wife and living in grand style in a manor house.

Even Lowell's mania was dynastic rather than merely
personal. In 1845, the deteriorating mental condition of

Harriet Lowell, the mother of his poetic ancestor, James Russell Lowell, forced the family to transfer her to McLean's mental hospital—where Robert would later be confined. James Russell Lowell's sister Rebecca also suffered from severe mental disorders and he himself experienced "gross and frightening depressions that continued to plague him his entire life. . . . They were accompanied by mental torpor, paranoia, unexplainable fears that he was going mad, pangs of guilt. . . . Frequently these episodes of melancholia gave way to their manic counterpart—great gushes of mental activity and physical exertion."[40] Lowell, who suffered the same oscillation between depression and mania, transformed his personal experience into a public and even universal statement.

In "Lady with Lapdog" Chekhov remarked: "civilized man [is] so anxious that his personal secrets should be respected." But the humiliation, grief and revolt of Ginsberg's *Howl* (1956), with its startling opening: "I saw the best minds of my generation destroyed by madness," increased the prestige of irrational behavior. As Leslie Fiedler noted: "Surely it is not the lucidity and logic of Robert Lowell or Theodore Roethke or John Berryman which we admire, but their flirtation with incoherence and disorder."[41]

The shockingly personal Lowell circle, more self-conscious of their wounds than previous writers, felt their poetry of personal tragedy and mental illness had to have the authority of the extreme. They helped to establish the dangerously fashionable notion that living at the edge of suicide—or falling over—was the most authentic stance, almost an absolute requirement of the modern sensibility. John Bayley observed that their menacing, morbid verse is "almost wholly interiorized, the soul hung up in chains of nerves and arteries and veins." Their poems are arrested by their own finality, "like a suicide hitting the pavement."[42]

Lowell and his friends sought salvation in art to compensate for the anguish of their existence. Though their misery was transformed, in their own obsessed fashion, into poetry,

these tortured souls rarely achieved serenity in their lives.
Lowell gave a grim, if oversimplified definition of his manic-
depressive states (which he portrayed in "Waking in the
Blue"), and blamed them on chemistry rather than on
hereditary or emotional factors: "Mania is extremity for one's
friends, depression for one's self. Both are chemical. In
depression, one wakes, is happy for about two minutes,
probably less, and then fades into the dread of day." Seamus
Heaney, who knew Lowell well in the 1970s, emphasized his
sacrificial aspect and agreed that "the madness, the disease,
really did nail him into suffering all his life."[43]

In his manic phase, Lowell identified with and exalted
tyrants like Napoleon and Hitler. He kept a copy of *Mein
Kampf* under the dust jacket of *Les Fleurs du Mal*. Jonathan
Miller recalled that Lowell saw the world "populated by a
series of tyrants and geniuses all jostling with one another,
competing with one another in knowledge or in sexual skill."[44]
Like Malraux with De Gaulle and Greene with Torrijos,
Lowell befriended, idealized and romanticized a charismatic
political leader, Eugene McCarthy.

Anne Sexton remembered that as a teacher Lowell worked
"with a cold chisel with no more mercy than a dentist."
Another student, who admired Lowell, but saw him as a
dangerous adversary, believed that his illness allowed him to
be unbearably rude: "The quixotic nature of his mental state,
and the excuse it gave him to attack at random if he wished,
kept people at a wary distance. . . . I often had the distinct
impression that Cal [Lowell], although pretending to be half-
mad, knew exactly what he was doing. He did not like rivals.
There was, despite the kindness and the humility, a caged
meanness that could spring out at any moment. . . . So alive to
the poetry of the 'greats,' Lowell also had the capacity for
extreme cruelty, where the living . . . were concerned. He
liked to pit student against student, friend against friend, to
draw the listener into the role of conspirator against the other,
less fortunate contenders for his favor."[45]

The twinned power of Lowell's creative and destructive

force inspired his poetry as well as the trail of desolation he left behind him: a dozen infatuated and victimized girls, two wives (Jean Stafford and Caroline Blackwood) driven to alcoholism and mental asylums. Lowell appropriated Delmore Schwartz's ex-wife when that poet was spiraling toward his doom. He seemed to encourage the impulses that fed the crack-up verse of his students, Anne Sexton and Sylvia Plath, and led directly to their suicides. After attending Lowell's poetry-writing class at Boston University, Sexton, Plath and George Starbuck would repair to the Ritz bar and perversely recall their attempts to kill themselves: "Often, very often," Sexton wrote, "Sylvia and I would talk at length about our first suicides; at length and in detail. . . . We three were stimulated by it, even George, as if death made each of us a little more real at the moment."[46] It is worth noting that Sexton adopted a "posthumous" voice, spoke as if their attempts had been successful and enjoyed the conversations because it placed her in the Lowellian tradition of mad poets.

When asked "For what fault have you most indulgence?" the tolerant Marcel Proust responded: "for the private life of geniuses." But these pitilessly dedicated men, permitted to become monsters in the name of art, passed the limits of tolerance and sacrificed many people for their poetry. In *Bartleby in Manhattan*, Elizabeth Hardwick, no doubt writing with Lowell in mind, noted that the artist's "drunkenness, infidelities, vanities, madness are looked at with a ruthless acerbic intimacy—looked at even by himself. His suffering is kept at a distance by distortion and parody"—though her suffering could not be assuaged by these techniques.[47]

These poets were well aware of what their friends and families had suffered. During their lucid periods, they re-played their guilt in the cruel daylight of the mind. Berryman adopted Miranda's "Oh! I have suffered / With those that I saw suffer" (*Tempest*, I.ii.5) as the epigraph to *Recovery*, though "With those I *made* suffer" would have been even more accurate. Lowell complained to J. F. Powers: "Everyone tells me I'm inhuman." In "Middle Age" he confessed: "I forgive /

those I / have injured!" and in "Dolphin" admitted: "my
eyes have seen what my hand did." Like his monstrous and
much-admired namesake, Caligula, Lowell could be cruel. If
he ever shed tears, he wept like a spider who watches his
trapped and struggling victims. Like his aesthetic hero
Flaubert, his "mania for phrases dried his heart."[48] His poems
were a grisly retribution for his life.

VI

Modern authors have always been intensely competitive.
Stephen Crane felt overshadowed by Kipling and complained:
"I'm just a dry twig on the edge of the bonfire." Berryman
noted that when Swinburne died in 1909, Yeats exclaimed to
his sister: "I am the King of the Cats"; and at Yaddo in May
1950, Roethke echoed Yeats and proclaimed: "*I'm king of the
cats* here." Frost told an interviewer: "I've always thought of
poetry as something to win or lose—a kind of prowess in the
world of letters played with the most subtle and lethal of
weapons."[49]

The American emphasis on immediate success, the idea of
art as a competitive business and the gladiatorial concept of
the writer, encouraged Hemingway to view literature as a
kind of boxing match: an aggressive struggle in which writers
were pitted against each other to see who would come out on
top: "I started out very quiet and I beat Mr. Turgenev. Then
I trained hard and I beat Mr. de Maupassant. I've fought two
draws with Mr. Stendhal, and I think I had the edge in the
last one. But nobody's going to get me in any ring with Mr.
Tolstoy unless I'm crazy or I keep getting better."[50]

The generation of American novelists who followed
Hemingway and were contemporaries of the four poets
imitated his aggressive attitude toward his fellow writers.
Mailer, Styron, Jones and Shaw had similar military experience, came out of the war battling and also saw art as a lethal
game. Mailer even competed with Shaw about who could lose

weight faster. When Mailer and Jones were discussing Styron
at a party "where all the writers were talking in terms of a
Hemingway competition, as if you get into the ring, ready to
knock out the existing champ, Jones was saying, 'I'm not sure
Styron's in our class.'" Mailer—who reminded himself, "get
off your ass, Norman, there's big competition around"[51]—
attacked all his contemporaries in *Advertisements for Myself*
(1959).

In 1966 Allen Tate ruefully noted that "the high civility of
Eliot and Ransom has almost disappeared from the republic
of letters. Its disappearance means the reduction of the
republic to a raw democracy of competition and aggression."[52]
The competitive and aggressive Lowell circle, keenly interested
in literary politics, also seethed with anxiety about their status
and reputations. Driven by fear and envy, by ambition and
the awareness of a shrinking audience, they each wanted to be
the major poet and always kept a shrewd eye on the
fluctuations of rank. These lonely poets, practicing a solitary
art, cultivated the ideal of a congenial collaboration. They
were capable of generosity in correspondence and reviews; but
were overcome, when they met, by the competitive spirit and
made dangerous attempts at domination.

Lowell was the master in this deadly competition, the sun
around which the other stars revolved. Seamus Heaney noted
that Lowell combined pedagogic, dynastic and poetic power:
"There had been a lineal descent, a laying on of hands, first by
Allen Tate and John Crowe Ransom, and then by T. S.
Eliot." Lowell spoke "with a dynastic as well as an artistic
voice . . . [and a] nimbus of authority ringed his writings and
his actions."[53] Lowell achieved immediate recognition when
his first two volumes of poetry were published in the mid-
1940s, but the other, older poets felt they had not received
their fair share of the major prizes, honors and awards. Lowell
won the Pulitzer Prize for *Lord Weary's Castle* in 1947;
Berryman did not win it (for *77 Dream Songs*) until 1965.
Roethke and Jarrell were not granted a major prize until, late
in life, the former got the National Book Award for *Words for*

the Wind in 1959 and the latter for *The Woman at the Washington Zoo* in 1961.

In 1967 the poet–critic Hayden Carruth observed that Lowell was the most envied American poet: he had reputation, influence and steady sales. Carruth believed that "Lowell has given us more than enough evidence of his firmness and integrity . . . to substantiate his moral fitness for the role" of leading poet of his generation. But other poets had grave doubts about his character, his ambition, his quest for fame and power. In 1966 Robert Bly warned of the dangers of fame and success: "The older poets [Stevens, Frost, Williams, Eliot] have all died in the last years; the publishing world feels lonesome without a great poet around. Robert Lowell is being groomed for this post. The result is evil, especially for Lowell."[54] Louis Simpson agreed that "Lowell may be a pacifist, but as a writer he is aggressive—he seems to be grappling with the world in order to subdue it." And Stanley Kunitz remarked that Lowell became a literary dictator and insisted that everyone recognize his pre-eminence.[55]

Lowell liked being famous, and felt that poets needed some kind of external power in order to succeed. He became a dangerous rival, a cold-blooded literary politician and a kingmaker who controlled reputations. Both friends and pupils agreed that he liked to manipulate his followers and mock his rivals. Stanley Kunitz stressed Lowell's obsessive denigration of his peers: "I have never known anyone so singularly immersed in writing as was Cal. Berryman and Roethke may have vied with him in this respect, but his concentration on the literary landscape was more unremitting. . . . The game of rating his contemporaries—the game he loved to play at parties, especially when inferiors were present—[was played] with high-keyed zest and malice." Lowell seemed to thrive on emotional turbulence and gladiatorial combats with his fellow poets: "Living in the imminence of an internal chaos that would have wrecked many lives, he so often seemed stronger and not weaker than the normal person."[56] Though the leader of a creative group, Lowell

dominated his friends by an overwhelming force of will and
led them to disaster and destruction.

But even Lowell, as he passed the age of fifty, became
weary of the intense competition. In 1970, after the death of
Roethke and Jarrell, he withdrew to England (as Jarrell
had withdrawn to North Carolina), began teaching at the
University of Essex and married Caroline Blackwood. He now
seemed to prefer a gentler atmosphere ("why should the agèd
eagle stretch its wings?") and used a military metaphor when
comparing England to America: "here there's more leisure,
less intensity, fierceness. Everyone feels that; after ten years
living on front lines, in New York, I'm rather glad to dull the
glare. . . . Our atmosphere sometimes bristles as if with little
bits of steel in the rain when it falls. It strikes mostly in the
mind, in argument, in our edginess."[57] Many poets were
relieved when he left.

Lowell had tremendous personal authority, was pre-
eminent in his circle and dominated the literary arena. Like
the grand lady in Henry James, he had "an air of keeping, at
every moment, every advantage." He had the most distinguished background, studied with the most influential
teachers, was the most talented poet, earned the most awards
and money, had the most powerful personality, attracted the
most devoted friends, married the most brilliant wives, had
the most impressive engagement in political events, established
the best public image, and survived to bury and elegize all the
other poets. Lowell also surpassed his competitors in negative
qualities. He had the most eminent lineage of insanity, the
most awful mother, the most high-minded refusal to fight in
the war, the most violent and brutal behavior, the most
destructive marriages, the most manic episodes, the most
shattering poetic revelations, the most profound guilt.

2

Robert Lowell and Randall Jarrell

Lowell and Jarrell came together as pupils of John Crowe Ransom: they absorbed the same lessons and shared the same goals. Their education provided the ideals and context for their work. It provided a hierarchical view of literature in which poetry was at the pinnacle and inspired an ambition to write poems which would assume their proper place in that hierarchy. The emphasis of New Criticism on the selection and scrutiny of the finest poetry in the language intensified the sense of competition that was inherent in American capitalism and culture. Highly praised by their distinguished poet-teachers and keenly aware of their abilities, these young writers became intensely ambitious. Lowell was fitted by background and by talent to be the greatest poet of his generation; Jarrell's gifts were more critical than creative.

The force of Lowell's powerful if disturbed mind and of his overwhelming personality was immediately apparent in the imaginative strength, rhetorical force and technical skill of his work. He virtually invented confessional poetry and had a profound influence on Snodgrass, Sexton, Plath and other poets. Jarrell was an extremely intelligent writer, a brilliant though eccentric novelist and the best poetry critic of his time. He wrote pioneering essays on Whitman, Frost, Williams and Auden as well as on Lowell; after forty years his judgments still seem unerringly accurate. Yet Jarrell lacked Lowell's rhetoric, Berryman's originality and Roethke's lyricism.

31

Though he had interesting ideas, he wrote limp, prosaic, unmemorable lines. He was too often fanciful and fey; too precious, dreamy and whimsical. His melancholy frequently merged with self-pity.

Since both poets were psychologically frail and suffered mental breakdowns that were closely connected to and expressed in their poetry, their rivalry was both dangerous and destructive. Jarrell obliquely expressed the anguish, pain and self-laceration that appeared openly in Lowell's confessional work, and his training and critical faculties led directly to his sad fate. Jarrell recognized and celebrated in Lowell the greatness he himself was unable to achieve.

Lowell and Jarrell first met in the spring of 1937 when Jarrell was a graduate instructor and Lowell a student at Vanderbilt University. They followed Ransom to Kenyon College that fall and shared an upstairs bedroom in their teacher's large house. In October 1937 the kindly Ransom wrote to his former pupil, Allen Tate, who had taught both Lowell and Jarrell: "Randall and Cal [Lowell] are pretty good company; both good fellows in extremely different ways. Randall has gone physical and collegiate with a rush; tennis is the occasion; good for him. Cal is sawing wood and getting out to all his college engagements in businesslike if surly manner; taking Latin and Greek and philosophy and, of course, English; wants to be really educated."[1]

Ten days later Lowell also emphasized their differences: Randall dapper, cavalier, abrasive, athletic; Cal slovenly, single-minded, surly and studious. He told the poet Richard Eberhart that Jarrell, who had majored in psychology, was "a complete abstraction who believes in Shelley, machines, [William Empson's] 'ambiguities,' and intelligence tests." And in an elegiac essay on Ransom, Lowell later recalled Jarrell's education, speech, dress, high spirits and intelligence:

> My friend Jarrell . . . was educated in the preoccupations of the Thirties, Marx, Auden, Empson, Kafka, plane-design, anthropology since Frazer, the ideologies and news of the

day. He knew everything, except Ransom's provincial
world of Greek, Latin, Aristotle and England. His idiom
was boyish, his clothes Southern collegiate. . . .

[Dr. Chalmers, the President of Kenyon,] watched
Randall going down a ski-crest in his unconventional,
unlovely clothes, crying, "I am an angel." Ransom suggested
that Randall had shocked Dr. Chalmers's belief. The
Aristotelian schoolmen had known no such enthusiastic and
inordinate angel.[2]

The uneasy and antagonistic friendship of the two young
poets was exacerbated by their contrasting personalities and
habits. Lowell soon transformed their room into utter chaos,
and they agreed to seek separate accommodation.

Lowell—big, strong, ruggedly handsome and well aware
of his aristocratic heritage—was fond of subtly degrading his
friend. Though sporty, Jarrell was thin and delicate, and had
a dark complexion that gave him what Lowell called a
"slightly South American" look. Lowell also said Jarrell had
Jewish blood. And when a German once asked Lowell's wife
"if it were true that Randall Jarrell was a negro, Lowell,
standing near, had [patronizingly] replied that if Jarrell *were* a
negro, he was the finest negro poet of all time." Stanley
Kunitz, a friend of both poets, thought Jarrell was rather
mysterious about his background, perhaps because, when
with Lowell, he was ashamed of it.[3]

Though both men had weak, absent fathers and oppressive, dominating mothers, Jarrell's childhood was marked by
dislocating poverty and neglect, while Lowell had all the
advantages of a wealthy and aristocratic background. Jarrell,
three years older than Lowell, was born in Nashville in May
1914, the second child (the first apparently died in infancy) of
a 19-year-old mother and a 20-year-old father, who was then a
bookkeeper. Soon after Jarrell's birth, his family moved to
Long Beach, California, where his father worked in a
photographer's studio. His parents separated in September
1925, when his mother and younger brother Charles returned

to Nashville, and Jarrell remained in Hollywood with his paternal grandparents and great-grandmother. Jarrell later recalled that when summoned to rejoin his mother "he hated to leave. 'How I cried!' he said. And he'd begged them so hard to keep him that when they wouldn't—or couldn't—he blamed them for being cruel and resolved never to think about them again."[4]

Jarrell's father soon remarried; his mother moved about frequently in Nashville, struggling to meet her financial obligations and to care for her two sons. Jarrell was forced to do what he considered "hellish" and humiliating jobs, like collecting money for newspapers and selling Christmas seals door-to-door: "*Imagine*, pestering people like that in their houses. Wasn't that a wicked thing to make a child do?" In 1926 the lonely, handsome boy posed for the statue of Ganymede on the bogus Parthenon in Centennial Park. "His mother said the sculptors had asked to adopt him, but knowing how attached to them he was she hadn't dared tell him. 'She was right,' Randall said bitterly. 'I'd have gone with them like *that*.'"[5] During his childhood Jarrell lost his mother three times: when Charles was born and replaced him as her favorite, when he was suddenly severed from both parents and brother in 1925, and when his mother remarried in about 1930. After his mother's second husband was killed in a car crash in 1940, Jarrell (whose brother had moved permanently to Paris) had sole responsibility for her.

Blair Clark's insight about Lowell applies with equal force to Jarrell: "He was struggling with two dynamos, one leading him to some kind of creative work, the other tearing him apart." Though destined (like Hart Crane) for the candy business, Jarrell was sent by a wealthy uncle to Vanderbilt, where he became the favorite pupil of the most respected and influential poets of the South: Ransom, Tate and Robert Penn Warren. These poets soon acknowledged his superior gifts, technical skill and formal mastery of verse. Tate remembered Warren "showing me some of the boy's poems. There was one beginning 'The cow wandering in the bare field' which struck me as prodigious: I still think it one of his best poems."[6] His precocious reputation as a "literary genius" led the youth to nourish great expectations.

Jarrell could be charming and gentle, but even friends like Elizabeth Bishop admitted that he "was difficult, touchy, and oversensitive to criticism." Berryman called him a "hard loser. He wasn't a man who liked to lose at all." In a late interview Tate angrily recalled: "Cal, as we called him, was easy to get along with; Randall was the most difficult human being I ever knew. His vanity was absolutely astronomical. He insulted everybody. He would sneer at people."[7] While Lowell's charm could captivate even those who knew his brutal side, Jarrell's arrogance alienated his friends and made many enemies.

Even Jarrell's close friend and admirer, Peter Taylor, mentioned his conceit, his intransigence, his primness and his repression: "Randall never in his life used a four-letter word. He couldn't stand a joke about sex. He wouldn't have it." Well aware of Jarrell's murderous wit, Lowell acknowledged: "He had a deadly hand for killing what he despised. . . . Both his likes and his dislikes were a terror to everyone." But, Taylor observed: "Cal was *determined to learn what he could from Randall.* . . . He wouldn't reject him the way other people did. Because Randall *was* hard to take." Lowell appreciated his friend's critical capacities, especially when they helped improve his own early work and to establish his literary reputation. Robert Fitzgerald believed that Jarrell was Lowell's master and retained that role throughout his life.[8]

Lowell was the American equivalent of the aristocratic Bertrand Russell. Jarrell, as conscious of Lowell's poetic genius as he was of his illustrious background, tried to defend himself against both. He once mocked Lowell's New England pedigree by exclaiming: "I'm sure the Lowells (the older Lowells, that is) have all sorts of Egyptian connections, were in the old days, Egyptians." And Elizabeth Bishop, who admired Lowell's poetic deployment of family traditions and personal history, expressed the envy Jarrell must also have felt

when she told Lowell: "All you have to do is put down the
names! And the fact that it seems significant, illustrative,
American etc. gives you, I think, the confidence you display
about tackling any idea or theme, *seriously*, in both writing and
conversation. In some ways you are the luckiest poet I
know!"[9]

Lowell portrayed himself as an aristocratic descendant,
bearing his personal genealogy like Aeneas carrying old
Anchises from the flames of Troy. With great subtlety, he
exploited as he repudiated his family tradition. His immediate
forebears were not impressive. His father, an aunt observed,
hadn't "a mean bone, an original bone, a funny bone in his
body!" Lowell's mother forced her husband to abandon his
undistinguished career in the Navy; and in his forties, his soul
went underground. Lowell's mother—who had a disturbing
affair with his sonneteering psychiatrist, Merrill Moore—later
observed of her marriage: "having to live in constant
companionship with this comparative stranger, whom [I]
found neither agreeable, interesting, nor admirable, was a
terrible nervous strain."[10] Her son felt that her very presence
made all the joy go out of existence.

At school Lowell acquired the appropriate, lifelong
nickname of Cal: part Caligula, part Caliban. Fascinated by
the world of tyrants and the moral stench of power, he soon
showed the boorish, berserk and brutal side of his character.
Lowell's biographer, Ian Hamilton, writes that he was
"remembered as dark, menacing, belligerent; always bigger,
stronger, shaggier than his contemporaries. . . . He was able
to establish his own local tyranny by regularly bloodying the
noses of schoolroom rivals . . . or by spraying enemy third-
graders with wet fertilizer. . . . People left him alone—
although they thought he was crazy—because he was so
strong." During a holiday in Nantucket in 1936, Lowell
ordered his friends to eat bizarre concoctions and to read
poems and plays all day. One of them remembered: "I
lacked the confidence to challenge him. One put up with his
bullying."[11]

Lowell instructed his first fiancée, Anne Dick, during their initial sexual encounter: "I've been to a whorehouse, twice. I can tell you what the whores do. I can tell you and you can try and do it." He once struck his father to the ground. While courting Jean Stafford, he drunkenly crashed his parents' car into a wall and smashed up her nose and head; after their marriage, he deliberately hit her in the face and broke the painfully repaired nose for the second time. In 1948 Lowell had an affair with Carley Dawson, which she found baffling and singularly joyless. He spent a good deal of time talking about bears (a private fantasy) and, during a discussion of Shakespeare, suddenly began to strangle her. He was a mental case in his teens. In 1939 Jung decisively told Lowell's mother: "If your son is as you described him, he is an incurable schizophrenic." In "St. Mark's, 1933," a poem in his final volume, *Day by Day*, Lowell confesses that his harsh unconscious will still drives him to torment his closest friends.[12]

Yet Lowell also had the same profound dedication and commitment to a poetic vocation as the young Milton and, like his predecessor, studied with the finest teachers of his time. He was taught at St. Mark's by Richard Eberhart, a disciple of I. A. Richards and William Empson; had a cool but salutary confrontation with Frost at Harvard; learned classics, history, philosophy and poetic technique from Ransom at Vanderbilt and Kenyon. The brilliant pupil pitched a tent for several weeks on the lawn of Allen Tate; became Ford Madox Ford's secretary at Olivet College; studied at Louisiana State with Warren and Cleanth Brooks.

After Kenyon, Jarrell taught English at Texas for three years and married his first wife, Mackie (who was also a professor), in 1940. Lowell taught for a year at Kenyon, worked at the Catholic publishers Sheed and Ward in New York, and in 1940 also married his first wife, the novelist Jean Stafford. The marriage to Stafford, a lapsed Catholic convert, coincided with his first period of religious mania, his own conversion to the Church of Rome and his cataract of Catholic verse. From that moment, according to Stafford, their life declined and sexual relations ceased. "I fell in love with Caligula," she said, "and am living with Calvin. He's become a fanatic. During Lent he starved himself. If he could get his hands on one, he'd be wearing a hair shirt."

When Lowell announced in 1946 that his affair with Gertrude Buckman, the former wife of Delmore Schwartz, marked the end of their marriage, Stafford went on a mad drinking binge and entered the Payne Whitney Clinic for a psycho-alcoholic cure. He demanded a divorce and left the Church, which had served its aesthetic as well as spiritual purpose. He rejoined the Catholic Church in 1949 after (he said) "receiving an incredible outpouring of grace"; and re-entered the Episcopal Church, with less flourish, in 1955. His religion, like his mania, went in cycles and inspired his poetry. Stafford, who had the tongue of an adder and a heart black with rage, poured out vitriolic reproach: "I know this, Cal, and the knowledge eats me like an inward animal; there is nothing worse for a woman than to be deprived of her womanliness. . . . I am sick now, I see no end and I wish, I wish, I wish, I wish to die."[13] "The Mills of the Kavanaughs" is a parable of their marriage.

During the war the paths of the poets radically diverged. Jarrell spent these years at army bases in Texas, Illinois and Arizona. Washed out of pilot training after going into a spin on a test flight, he became a ground instructor in a model airplane that simulated flying conditions. The atmosphere of pervasive pettiness in the army made him feel like an orphan in a Dickens novel, and he escaped during leaves to the library of the University of Illinois. In 1943 he shrewdly observed: "I believe nationalism, so far from dying out as people once believed, is going to reach heights it's only in isolated cases attained before."[14] Jarrell, the only major poet to serve in the armed forces, did not go overseas or experience combat. But he established his reputation as a war poet, and wrote many of his finest poems about the effect on both soldiers and victims of the murderous acts that were committed in the name of civilization: the death of pilots flying from bases and carriers, the victims in field hospitals, the bombing of civilians in German cities, the suffering of children and the fate of the Jews in concentration camps.

Lowell at first said: "If the war comes and they want me, I'll gladly go." He had volunteered for the army and been rejected because of defective vision, but then changed his mind about the war. Instead of appearing before his draft board and explaining his beliefs as a combative conscientious objector, he refused to report and forced the authorities to prosecute him. His first political act was a letter of September 7, 1943 to President Roosevelt ("the Lowells speak only to God") which stated his refusal to participate in an unjust war whose goal, he believed, was the permanent destruction of Germany and Japan. His quixotic but defiant gesture earned a light sentence of one year in prison and a parole after four months. In West Street Jail, the gangster Louie Lepke said, "I'm in for killing. What are you in for?" and was told: "Oh, I'm in for refusing to kill."[15] Though few people would have agreed with Lowell's attitude about the war against the Nazis and many would have regarded it as shameful, he managed to synthesize it in a witty anecdote that made Jarrell's worthy experience in the air force seem quite banal.

Both poets began to publish during the war. Jarrell kept close watch on Lowell's progress, retaining his proprietary attitude (which derived from their days at Kenyon) while delighting at his friend's success. Jarrell appeared with John Berryman in the leading avant-garde anthology, *Five Young American Poets*, published by New Directions in 1940. Lowell had his own book, *Land of Unlikeness* (1944), published by the small but prestigious Cummington Press, with an introduction by Allen Tate. The Press, founded in 1939 by Harry Duncan in western Massachusetts, specialized in modern American literature and later brought out poetry by Blackmur, Stevens, Tate, Warren, Williams and Winters. In August 1943 Jarrell told his wife: "There are five or six poems by Cal Lowell (original and goodish, though unsatisfactory and queer) in the latest *Sewanee Review*; the nicest one is about a Boston boy dying of cancer—full of local detail ["Arthur Winslow: Death from Cancer"]. They look so much better than Berryman's two printed by their side ["Farewell to Miles" and "Ancestor"] that it's funny."[16]

James Dickey believed that Jarrell was more ambitious about Lowell's reputation than about his own. In March 1945 Jarrell told Tate he had received Lowell's first book. It exuberantly portrayed the puritan heritage of New England, zealous Catholicism (inspired by Hopkins) and his opposition to the blind and bloody war, and would become a considerable critical success. Jarrell, who wanted to praise the book and was not sure other reviewers would do so, wrote with great enthusiasm about a major poetic talent in the *Partisan Review* (Winter 1945):

> Some of Mr. Lowell's poems are so good ("The Drunken Fisherman" is the best poem in any of these books) and all are so unusual that it makes reviewing his book a pleasure. . . .
> He has succeeded in making salvation seem as real, and almost as frightening, as damnation. . . .
> At his best Mr. Lowell is a serious, objective, and extraordinarily accomplished poet. He is a promising poet in this specific sense: some of the best poems of the next years ought to be written by him.[17]

In August 1945 Jarrell told Lowell he was "the only good friend of my own age," and identified with his work: "when I read your poems I not only wish that I had written them but feel that mine in some queer sense are related to them." Jarrell felt he had participated in their creation because of their shared teachers and poetic tradition, and his expert, word-by-word, line-by-line criticism of Lowell's unpublished work. Jarrell also identified with his friend by publicly acknowledging his merit.

Jarrell's private letters to Lowell about *Lord Weary's Castle* (1946), written while the poems were being composed, are very close to (virtually drafts of) his review of the book in the *Nation* of January 1947. After reading the manuscript, Jarrell claimed, with characteristic acuity: "it will be the best first book of poems since Auden's *Poems*. . . . 'Mr. Edwards and the Spider' is tremendously effective the way it is now. It's an awfully good poem. . . . 'Where the Rainbow Ends' is one of your very best poems from every point of view: one of the best religious poems in hundreds of yers. . . . I think they are some of the best poems anybody has written in our time, and are sure to be read for hundreds of years. . . . I think you're potentially a better poet than anybody writing in English."[18]

Jarrell's long and extremely influential review—which contained the kind of enthusiastic and quite unusual admiration that he usually reserved for Whitman, Frost, Williams and Auden, and rarely bestowed on a contemporary—rightly predicted that Lowell would become an influential poet: "No one younger than Auden has written better poetry than the best of Robert Lowell's. . . . It is hard to exaggerate the strength and life, the constant richness and surprise of metaphor and sound and motion, of the language itself. . . . One or two of these poems, I think, will be read as long as men remember English."[19] *Lord Weary's Castle*, which had absorbed the best poems of *Land of Unlikeness*, immediately established Lowell as a major poet. During 1947–48, he won the Pulitzer Prize, the American Academy of Arts and Letters Prize and a Guggenheim Fellowship, and was appointed Poetry Consultant at the Library of Congress. Jarrell was Consultant ten years later, but never won any of these awards. His slow climb to recognition, and sharp decline when he had achieved it, provided a powerful contrast to Lowell's meteoric career.

Jarrell's review appeared when he was literary editor of the *Nation*; and during 1946–47 he saw a good deal of Lowell in New York, published twelve of his poems as well as his review of Wallace Stevens' *Transport to Summer*. The poet and translator Robert Fitzgerald first met Lowell in Jarrell's company. Lowell was "tall, big-boned, shy, earnest, funny, bareheaded in all weathers; a Catholic, as I was—in both cases, to Randall, a matter for respectful but suspicious attention." Jarrell told Fitzgerald that Lowell was living "a hermit's life" after the break-up of his marriage to Jean Stafford. But Lowell, not an absolute anchorite, was having an affair with Gertrude Buckman, who carefully observed his relationship with Jarrell. Buckman did not find the guarded and prim Jarrell sexually attractive. He resembled a man in an Arrow shirt ad, and seemed to prepare a face to meet the faces that he met. She felt that Lowell revered Jarrell, who in turn was encouraging and protective. Lowell thought of himself as unique and believed Jarrell's talent was unequal to his own, but he respected Jarrell as a great mind and a great critic.[20]

Jarrell cultivated a quiet provincial life. In August 1947 he settled down to teach in a small women's college in Greensboro, North Carolina. After visiting Jarrell in December, Lowell told the novelist J. F. Powers that it was "an easy-going dingy place . . . [with] no intellectual excitement," and criticized Jarrell's mawkish attachment to pets: "All my friends have children except Randall, who has a cat."

When Jarrell's second wife, Mary, met him during a writer's conference in Boulder in 1951 (Lowell had met Stafford at a Boulder conference in 1937), she was quite taken by his saddle-shoes, cable-knit sweaters and what she fondly called his "French aviator's moustache." But W. D. Snodgrass, Jarrell's student that summer, recalled: "His girlish manner astounded everyone. One would find him lounging about on a stone wall somewhere wearing elegant tennis shorts and exclaiming, 'Gee! Golly! Don't you just *love* it here! I think it's just dovey!!!' "[21]

In December 1948 Lowell met Elizabeth Hardwick at the writers' colony, Yaddo, in Saratoga Springs, New York. Three months later, after providing Tate's wife with a list of Tate's mistresses and suspending the poet outside an apartment window while he recited the "Ode to the Confederate Dead" in a bear's voice, he had his first major breakdown and exposed his friends to the daunting impact of actual madness. He talked like a machine gun, with blazing eyes, became violent and homicidally hallucinated, suspected he was the reincarnation of the Holy Ghost, and was bound with leather straps in a padded cell. Tate shrewdly observed that Lowell had abandoned Stafford, the Church and poetry: his three defenses against disintegration.

Lowell had not reviewed Jarrell's *Blood for a Stranger* (1942), *Little Friend, Little Friend* (1945) and *Losses* (1948), but he did write a notice of *The Seven-League Crutches* in the *New York Times Book Review* of October 7, 1951—perhaps to reciprocate Jarrell's fine review of *The Mills of the Kavanaughs* in *Partisan* the following month. In May 1949 Lowell wrote Jarrell, with ambiguous qualification: "I've been thinking that you're perhaps the best poet in America (where are there better poets?)—unless I am."[22] And in his review of Jarrell's verse, the 34-year-old Lowell was careful to emphasize Jarrell's status as a literary man rather than a poet: "Randall Jarrell is our most talented poet under forty. . . . He is a man of letters in the European sense, with real verve, imagination, and uniqueness." He briefly traced Jarrell's career, erratically rated his war poems above those of Wilfred Owen, skimmed over his faults ("idiosyncratic willfulness and eclectic timidity"[23]) and, as Jarrell often did in his own reviews, listed the best poems in the book. Jarrell was pleased with the review and said: "It was far and away the best thing anybody's written about my poems."

In November 1951, the month he received Lowell's allegory on the disintegration of his cataclysmic marriage to Stafford, Jarrell reticently announced the conspicuously quiet end of his marriage to Mackie: "We'd been getting further apart every year, we had almost none of the same interests, [she more and more disapproved of me and I more and more felt impatient about her—] it was bad for us and getting worse, and I know we'll both be a lot better off apart."[24]

Jarrell began his review by praising *The Mills of the Kavanaughs*, then noted the quite radical flaws in the title poem, and concluded by ignoring the faults and praising the book:

> *Very* few living poets have written poems that surpass these. . . . [It] is an interesting and powerful poem; but in spite of having wonderful lines and sections—many of both—it does not seem to me successful as a unified work of art. . . . The people too often seem to be acting *in the manner of* Robert Lowell, rather than plausibly as real people act. . . . Occasionally, for a few lines, the poem becomes so academic and clumsy that one is astonished. . . . [Yet] it is a powerful and impressive poem, with a good many beautiful or touching passages and a great many overwhelming ones, one of the better poems of one of the best of living poets.[25]

Despite their friendship, there was a troubled undercurrent in their relations. Jarrell's genuine admiration clashed with his inward bitterness about the enormous success of his younger rival. He feared Lowell would be angry about the review and Lowell feared "ugly treatment"—perhaps because of his own insecurity about the poems, his anxiety about offending Jarrell in his notice of *The Seven-League Crutches*, their covert but intense competition and Jarrell's savage reputation as a critic. But Lowell's response to his friend's review was as positive as Jarrell's to his own. He somewhat defensively told Jarrell, the month the notice appeared: "I agree with most of what you say, except the heroine is very real to me and in a freakish way the poem has much more in it than any of the others. Anyway, I'm delighted . . . and have read it many times out of vanity. Perhaps I agree with it all."[26]

As the poets measured each other's faults as well as strengths, Jarrell began to reveal his poetic debts to Lowell. This influence was obvious to both poets, who began to mock each other publicly, if not in print. The title of Lowell's "Where the Rainbow Ends" (1946) reappeared in Jarrell's "The End of the Rainbow" (1954). Lowell's "Falling Asleep

Over the Aeneid" (1948), in which a man dreams he is
Aeneas, was followed by Jarrell's "A Girl in the Library"
(1951), in which the dreaming girl is compared to Tatyana in
Pushkin's *Eugene Onegin*. Most significantly, Lowell's
compressed personification of death in his "Aeneid" poem—

Their headman's cow-horned death's-head bites its tongue

—resurfaced in Jarrell's "The Knight, Death, and the Devil"
(1951) as the more prosaic

Cowhorn-crowned, shockheaded, cornshuck-bearded,
Death is a scarecrow.

Lowell would caustically mimic both Tate and Jarrell.
Randall would make up wickedly witty parodies of the
eccentric trust-fund Lowells and of Cal's favorite morbid-
Catholic effects, "full of sabbaths, sermons, graveyards,
ancestors."[27]

After his first mental breakdown in 1949, Lowell's manic
episodes recurred with terrible regularity nearly every spring
—in Salzburg, Cincinnati, Boston and Buenos Aires—and he
had suffered fourteen or fifteen attacks by 1968. He was given
electro-shock treatments—"like a trolley-pole sparking at
contact." Artaud, Hemingway and Sylvia Plath (who described her experience in *The Bell Jar*) also endured this ghastly
process, which produced convulsions and coma. These
shocks, Artaud explained, "make me despair, take my
memory away, numb my thinking and my heart, make me
absent and aware of myself as absent. I see myself as pursuing
my own existence for weeks, like a dead man at the side of a
living man who is no longer himself."[28] But they seemed (at
least temporarily) to help Lowell. He married Hardwick in
July 1949 and spent his honeymoon in Stafford's alma mater,
the Payne Whitney Clinic. Despite his horror of babies, their
daughter Harriet was born in 1957. Lowell predicted her first
words would be *"Partisan Review."*

Lowell's acute mania was accompanied by love affairs with young girls that sparked the jerky graph of his heart, by fantasies of rejuvenation and rebirth, and by a desperate need to have his wife and mistresses competing for his favor. Hardwick's surpassing love, frenetic fidelity, devotion merging into martyrdom, humiliating masochism, unlimited capacity for suffering and endurance made her the tragic heroine of Lowell's life. It is not clear why Hardwick was always willing to take him back after he had left her, for (echoing Stafford) she had expressed her "utter contempt for . . . you for the misery you have brought to two people who had never hurt you." Nor is it clear if she contained or contributed to his illness. His incompetent therapist provided very little insight about his illness and, when her patient became obstreperous or violent, actually said to him, with a self-pity notably absent in Hardwick: "Cal, how can you do this *to me?*"[29] Though his disease was incurable, lithium finally held off his attacks for as long as four years.

In September 1956 Jarrell wrote with apparent objectivity and slight irritation to their mutual friend, Elizabeth Bishop, about his first embarrassing encounter with Lowell's mania and emotional entanglements:

I see very little of Cal. When he was in love with that Italian girl [Giovanna Madonia] he wrote that he was going to be divorced and wanted to visit us; he did, fairly along in a manic stage—then while he was in the hospital I had to do quite a bit of difficult corresponding with the Italian girl, since he'd named me, in letters, as the American friend to correspond with; also he'd shown Elizabeth Hardwick my letter saying I was glad he was being divorced. . . . We saw them a little last summer; she was very cordial, poor disingenuous thing! and Cal was joylessly being good, the properest Bostonian imaginable.[30]

Though he was kind and loyal to Lowell, most people still found Jarrell "hard to take." His prickly personality and savage reviews certainly hurt his career. By contrast, Lowell's behavior, no matter how outrageous, could always be justified by his madness, which, in turn, inspired the protective sympathy of his friends. As early as 1938 in Kenyon, the mild and moderate John Ransom had commented on Jarrell's "rather untactful manners and unimpressive public speech." And in 1957, when Jarrell was being considered as Ransom's successor and editor of the *Kenyon Review*, Ransom, in a letter to Tate, objected to Jarrell's contentious character and noted the prosaic limitations of his verse: "Jarrell is too polemical and stylistically too journalistic and personally too fond . . . of having enemies to be acceptable. . . . His way of life in a small community would make a riffle, and there would be many incidents. . . . Randall has a great journalistic or publicist flair. . . . He is more or less sensational. . . . What he has done is impressive if you look only at his *Selected Poems* . . . but it is imperfect, and always verging into prose." Surprisingly, Ransom's doubts about Jarrell's personality and poetry were overcome, and he was persuaded to offer his pupil the job. But Jarrell chose to remain outside the power structure and refused it. "After his unhappy childhood and previous existence generally [i.e. his first marriage]," Ransom (echoing Jarrell) explained it to Tate, "he at last is in bliss, with a congenial job, a home which he owns, and a honeymoon still going on with his new wife, so why should he give all that up?"[31]

Lowell, whose chaotic life and restlessness were a strong contrast to Jarrell's happiness and stasis in California, continued to visit his friend. Writing to Berryman in March 1959, Lowell evoked a tragic theme that would recur in the poems of the survivors after the unexpected deaths of Roethke, Jarrell and Schwartz: "I'm just back from Greensboro, where Randall and I enjoyed ourselves lamenting the times. It seems there's been something curious[ly] twisted and against the grain about the world poets of our generation have had to live in. What troubles you and I, Ted Roethke, Elizabeth Bishop, Delmore, Randall—even Karl Shapiro—have had."

Two years later, recalling that visit to Jarrell, Lowell contrasted the focus of their anxieties: "I remember once, the last time at Greensboro, I think, when you came into my room and began talking out of a blue sky about the ills of our culture, and Mary [Jarrell] said that I worried about personal matters while you were upset about the world."[32] Mary's observation, however, was more ironic than accurate. Both poets had rejected the conservatism of the Fugitives and Southern Agrarians, led by Ransom and Tate, and held liberal views. But it was Lowell rather than Jarrell who achieved national prominence in the 1960s by engaging in politics and trying to cure the ills of the world.

Unlike Hemingway, whose artistry was eventually submerged and destroyed by his public image, Lowell had a fine ability to project and manipulate himself as an authoritative public figure. He emerged as a political personage in a highly publicized letter to President Johnson on June 3, 1965 (which recalled his earlier letter to President Roosevelt) refusing, because of the Vietnam War, to attend the White House Festival of the Arts. He marched on the Justice Department in 1967 and on the Pentagon in 1968, and was immortalized in Norman Mailer's *Armies of the Night* (1968). He formed a close friendship with Senator Eugene McCarthy and distracted him from serious political responsibilities during his ill-fated presidential campaign.

During the early 1960s, Lowell and Jarrell continued their critical dialogue and mutual appreciation in person, in letters, in interviews and in print. Lowell won the National Book Award for the innovative and influential *Life Studies* in 1960 and the following year Jarrell won it—his first major prize—for the less impressive *Woman at the Washington Zoo*. Lowell, who had been previously elected, nominated Jarrell for membership in the National Institute of Arts and Letters in 1960. It was cruelly ironic that Jarrell had virtually stopped writing poems when Lowell reached the height of his powers.

In his much-publicized and frequently reprinted interview with the *Paris Review* in the spring of 1961 (Jarrell's

conversation was never recorded by that journal), Lowell
thrice referred to Randall. Lowell rightly called him "the most
brilliant critic of my generation" (though this was not the field
in which Jarrell wished to excel), said he used to submit his
poems to Jarrell before publishing them, and closed with a
more generous though carefully qualified judgment of his
friend's wide range of interests, intellect, critical acumen and
war poems: "Jarrell's a great man of letters, a very informed
man . . . the best professional poet. He's written the best war
poems, and those poems are a tremendous product of our
culture." In his less distinguished interview in *Analects* (Spring
1961), obscurely published in Greensboro, Jarrell returned the
compliment and repeated what he had often said in print:
"Robert Lowell is another of the poets that I like best. He is an
extremely powerful, and often quite overwhelmingly intense
and forceful poet."[33] Lowell, maintaining a polite stance, again
stressed Jarrell's professionalism and literary status, and
praised his early rather than his current work. Jarrell, speaking
more honestly, described Lowell's personal impact as well as
the force of his poetry.

In November 1961, Lowell confessed to Jarrell: "You are
one of the very few people I feel deeply enough in with to talk
deeply with." Early in 1962, for the second time in Jarrell's
lifetime, Lowell—who had been largely responsible for estab-
lishing Elizabeth Bishop's reputation—gave a rare but useful
puff on the dust wrapper of the wistfully titled *A Sad Heart at
the Supermarket*. As usual, he stressed his friend's cultural
rather than creative importance: "Randall Jarrell is a wit and
the last of our great poet–critics. These essays speak with
prophetic distress about our culture. They are their author's
Culture and Anarchy. I know I am making an immense claim,
but I think no one since Arnold has written on this subject
with more humor, intuition and authority."

The following year, in his extensive survey "Fifty Years
of American Poetry" in Karl Shapiro's *Prairie Schooner*, Jarrell
noted that Lowell "always had an astonishing ambition"
(Berryman said the same thing about Jarrell), referred to his

public image and (during his own period of sterility) emphasized Lowell's extraordinary growth: "Robert Lowell is the poet of shock . . . perhaps because his own existence seems to him in some sense as terrible as the public world. . . . He is a poet of great originality and power who has, extraordinarily, developed instead of repeating himself. His poems have a wonderful largeness and grandeur, exist on a scale that is unique today."[34] Jarrell's final judgment of Lowell appeared in the last part of the last chapter of his last book of criticism.

In an important *Observer* interview with his disciple, A. Alvarez, in July 1963, Lowell referred to Jarrell's 1947 review of *Lord Weary's Castle* and reinforced Jarrell's more recent comment that he had indeed moved from repetition to development: "When my second book came out the most interesting review of it was by Randall Jarrell. Though he liked the book, he made the point that I was doing things I could do best quite often, and I think he quoted Kipling— when you learn how to do something, don't do it again."[35]

In January 1964, aware that Jarrell's poetic decline coincided with his own achievement, Lowell tried to cheer up his old friend with a bit of comforting praise that applied to the earlier rather than the present phase of Jarrell's life: "You stay young, and it's good to think of you, still so honest and hopeful and full of brilliant talk and knowledge, able to judge and make. Your great parade of women [in the poems] have a delicate splendor." Jarrell, depressed by his present failure, may well have taken "you stay young" to mean that he had failed to develop as an artist and was now writing children's books that signaled a regressive retreat from adult concerns. His almost feminine "delicate splendor" seemed a weak contrast to the "largeness and grandeur" he had praised in Lowell.

In a *Newsweek* interview of October 12, 1964, to mark the publication of *For the Union Dead* (Jarrell did not make *Newsweek* until his suicide was reported the following year), Lowell praised his pedagogy: "Most poets today live by teaching and Lowell remembered Randall Jarrell's line—

'God who took away the poet's audience gave him students instead.'"[36] Jarrell's students were at a girls' college in Greensboro, Lowell's (when he chose to teach) were at Harvard. Lowell's private income, substantial royalties and lucrative lecture fees obviated the need for the salary and security of a regular academic position.

Jarrell, who came north to attend the premiere of *The Old Glory*, was passionate about the plays that were dedicated to him and to the English director, Jonathan Miller. During the actual performance, he exclaimed aloud: "Oh, that's so clever. That's so like Cal. . . . Cal can do this kind of thing in his sleep!" W. D. Snodgrass, a brilliant pupil of both Lowell and Jarrell, who had won the Pulitzer Prize for *Heart's Needle* in 1959, also attended the first night and recalled that when Lowell's play "appeared at the American Place Theater in New York, Jarrell came to me on the stage afterwards and said, 'That's the best play ever written in American, isn't it?' I ventured to say that I thought it was a very fine play but not so great as that and received a most vicious insult."[37] Snodgrass felt Jarrell "was personally jealous of Lowell and so overcompensated"—perhaps because he was so personally involved in Lowell's life and art.

Though he had some serious reservations about the verse play, Jarrell also defended it against the lukewarm response of the critics in a letter of November 29, 1964 to the *New York Times*: "I have never seen a better American play than 'Benito Cereno,' the major play in Robert Lowell's 'The Old Glory.' The humor and terror of the writing are no greater than those of the acting and directing; the play is a masterpiece of imaginative knowledge." No wonder that Lowell, during his interview with *Life* in February 1965, repeated: "Of poets alive now my favorites are Elizabeth Bishop and Randall Jarrell."[38]

The two poets had always, since their days at Kenyon, been extremely competitive. Berryman retold Jean Stafford's revealing story of how Jarrell, after playing and losing a game of croquet with his friends' children, was seen, early next

morning, advantageously "studying the ground—changing
the wickets." Robert Fitzgerald remembered that Jarrell
invented games with Lowell, who had a real, balloon-like
animal bladder on a stick. When one of them made a mistake
with a quotation or a date, the other could beat him with the
bladder. Jarrell, fierce in his admirations, learned to make
lists with Lowell and put himself on the line about poets' best
works.[39] (In his obituary of Jarrell, Lowell recalled: "Woe to
the acquaintance who liked the wrong writer, the wrong poem
by the right writer, or the wrong lines in the right poem!") But
Karl Shapiro saw the more sinister side of their competitive
struggle: "The game was Who's First and it was Lowell's
game. The idea is to grade the poets until the downgrading
wipes most of the competition off the board. Two or three
remaining contenders then engage in a death struggle. Jarrell
played this game with a will but his winning instinct was no
match for Lowell."[40]

Jarrell got the worst of the struggle because Lowell had the
greater talent, greater fame and greater influence. Peter
Taylor's wife Eleanor thought Jarrell's public reputation fell
cruelly short of what he felt he deserved, that he "suffered
sometimes, in rare moments, at certain worldly honors
appropriate to him he never got." In his obituary notice,
Lowell, who had an international reputation and knew every
important cultural figure in America and Europe, emphasized the modest compensation of purity and obscurity in
Greensboro: "He once said, 'If I were a rich man, I would pay
money for the privilege of being able to teach.' . . . There his
own community gave him a compact, tangible, personal
reverence that was incomparably more substantial and
poignant than the empty, numerical, long-distance blaze of
national publicity." Jarrell, nursing his modest flame,
undoubtedly longed for a blazing bit of national attention.
And his jealousy of Lowell even destroyed his old friendship
with Allen Tate. "He turned against me," Tate said. "He dedicated his first book to me, and asked me to make selections for
it. But he turned against me after that. . . . Robert Lowell

came along and Randall thought I preferred Robert to him."[41]

Jarrell had been briefly exposed to Lowell's madness, which he saw as a foreboding of his own. And Lowell gratefully acknowledged Jarrell's (long-distance) sympathy during his troubled times: "Randall had an uncanny clairvoyance for helping friends in subtle precarious moments— almost always as only he could help. . . . Twice or thrice, I think, he must have thrown me a lifeline." But Jarrell failed to help Lowell at the most crucial moment. Though trained in psychology, Jarrell became terrified when confronted with Lowell's mania during his friend's visit to Greensboro in 1954, lost all Freudian insight, abandoned clinical objectivity and "found it distasteful to be even minimally involved in this crisis." After Lowell had telephoned to report he had been hospitalized for mania, Jarrell, half-stunned, said ruefully: "So that's what it was. He was manic. . . . As any fool could plainly see . . . but me. . . . Oh, Randall, you're so dumb. . . . How really stupid of me. . . . Poor old Cal."[42]

Lowell, by contrast, "had always thought of [Jarrell] as invulnerably rational, somehow protected by cleverness from any serious psychic upheavals." But he was more frail and vulnerable than Lowell suspected. When James Dickey first met Jarrell in 1961, he was taken aback by the poet, who did not match his high expectations. He looked much older than forty-seven; he was fragile, unathletic and showed parchmenty eyelids. Stanley Kunitz recalled that when he met Jarrell, just before his death in 1965, "I saw for the first and last time the naked vulnerability of his countenance."[43] Jarrell had always succeeded at everything he had ever done, so relative failure— the recognition at the end of his life that he was, compared to Lowell, a failure—was more difficult to accept. He had to be a great, perhaps the greatest poet—or he was nothing. Lowell wrote poems about his depression while depressed; Jarrell merely lapsed into sterility and silence.

After Jarrell had broken down and slashed his wrist in January 1965, Lowell tried—in one of his finest letters—to comfort his friend with insight, based on his own mental illness, about dissociation from the mad self: "What looks as though it were simply you, and therefore would never pass, does turn out to be not you and will pass. Please let me tell you how much I admire you and your work and thank you for the many times when you have given me the strength to continue. Let me know if there's anything I can do. Courage, old friend."[44] Ten months later Jarrell was dead at the age of 51. Dressed entirely in black and walking at night along a four-lane highway, he lunged into the path of a car.

Lowell was one of the pallbearers at Jarrell's funeral at Greensboro on October 17, 1965. Though he published only one review and a blurb about his friend during his lifetime, he wrote more—and more positively—about him after death had removed his poetic rival. Lowell's important obituary–essay appeared first in the *New York Review of Books* on November 25, 1965, then as an "appreciation" in the paperback edition (1966) of Jarrell's last book, *The Lost World*, and finally in the memorial volume that Lowell edited in 1967 with Peter Taylor and Robert Penn Warren. Lowell's tribute, composed in a series of sketches, portrayed Jarrell as a student, an aviation instructor, an inspired teacher, a critic whose frankness department chairmen (like Ransom) found "more unsettling and unpredictable than the drunken explosions" of a Dylan Thomas, an underrated poet (though *The Lost World* is certainly not his "best book"), a sympathetic friend, a "noble, difficult, and beautiful soul." Recalling their days at Kenyon, Lowell mentioned his rebarbative qualities and said Jarrell was "upsettingly brilliant, precocious, knowing, naive, and vexing." He acknowledged Jarrell's intellectual rather than poetic talents: "His gifts both by nature and by a lifetime of hard dedication and growth, were wit, pathos, and brilliance of intelligence." And he concluded with a lively and sympathetic description of Jarrell's looks, tastes and interests that tried to penetrate his careful mask:

Poor modern-minded exile from the forests of Grimm, I see him unbearded, slightly South American-looking, then later bearded. . . . Then unbearded again. I see the bright,

petty, pretty sacred objects he accumulated for his joy and
solace: Vermeer's red-hatted girl, the Piero and Donatello
reproductions, the photographs of his bruised and merciful
heroes: Chekhov, Rilke, Marcel Proust. I see the white
sporting Mercedes-Benz, the ever better cut and more
deliberately jaunty clothes, the television with its long
afternoons of professional football, those matches he
thought miraculously more graceful than college football.[45]

It is not clear whether Lowell recognized himself and his
wife in *The Lost World* and chose to ignore it or whether he was
blissfully unaware of the satire in the volume that contained
his "appreciation." For a "Well-To-Do Invalid" is an extremely bitter poem that attacks Hardwick as nurse–mother
to Lowell and mistakenly predicts he will survive her. Jarrell's
dramatic monologue expresses the rivalry between old friend
and new wife (who was a fellow Southerner) and portrays her
as ingratiating, insincere, domineering, dishonest, self-serving.
Lowell's governess and mother is as attractive as a nurse in
her near-white clothes, and she has forgiven many sins in her
overgrown child. Whenever there is an emergency, she always
calls in the right specialist. She has adopted him as her
natural disaster and is as loyal as a plaster saint. But the poem
deliberately ignores the depths of Hardwick's disinterested
suffering and fails to give her credit for holding Lowell's life
together. It is also cruelly ironic, for Jarrell himself soon
became a patient, cared for by Mary, his own nurse–mother.
Like Hardwick with Lowell, she survived him, reaped the
benefits of his career, tried to influence his posthumous image
and to control his reputation. Jarrell's wife noted that
"Elizabeth Hardwick was not [his] type, and he even
[prematurely] congratulated Lowell for leaving her."
Hardwick, after seeing Jarrell's officious letter, maintained
polite relations but did not come to Greensboro. Jarrell's
dislike of Hardwick, combined with Lowell's mania and his
own poetic sterility, may have contributed to the coolness in
their friendship after 1950.

Ian Hamilton observed that "the death of Randall Jarrell

had removed the one critical voice that Lowell was in fear of—What will Randall think of *this*? had always been one of his first worries."[46] And Jarrell's death may also have contributed to the looser style of Lowell's *Notebook* (1969; revised 1970), in which his two elegies of Jarrell—a fascinating complement to the obituary–essay, which did not mention the suicide—first appeared.

Lowell had no doubts about Jarrell's suicide[47] (officially described as an "accident"), and in "Ten Minutes" thinks he might end his loneliness in the same way as his friend did. He too, late at night, sees suicidal headlights that burn and vanish on the highway. In one elegy, Jarrell holds his slashed wrist as he had once held his black Persian that had also been killed by a car. In another elegy, Jarrell (called "Child Randall" to suggest nobility and innocence) dressed entirely in black, walks in a trance on the highway, seeks death and lunges on the windshield.[48]

In a series of interviews during the last decade of his life, Lowell frequently referred to Jarrell, who became both a nostalgic memory and a moral touchstone. In March 1967 Lowell repeated a favorite quote he had used in the obituary–essay and told the drama critic, Michael Billington: "My old friend, Randall Jarrell, once said that he liked teaching so much that, if he were rich enough, he'd pay to be a teacher." Speaking to the classicist D. S. Carne-Ross the following year, he recalled Jarrell's private but severe criticism of his verse play *Benito Cereno*, and his ideas on translation: "My old friend Randall Jarrell suggested to me it would have been better if *Benito* had been printed as prose—not changing a word but printing it in paragraphs rather than lines. And quite likely he was right, but it seemed to make very little difference.... I remember a wonderful crack of Randall Jarrell's about translation. He said nobody thinks that some professor of Lithuanian could have written *Anna Karenina*, but everyone thinks he is the ideal man to translate it."[49] For Lowell, translation was a complement to his original poetry; for Jarrell, it was a poor substitute.

In September 1969 Donald Newlove reported Lowell's now familiar judgment of his friend: "He was our best critic and wrote our best war poetry. . . . Now Jarrell, he was so enthusiastic, and a great quoter. You wanted to read whatever he was writing about. That's the mark of a great critic— enthusiasm." This quality was notably absent in Lowell's comments about Jarrell.

Two years later—still stressing Jarrell's superb criticism, much of it in praise of himself—Lowell observed that his friend was the epitome of the New Criticism: "Jarrell's evaluations were often more imaginative than his authors. We began in the age of the New Critics. . . . That age has passed: its last spirit was Randall."[50] In May 1976, writing about their mutual friend Hannah Arendt in the *New York Review of Books*, Lowell again emphasized Jarrell's role as teacher and his ability to praise rather than condemn: "Years earlier [in 1951] Randall Jarrell had written me in Holland that if I wanted to discover something big and new, I would read Hannah Arendt's *Origins of Totalitarianism*. Randall seldom praised in vain."

In his obituary of Lowell in October 1977, Stanley Kunitz noted that Jarrell, Tate, Bishop and Peter Taylor had been placed in Lowell's Pantheon, "had already been elevated, alive or dead, to angelic company. To him their works were sacred texts." And Kunitz recorded that Lowell, commenting on his tendency to revise and reorder his poems in subsequent volumes, revealed that Jarrell remained, to the very end of Lowell's life, the severe but sympathetic mentor of their Kenyon days ("What will Randall think of *this*?"): "Once the ghost of Jarrell appeared in a dream to him, scolding, 'You didn't write, you *re*-wrote.'"[51]

Jarrell was the ideal reviewer of Lowell's poetry, the perfect Ganymede to Zeus. He was a close friend, shared his teachers and tradition, was familiar with the personal experiences that inspired the poems, had read the works in manuscript, discussed them with the author, had a keen understanding of the themes and techniques, was greatly respected as a critic and eager to commend the poems in influential journals.

The tenor of Lowell's magisterial comments during Jarrell's lifetime were both deferential and arrogant, faintly patronizing, subtly deprecating, undermined by conde-scending qualifications. Karl Shapiro's belief that Jarrell wrote obsequiously about Lowell, as if he were afraid of him, and that Jarrell was "killed" by competition with Lowell—a monster and a bully—is exaggerated, but it does contain an element of truth.[52] Lowell said just enough to affirm his loyalty, but not quite enough to enhance Jarrell's reputation. In Kenyon, the naive and vexing Jarrell, despite brilliant qualities, seemed limited by boyishness, unlovely clothes and abstract (rather than intuitive) intelligence. He did not quite fit in—as the Lowells always did—and might even have been Negro, Jewish or South American. He lived quietly in remote and boring Greensboro, far from the blaze of public acclaim, and cultivated cats instead of children. (Lowell had a daughter and a son.) He was a difficult man, a savage but superb critic. He wrote the best war poetry (which wiped out Karl Shapiro and did not compete with Lowell's pacifist work), but did not equal Elizabeth Bishop, let alone Lowell himself. Reduced to a series of aphorisms and anecdotes, and relegated to the realms of prose, Jarrell was, as Shapiro observed, no match for his powerful rival. Though Jarrell had some initial advantages—he was older, had a wider range of learning and published his first book four years earlier—Lowell quickly outdistanced and demolished him.

3

Randall Jarrell and John Berryman

I

Berryman's background was less distinguished than Lowell's but more genteel than Jarrell's. Born (like Jarrell) in 1914, Berryman grew up in small towns in Oklahoma and Florida before moving to New York City when he was twelve. Berryman attended South Kent School in Connecticut, Jarrell went to a public high school in Nashville. Berryman graduated from Columbia and Clare College, Cambridge; Jarrell from Vanderbilt and Kenyon. Berryman's teachers were Mark Van Doren and his Princeton colleague, Richard Blackmur; Jarrell's were Ransom, Tate and Warren. Berryman's closest friends were Jewish writers, Delmore Schwartz and Saul Bellow; Jarrell's were Lowell, Peter Taylor and Robert Fitzgerald. Both men were extremely learned (though Berryman never finished most of his major projects); but Berryman was the more daring and impressive poet.

As poetry became part of American academic life after the Second World War, the typical contemporary poet–critic associated himself with established values and sought patronage and honors that would support his work and verify his artistic stature. Though the unstable poet often seemed a dubious candidate to the institutions that funded the arts, Berryman won fellowships from the Rockefeller and Guggenheim foundations, from the National Endowment for the Arts and the National Endowment for the Humanities, and was a United States Information Agency lecturer in India. Jarrell lectured at the Salzburg Seminars and was Poetry Consultant at the Library of Congress.

The two poets had very different temperaments. Jarrell led an orderly and integrated life (until 1964), was unusually prudish and repressed, "didn't drink or smoke, disapproved of gossip and sexual innuendoes in conversation, and had no tolerance for small talk." Berryman (like Lowell) led a chaotic and fragmented personal life: he was wild and uninhibited, a chain-smoker and alcoholic, a compulsive womanizer, a great literary gossip. Friends like Taylor, Tate, Snodgrass and Lowell, who felt that Jarrell was arrogant and abrasive, also found Berryman unpleasant and even unbearable. Snodgrass thought that any sort of conversation with Berryman was "'incredibly valuable,' yet 'he did turn those sessions so painful that you finally fled howling.'" Lowell agreed that "hyperenthusiasms made him a hot friend, and could also make him wearing to friends . . . no one had John's loyalty, but you liked him to live in another city."[1] Both Jarrell and Berryman grew long, mask-like beards toward the end of their lives as they changed their public images and developed their public personae. The witty and elegant Jarrell, smartly dressed in an expensive suit and homburg hat, was photographed by Philippe Halsman behind the steering wheel of a Mercedes-Benz. The eccentric and unkempt Berryman, his eyes as wild as his beard, was portrayed in *Life* magazine holding forth in Dublin pubs and making vatic pronouncements amid crumbling stone ruins.

The most traumatic event in Berryman's life and most obvious reason for his emotional turmoil was the suicide of his father, John Smith, in Tampa in June 1926. Berryman obsessively returned to his father's grief and fear, and to his own feelings of desolation and rage, in his late works: *The Dream Songs* (1969), *Recovery* (his novel about alcoholic rehabilitation, published posthumously in 1973) and *Henry's Fate* (1977). In the last he regretted the emotional es-

trangement and powerful death wish that prevented the
father from loving the son, the son from helping the father.

In one Dream Song he objectively suggested that self-
murder was inevitable, that early one morning, his father took
his gun, went outside near Berryman's window and did what
he had to do. In another he sadly accepted his father's fatal
legacy:

> in a modesty of death I join my father
> who dared so long agone to leave me.
> A bullet on a concrete stoop
> close by a smothering southern sea.

But Berryman was brutally honest about his own degradation
and desire for vengeance in a journal entry of 1954, which
described how his father posthumously but deliberately
mocked and then eliminated his son like a piece of excrement:
"So [my] dream is my bloody father looking down at me,
whom he's just fucked by killing himself, making me into a
shit: and taunting me before he flushes me away."[2] Berryman's
psychotherapy encouraged not only a recollection and
interpretation of dreams, but also—thirty years after the
event—an element of self-pity. He subjectively shifted the
emphasis from his father's real suffering to the effect of the
suicide on himself, and attributed to his parent vengeance,
hostility and malign intent. The degrading dream shows that
he was never able to accept his father's death, and this
unresolved conflict formed the core of his art. As with the
other three poets, the loss of the father and fractured family
was a dominant theme in Berryman's work.

His father's suicide inevitably poisoned his relations with
his mother and his wife. He believed his mother had driven his
father to kill himself and was now free to focus her malign
influence on himself. And he made his wife (a substitute
mother) share his suffering during periods of depression and
mania.

Martha Berryman married her friend, and perhaps lover,
John Angus Berryman, only two and a half months after her

husband's suicide. Her son dropped the plebeian Smith, adopted his stepfather's name and later told his first wife: "This act of disloyalty I will never, never be able to repair." In order to eliminate his guilt and release himself from the stranglehold of his "unspeakably powerful possessive adoring MOTHER," Berryman (when drunk, and in a far-fetched fashion) blamed her for the death of his father and for the destruction of her sons. He also rationalized the suicide by placing himself in the Hemingway tradition and realizing the literary potential of family tragedy: "she helped destroy my father . . . affairs . . . [intermittent heavy drinking]; horribly weakened my [younger] brother; would never, and *still* hasn't let go of me in *any* degree—e.g., *in*terminable letters, clips, incessant battering harangue. SEDUCTIVE. . . . Did I myself feel any *guilt* perhaps—long repressed if so, and mere speculation now (defence here)—*about Daddy's death*? (I certainly picked up enough of Mother's self-blame to accuse her once, drunk and raging, of having actually murdered him and staged a suicide.) . . . Gun-death at dawn, like Hemingway's, imitating his father."[3]

Berryman was never able to resolve his Oedipal conflicts. He had got rid of his father and sexual rival, but found that John Smith was immediately replaced by an even more formidable antagonist. He could neither shift the feelings of disloyalty and guilt about his father's death on to his mother nor deal with his profound disgust about Martha's sexual relations with his new stepfather.

Berryman's emotional turbulence continued at school and during his first marriage. In 1931, while at South Kent, he attempted suicide by throwing himself on railroad tracks as a train approached and was pulled off just in time. In 1942 he married the "sandy-haired mild good and most beautiful / most helpless and devoted" Eileen Mulligan. "He was," she said, "her closest relative: the father who had died when she was a child; the brother she never had; and most binding of all, the teacher who had formed her." In the summer of 1943, at a despairing point in his life, when Berryman failed to get reappointed at Harvard and had to sell encyclopedias to the occupants of Harlem tenements, he leaped onto a high ledge and threatened to jump. With Berryman impatient for death, suicide became Eileen's adversary: "John's life had become a high-wire act. He was flirting with his subtle foe in the certainty that there was an invisible net, held by me, which would catch him should he lose his footing."[4] By demanding that Eileen succeed where his mother had failed and protect him from death Berryman subjected her to a constant and unbearable strain.

Their next major crisis occurred in Princeton in 1947 when Berryman had his first adulterous love affair with the golden-haired, heart-breaking and inspiring "Lise," the wife of a colleague, whom he later celebrated in *Berryman's Sonnets* (1967). He began drinking heavily with his mistress, kept on after the affair ended and eventually became an alcoholic. But he refused to accept blame for his infidelity and told Eileen that he had actually experienced more suffering than satisfaction: "Surely you must see that there is little pleasure to be had from all this. It's a disease, an *illness*." He used his illness to justify his behavior and achieve sexual freedom, but his suffering came more from the torture of love and the loss of Lise than from his guilt about Eileen.

Berryman later denied his own responsibility for drinking in another disingenuous comparison with physical illness: "an alcoholic is not more responsible for his vices than the gangrene victim for his stench. Both offend, innocent, feeling ineradicable guilt, with shame and rage." In *Recovery*, Berryman blamed the break-up of their marriage on "liquor and bad sex." Eileen confirmed that "both had made life intolerable off and on during the second half of our marriage. But it was more his need to live in turbulence . . . that finally forced me to make my decision." The emotional turbulence that stimulated Berryman's poetry also drove Eileen to the breaking point. In the fall of 1953, after they had returned from a summer in Europe, she told Berryman she was leaving him and he accepted "'the worst words ever spoken to him' with 'horror and assent.'"[5]

In her novel *The Maze*, published three years after
Berryman's death, Eileen Simpson (who had become a
psychotherapist) explained the principal reasons for the
dissolution of their marriage: his selfish demands, emotional
dominance, childish dependence, reckless drunkenness and
sexual infidelity. An admirer summarizes their relations when
he tells Benjamin Bold's wife, Roxana: "He's the great man.
He makes a mess. You clean up after him. Why? Is the care
and feeding of poets so damned interesting? I doubt it. And as
for his compulsive sleeping around. . . . You've completely
submerged your personality to his. . . . He tries to hold you by
whipping up excitement about his work. When that fails, he
reminds you how much he needs you."

When Benjamin becomes drunk and violent, Roxana is
terrified and sees him as a wild and dangerous animal: "His
eyeballs looked as if they had floated loose from their sockets.
His lips were drawn back in a gash, his teeth bared in a
grimace of pain. He looked like a frantic horse tethered in a
burning barn. . . . With a tongue honed to a rapier sharpness,
and a pen to serve his animus and rage, he had never, until
now, needed physical violence." In the novel, Simpson also
portrayed Berryman's belief that the artist must seek and
suffer misery in order to pay for and to stimulate his poetic
gift: "Benjamin courts, even collaborates with disaster. He has
a very limited tolerance for happiness. I sometimes think that
if he felt he wasn't paying a high enough price for his gift he
would get panicky, afraid that his talent might dry up. So he
keeps the turbulence going all the time." Lowell expressed the
same idea in "The Severed Head" when he described how a
desperate writer tried to complete his manuscript with his
own blood, which dripped like red ink from a plaster tube in
his heart.[6]

The role of poetry was paramount in Berryman's life and
he was driven by ambition to achieve pre-eminence in this art.
But his extraordinary achievement could never be adequately
recognized by a materialistic society that remained profoundly
indifferent to literature. Forced to lead an economically and

emotionally precarious existence during his marriage to
Eileen—who was the one stable point in his life—he became
desperate to gain recognition from the poets he respected.
Like the other three poets, Berryman equated creation with
suffering so that he could find some positive value in his
tormented life. Once he discovered that readers were fascinated
by his private grief and agony, he began to channel his
anguish into his poems.

II

Berryman was notorious for his fanatical jealousy and intense
competitiveness toward other poets. "Crane's bad luck under
Kipling," he said, "mine no doubt under Lowell." He wanted
his friends to succeed but feared his literary rivals would
threaten his own career, and felt guilty for envying instead of
admiring their success. Speaking, in a late interview, of his
early lack of recognition (and thinking of Lowell's early fame),
Berryman admitted: "I overestimated myself, as it turned out,
and felt bitter, bitterly neglected."[7] He knew his early work
did not deserve to be praised, but felt nevertheless that he
ought to be admired.

Berryman and Jarrell extended their competition to every
aspect of life, including the relatively trivial yet revealing area
of sport. Tennis, for example, provided an outlet of aggression
and a relief from the torments of art, and expressed their social
and sexual conflicts, their individual ambitions and their
narcissistic drives. They inevitably carried their inflated egos
from the study to the court and competed as ruthlessly in
sporting as in literary life.

For Berryman and Jarrell, the introspective sport encouraged self-analysis and self-laceration, for both wanted to be
much better than they actually were. In one of his Dream
Songs, Berryman observed: "This world is a solemn place,
with room for tennis." But he talked about the game far better
than he played it. As an awkward fifteen-year-old prep-school

boy, he had confessed not only to double but also to multiple faults: "I judge bounces very poorly, my foot work is terrible, I don't watch the ball closely enough, I am late getting in position, my strokes are incorrectly produced, my service is a series of double-faults, etc. In fact, I'm ashamed to appear on the court."[8] And in "Tennis in Middle Age," he lamented that he was always beaten by an inferior player (his wife).

But he disguised and compensated for his defeats by engaging in verbal contests with Jarrell. Eileen described "how they bragged! John, who ached to play well (but was temperamentally rather than physically unsuited to the game), bragged that he had once been ballboy for Helen Wills at Forest Hills. Randall could top that and did. They recalled games they'd seen, exchanged stories about memorable shots. Listening to them was like watching a match."[9] These poets—in their lives as in their work—were egoistic, aggressive, even violent: eager for victory and angry in defeat.

In 1939, before Berryman and Jarrell had met, and before Lowell had begun to publish his mature poetry, Tate stimulated the competition and presciently told Berryman: "you and Jarrell are the best of your generation." The two poets appeared together (with twenty poems each) in their first book, *Five Young American Poets*, published by New Directions in 1940. Both wrote a "Note on Poetry" to preface their verse. Berryman somewhat self-consciously and pedantically proposed "to paraphrase the poem called 'On the London Train' and examine some of the differences between the methods of prose and of verse." Jarrell, much more confident and sophisticated at this stage of their careers, stressed "the fundamental kinship of modern and romantic poetry,"[10] an argument he would refine and recycle in "The End of the Line" (*Nation*, February 1942).

In Ransom's vitally important evaluation of their poems in the *Kenyon Review* (Summer 1941), Jarrell received one and a half pages of qualified praise while Berryman got only half a paragraph. Perhaps recalling Jarrell's exclamation while skiing at Kenyon: "I feel like an angel," Ransom stated: "I think Jarrell is quite the most brilliant of the five. . . . He has an angel's velocity and range with language, and drops dazzling textures of meaning done up in a [consistent] phonetic raggedness." But Ransom was much less enthusiastic about Berryman, who was then unknown to him, and used an adjective that would never again be applied to Berryman's work: "The most technically balanced and artistically satisfactory are Berryman and [George Marion] O'Donnell. . . . Berryman is the more reliable, and also seems to have the bigger and wholesomer [!] range of interest."

In the *Partisan Review* (May–June 1941) Tate briskly noted that "Mr. Jarrell's introduction is easily the best. . . . Mr. Berryman's self-scrutiny is intelligent but unnecessary"— because the poems had to stand on their own and be judged by others. Like Ransom, Tate thought Jarrell was the better poet and seemed to praise Berryman without actually doing so: "At present even Jarrell and Berryman, the most brilliant of the five, do not quite come off. . . . Nevertheless, so far as I can see, Jarrell is the best we have to offer as a white hope for poetry in his generation. He has written three or four poems that can compete without embarrassment with the best of our time. At a glance Berryman looks still better, and he may actually be better; though I doubt it. . . . His line has more firmness and structure than Jarrell's. . . . So in his way he is bolder than Jarrell, line by line, but within a structural timidity of feeling which I believe comes of his too great reliance upon Yeats."[11] Tate suggested that Berryman perhaps had greater potential talent than Jarrell and that if he could free himself from the inhibiting influence of Yeats, he might eventually surpass his rival.

Jarrell, himself a keen competitor, agreed with the judgment of his mentors and disparaged his young rival in a letter to Tate: "I think Berryman has a pretty inferior feel for language for one thing; and to talk about your old favorite, the poetic subject, he's obviously not really found his." Jarrell— who evaluated all the poets of his time and was expert in exposing their weaknesses—confirmed this opinion in a mocking review of the *New Directions: 1941* anthology, which justly emphasized Berryman's lack of originality and awkward early style: "John Berryman's 'Five Political Poems' have lots of Yeats, lots of general politics, a 1939 reissue of *1938*, and a parody of 'Lord Randall' ['Communist'] that—but nothing can make me believe that Mr. Berryman wrote this himself, and is not just shielding someone."[12]

The anthologist and poetaster Oscar Williams also reviewed the collection of five poets and disagreed with the ex-cathedra judgment of Ransom and Tate. Williams' statement that Jarrell had a forced rather than a natural talent started a war with Jarrell that lasted for the next five years: "The volume is at its best in John Berryman and at its worst in Randall Jarrell. . . . Jarrell is the re-write man, the will-to-be-a-poet with no talent. But his intolerable cleverness bores me." There was an element of truth in Williams' criticism, but it was hard for Jarrell to accept it from a third-rate hack writing in an undistinguished magazine.

Jarrell waited until 1946 for his revenge and then retaliated with devastating effect. Reviewing Williams' *A Little Treasure of Modern Poetry* for the *Nation* (February 1946), Jarrell ironically noted: "The book has the merit of containing a considerably larger selection of Oscar Williams' poems than I have ever seen in any other anthology. There are nine of his poems—and five of Hardy's. It takes a lot of courage to like your own poetry almost twice as well as Hardy's."[13] And Jarrell produced the definitive and fatal condemnation when he wittily declared that Williams' verse "gave the impression of having been written on a typewriter by a typewriter." Though Williams' slight reputation was permanently wrecked, he was also a power in the poetry world and managed to strike the last blow. As Jarrell, coolly feigning indifference, explained to Berryman in September 1946, Williams also deleted Jarrell's work from later editions of his anthologies: "I didn't know about the Little Treasury, though I could have predicted it—I knew that my reviews meant never being put in another Williams anthology, but I didn't know he'd even get to work on the old ones. Poor thing, he doesn't know any better—it's such an innocent response."[14]

III

Berryman was poetry editor of the *Nation* in 1938–39, Jarrell literary editor in 1946–47. During Jarrell's tenure Berryman reviewed Herbert Grierson's *A Critical History of English Poetry* and Cleanth Brooks' *The Well-Wrought Urn*. The poets first met in May 1946 when Margaret Marshall gave a party to introduce Jarrell, her substitute editor. Berryman's wife wrote that he and Jarrell "had corresponded at the time *Five Young American Poets* was published, and knew each other's work intimately, but had never met. John was so eager to talk to the poet he admired, the poet–critic he thought was the most original of their generation." But Berryman (like W. D. Snodgrass) was surprised to find that the sophisticated Jarrell naively "studded his conversations with italics and out of date expressions like 'Gol-ly!,' 'Gee whiz!' and (my favorite) 'Ba-by doll!'—all delivered in a high-pitched twang."[15] He seemed to combine ferocity and malice with vulnerability and childlike sweetness.

In about September 1946, shortly after Jarrell and Berryman had written laudatory reviews of *Lord Weary's Castle*, Lowell, eager for the poets to be friends, came down from New York with Jarrell to dine at the Berrymans' in Princeton. This disastrous pilgrimage was described by Berryman (1965), by Lowell (1972) and by Eileen (1982), but is not mentioned in the biographies of the poets.[16]

Berryman gives the most positive—and defensive—account of the meeting in the memorial volume (edited by Lowell) on Jarrell. The first problem was that Jarrell, the only poet "in the universe" who did not drink, arrived with a hangover from a poisoned canapé. Miserable and malicious, Jarrell directed his venom at Lowell and invented an apocryphal poem "full of characteristic Lowell properties" (including his grandfather and Charon), which Lowell did not find amusing. In Berryman's description, the evening at his house ended harmoniously, with Jarrell, the pampered invalid, comfortably covered on the couch and looking at a book: "While the rest of us had dinner, he lay there and made witty remarks about the photographs of the Russian ballet."

Lowell's more honest and incisive account of the "mis-encounter" in his obituary of Berryman admitted that the "two talents with so much in common failed to jell. . . . John was a prodigy; compared with Randall, a slow starter." Lowell, who did not mention Jarrell's "hangover" and referred only to his chills and fever on the way home, put the blame more on Berryman's awkwardness than on Jarrell's arrogance. Berryman "jarred the evening" by playing his favorite records. When this failed to animate his guest they switched to discussing ballet. Jarrell, whose greater authority was based on "forty, recent, consecutive nights of New York ballet," demolished Berryman's judgments with his own cool, odd and undoubtedly condescending evaluations. When Berryman complimented Jarrell on his review of *Lord Weary*, he accepted with a "glib croak" and did not return the flattery. On the way home Jarrell, who had a high, keyed-up voice, "analyzed John's high, intense voice with surprise and coldness."[17] Berryman, the insulted and injured, recovered sooner than Jarrell, who was coddled and covered by Lowell's coat (as he had been on Berryman's couch) on the slow train back to New York.

In Eileen's memoir, which adds valuable details and comes closest to the truth, Lowell found Jarrell's canapé hangover hilariously funny. Jarrell could not face food and listlessly participated in the conversation. But when Berryman tried to distract and amuse him, the invalid turned peevish. He criticized Berryman's taste in music as well as in ballerinas (whom, Lowell said, Jarrell had never seen): " 'You don't really like X, do you? She's *so* awful.' Or with mock compassion, 'Poor old Y. She was no *real* good.' " Eileen blamed the disaster on "what Cal called Randall's disconcerting habit of not

Randall Jarrell and John Berryman

distinguishing between what he said to one's face and behind one's back"; and added (as Lowell later told her) that Jarrell's invective continued after they had left Princeton: "All the way to New York, Randall kept up his abusive attack on John, convincing Cal that, far from bringing his two friends together, he had driven them apart." Eileen revealed that the "monumental flop" plunged Berryman into gloom for a whole week. He was unable to work, crushed by doubts and deeply depressed by Lowell and Jarrell's "façade of iron self-confidence."[18]

Berryman's version suppressed the meanness that had hurt him so deeply and pretended it had been quite a pleasant evening. Lowell's account left out his own malicious delight in Jarrell's illness and Jarrell's mockery of his poems. Lowell loyally diminished Jarrell's nastiness and claimed that it did no harm to Berryman. Though he portrayed himself as Cal the Peacemaker, he actually got intense pleasure from pitting the poets against one another and having them compete for his favor. Eileen's more objective description, when read in conjunction with the earlier ones, suggests that Jarrell, anxious to protect his friendship with Lowell against a threatening rival, used his illness as an excuse to attack both Lowell's poetry and Berryman's taste in ballet. His brilliant display during dinner, like his vituperation on the train, was intended to demolish the defenseless Berryman and to make Lowell feel guilty about praising their host. Though Jarrell dominated the dinner, he behaved very childishly, demanded all the attention and forced others to accept his dogmatic views. Lowell coped with this by mild ridicule and refused to be bothered by Jarrell's prima donna performance. But Berryman, too polite and insecure to defend himself against Jarrell's malicious remarks, became the real victim of the evening. The tri-focal incident reveals that the poets' friendship was extremely precarious, that every well-intentioned meeting took place on a minefield where anxiety about status and anger against rivals could always explode.

Berryman admired Jarrell's work more than Jarrell

admired his, just as Jarrell esteemed Lowell's work more than Lowell esteemed his. In both cases the most admired poet held the power. In a composite review of ten poetry books in *Partisan Review* (February 1948), Berryman (knowing his own book was about to appear) referred to Jarrell as a "sensitive and experienced critic" and said he had been re-reading his "favorite sestinas from Arnaut to Jarrell." (Daniel Arnaut, the Provençal troubadour and one of Pound's great enthusiasms, was rather exalted company for Randall.) No wonder, then, that Jarrell sent a generous letter praising the review. Berryman, whose emotional barometer fluctuated with the mood of the moment, was immensely gratified and—willfully ignoring the fact that his own flattery had lubricated the friendship—exclaimed: "If I can excite Jarrell by what I write, anything is possible."[19]

Vacillating between overweening confidence and debilitating despair, Berryman waited anxiously for Jarrell's influential judgment of his second book, *The Dispossessed*. In the *Nation* (July 1948) Jarrell took the tone of a teacher toward a pupil, repeated (with a pun on the title of the book) that Berryman was too strongly influenced by Yeats, praised "Winter Landscape" (the poem inspired by Brueghel's painting, which had originally appeared in *Five Young American Poets*) but criticized most of the book. He rightly saw Berryman as a promising and developing, though not yet fully mature poet: "John Berryman is a complicated, nervous, and intelligent writer whose poetry has steadily improved. At first he was possessed by a slavishly Yeatsian grandiloquence which at best resulted in a sort of posed, planetary melodrama, and which at its worst resulted in monumental bathos. . . . A good critic, he had felt, understood, and remembered only too well the effects of half a dozen contemporary poets, and these effects kept cropping up in his own poems; but without them, he could write as impersonal and nostalgic a poem as 'Winter Landscape'. . . . The style—conscious, dissonant, darting; allusive, always over- or undersatisfying the expectations which it is intelligently exploiting—seems to fit Mr.

Berryman's knowledge and sensibility surprisingly well, and ought in the end to produce poetry better than the best of the poems he has written so far in it." But Berryman, desperate for unqualified praise, felt that Jarrell and Lowell, protected by their self-confident façade, were "withholding from him their 'indispensable' approbation."[20] He feared he could not compete with them on equal terms, and believed the personal and critical approval of the only peers he recognized was essential to the realization of his poetic achievement, his literary reputation and his worldly career.

Jarrell and Berryman met in New York in December 1948, shortly after Eileen had fallen off her bike and badly hurt her back. A poor judge of mental illness, despite his training in psychology, Jarrell told Lowell that "Berryman seemed very nervous and hurried, because of his wife's illness I'm sure." But when they both had temporary jobs teaching writing at Princeton during 1951–52—Berryman still married to Eileen but Jarrell alone after the dissolution of his first marriage— they found each other stimulating and entertaining. Jarrell's letters to his fiancée, Mary, allow us to chart the development of their friendship.

In September 1951 Jarrell defined Berryman's essential characteristics and said: "John's nice, too, but thoroughly neurotic." The following month he mentioned Berryman's praise of his work (as Berryman had mentioned Jarrell's praise to Eileen): "I had a very nice time with the Berrymans at dinner at their house: stayed till late. Berryman was very complimentary about my . . . Auden pieces. . . . I agree with what you said about Berryman's poems. But he's very intelligent and nice and Disinterested: and believe me, *that's* rather rare among Our Intellectuals. One thing that ought to endear him to you and me: he's almost the only poet I know of who has written one or two poems influenced by mine."[21] Gratified by Berryman's flattering praise of his work, which he mistook for disinterestedness, Jarrell began to feel that Berryman's poetic defects were more than balanced by his admirable personal qualities. Jarrell's influence on Berryman, which he claimed but did not specify, remains vague and unconvincing. Lowell, by contrast, had a clear and potent influence on both his contemporaries and his disciples.

In the following months Jarrell, with mock modesty, reported Berryman's commendation of his criticism, again praised his generosity and his learning, and began to discover a sympathetic companion under the prickly surface: "Berryman astonished me by saying he thought and had thought for many years that I was the best reviewer of poetry alive. Was I dazzled and grateful. . . . Berryman has such a nice feeling of dis-interestedness and consciousness-of-the-centuries-and-other-lands. . . . [At a party,] mostly I talked to John Berryman, some to his wife, I certainly do like him. He's a quite touchingly modest person under the surface." But in May, when he heard rumors of Berryman's sexual boasts and adventures, the prissy Jarrell (who remained chaste while awaiting his second marriage), began to mock his friend. Mutual acquaintances "told me some unimaginably funny stories," he said, "about John Berryman as The Great Unappreciated Theoretical Lover."[22]

Berryman's review of *Poetry and the Age* in the *New Republic* (November 1953) generously confirmed in print what he had been saying in person. He placed Jarrell with the first critics of poetry, noted his unerring judgment and discernment of quality, and praised his frank, pragmatic method, which concentrated (like the best of the New Critics) on the meaning and merits of the poem: "This is, I believe, the most original and best book on its subject since *The Double Agent* [1935] by R. P. Blackmur and *Primitivism and Decadence* [1937] by Yvor Winters. . . . It exhibits fully the qualities that made Jarrell the most powerful reviewer of poetry active in this country for the last decade. . . . A salient truth about Jarrell, for the present reader, is that he is seldom wrong. . . . One cannot but remark on the healthy breadth of Jarrell's taste. . . . His neglect to theorize about poetry, to theorize above all about criticism, is one of the most agreeable features of a prepossessing and engaging book."

Berryman and Jarrell were two of the stars of the National Poetry Festival in Washington in October 1962, when Delmore Schwartz went berserk and Berryman loyally rescued him from jail. (Jarrell, self-absorbed and preoccupied with the conference, was completely unaware that anything unusual had happened.) Their last communication took place in June 1963 when Berryman wrote an enthusiastic letter to Jarrell, who had perceived the elusive unity of the Dream Songs, insisting that "there's one thematic norm, one personality, one diction, one set of dramatic arrangements."[23]

IV

Jarrell had published five volumes of poetry between 1940 and 1951, but there was a nine-year gap before *The Woman at the Washington Zoo*, one-third translations from Rilke, appeared in 1960. In the 1960s, as his poetic inspiration diminished, he concentrated on translations, anthologies, criticism and children's books. In his essay on Wallace Stevens, written when he was 37, Jarrell observed that poets have no choice about waiting for the spark of heaven to fall: "A good poet is someone who manages, in a lifetime of standing out in thunderstorms, to be struck by lightning five or six times. . . . A man who is a good poet at forty *may* turn out to be a good poet at sixty; but he is more likely to have stopped writing poems." And his second wife wrote: "The half-alive poet/artist may reckon with arid and idea-less attacks as Randall did, saying for a while, 'It's cyclical,' and writing 'Believe, my heart, Believe!' on scraps of paper all around the house. Also, he can read—as Randall did—all that the Germans have to say about the crisis in the poet's ego that causes his creative paralysis." But these desperate attempts at resignation, incantation and reflection did very little good when inspiration failed. Jarrell suffered from that "morbidness which not infrequently casts a shadow on the mind of the ignored innovator."[24] In the mid-1960s he feared he might never recover his creative powers.

Jarrell's morbid depression was all too apparent to close friends who met him in 1965. Hannah Arendt recalled: "When I last saw him, not long before his death, the laughter was almost gone, and he was almost ready to admit defeat." Although Jarrell had been severely damaged for several years, Mary was too close to her husband to foresee the disaster that occurred in January 1965 and confined Jarrell to a private hospital in Chapel Hill: "Randall's nervous breakdown was showing signs that all but we could see. . . . Before it was through with us, this ordeal called forth a desperate valor we'd never known we had. . . . When the doctors let him come home again, Randall was not as good as new, but he was recovering."[25]

The reviews of *The Lost World*, which appeared while Jarrell was in the psychiatric ward, must have intensified his depression. Friends like Philip Booth and William Meredith praised the book; Jean Garrigue, Samuel Moon and W. J. Smith also wrote favorable notices. But the negative reviews, which repeated the old charges of sentimentality and self-pity, had a greater emotional impact on the hypersensitive invalid who had written so many cruel reviews. Joseph Bennett wrote in the widely read *New York Times Book Review*: "His work is trashy and thoroughly dated; prodigiousness encouraged by an indulgent and sentimental Mamaism, its overriding feature is doddering infantilism." This savage judgment was re-inforced by the more persuasive and influential critics, Paul Fussell and Roger Sale, and by Jarrell's younger rival, James Dickey, who had come up to Vanderbilt when Jarrell was still the prototype of the brilliant promising poet. In the *American Scholar*, Dickey exposed the crucial weaknesses of his poetry: "In Jarrell there is a pervasive and disquieting flatness. . . . He generally does not hold out long enough for the truly telling phrase, for the rhythm that matches exactly the subject, the image, the voice."[26]

Jarrell resumed teaching at Greensboro in the fall term but returned to Chapel Hill for further medical treatment on October 10. Four days later, while walking alone at night on a busy highway about a mile and a half south of town, he was struck by a car. The front page of the *Chapel Hill Newspaper* of October 15, 1965, which had a photograph of the damaged car, reported: "Jarrell was walking south, facing oncoming traffic, when the accident happened at about 7:30 p.m. Graham Wallace Kimrey, 42, of Sanford, was identified as the driver of the car. Jarrell's head struck the right side of the windshield, breaking a large hole in the glass, and threads of his dark clothing were imbedded in the pane on the side of the car, the patrolman reported. Both Kimrey and his wife told the patrolman the victim seemed to whirl, 'as I approached he appeared to lunge out into the path of the car.'"

The *New York Times* of October 15—where most of the literary world read about Jarrell's death—emphasized the mysterious circumstances and was the first newspaper to state it was a suicide: "[Jarrell] was struck by an automobile as he walked along the heavily traveled Chapel Hill bypass, U.S. 15–501. There was no immediate explanation for Mr. Jarrell's presence as a pedestrian on the highway. State Trooper Guy C. Gentry, Jr. said: 'We are going on the assumption that it was a suicide.' He said witnesses reported that the victim 'had lunged into the side of the car that struck him.' No charges were placed against the driver."

The 18-page report of Jarrell's autopsy, authorized on October 15, explained his psychiatric history and the injuries sustained on the night of October 14. The pathologist, Dr. Fred Dalldorf, abstracted his findings in a clearly written two-page "Summary of Case": "The patient had been seen at the North Carolina Memorial Hospital previously for psychiatric difficulties. He had been last hospitalized here [in May] approximately 5 months prior to his death with a manic depressive psychosis, and [in January] just prior to that hospitalization, he had attempted suicide by inflicting multiple cuts on his left arm. At the time of his death, he was receiving outpatient treatment here for these wounds."

Dr. Dalldorf gave the precise diagnosis of Jarrell's mental illness, revealed that he had attempted suicide in January 1965 by deeply slashing the bend and wrist of his left arm (the diagram on the first page of the autopsy report showed "two 4 cm scars left antecubital fossa" and "multiple 4 cm scars left wrist"), and explained that he was at the Chapel Hill Hand Rehabilitation Center in October to repair these severe wounds and restore the use of his left hand—which necessitated a skin graft and "physical therapy for a nerve regeneration pain."

Many factors contributed to Jarrell's suicide: his unhappy childhood, the break-up of his marriage to Mackie Langham in 1951, worries about the health of his mother (who had entered a nursing home in 1965), periods of sterility, fears that he would lose his poetic powers, hostile reviews of his last book of poems, division between his personal life and his poetic ideal, realization that he had not fulfilled his brilliant promise and impossible hopes, marriage problems, severe nervous breakdown, manic-depressive psychosis and the earlier attempt to kill himself. Jarrell's uncharacteristic involvement of the driver and his wife, which risked their lives as he destroyed his own, was probably an attempt to make his suicide seem like an accident. Jarrell had always been an extremist: a man of passionate enthusiasm and intense hostility. These traits were reflected in his all-or-nothing habits, friendships, marriages, criticism—in his life as in his death. Jarrell was apparently not in full control of his mind and body when he lunged into the car on that dark night. But it was will, not fate, that determined his death.

V

The suicide of Jarrell—who died at 51, the same age as his gentle, vulnerable heroes, Proust and Rilke—had a powerful impact on Berryman. He recalled the recent deaths of Frost, Roethke and MacNeice; confessed that "Jarrell's death hit me very hard"; and told their mutual friend William Meredith to convey his feelings of shock and sorrow to his colleague,

Mackie Jarrell. Berryman at first thought Jarrell's self-confidence and childlike quality would have prevented him from killing himself. But he later accepted the *New York Times* report that had called it a suicide.

After acknowledging the truth about Jarrell's death, Berryman placed him in the tradition of alcoholic and suicidal poets who seemed to foreshadow his own fate: "The record is very bad. Vachel Lindsay killed himself. Hart Crane killed himself, more important. Sara Teasdale—quite a good poet at the end, killed herself. Then Miss Plath recently. Randall—it's not admitted, but apparently he did kill himself—and Roethke and Delmore might just as well have died of alcoholism. They died of heart attacks, but that's one of the main ways to die from alcoholism. And Dylan [Thomas] died in an alcoholic coma."[27]

Berryman's obituary essay on Jarrell described his personal reaction to Jarrell's death, their long friendship which began with a correspondence about who else should be included in *Five Young American Poets*, his recollection of the Lowell–Jarrell visit to Princeton in 1946, Jarrell's public quarrel with the sweet-souled Conrad Aiken which "did go beyond the limit" and Jarrell's terror as a reviewer. Though Jarrell's exalted standards frequently allowed him to indulge in savage and apparently pleasurable condemnations, Berryman charitably excused—or forgave—him and explained: "He was immensely cruel, and the extraordinary thing about it is that he didn't know he was cruel." Recalling Jarrell's attitude toward tennis and ignoring the period of sterility at the end of his life, Berryman self-reflectively concluded: "It's a good thing that he had a very successful career, as he did, because he was a hard loser."[28]

The shade of Jarrell wandered restlessly through the Dream Songs, illuminating the themes of bodily decay, loss, fear, guilt and suicide. In song 198 Berryman stated: "I wish all well, / including Mrs. Randall Jarrell," as if to forgive her or compensate for her suffering at Randall's death. In song 7 he mentioned the silent film of 1925 (based on a story by

Conan Doyle) that provided the title of Jarrell's final volume
of poems. In the relatively weak song 121, Berryman called
Jarrell a "bearded corpse" (though he had shaved his beard
shortly before his death), over-praised *The Lost World*, alluded
to his translations from the Brothers Grimm and imagined his
friend's desperate resolution as the death car sped down the
highway.

In his formal elegy, song 90, Berryman portrayed Jarrell's
self-devouring torment and fearful panic as well as his driving
ambition. Berryman also suggested that he would soon give
his friend (who addresses Berryman as "Pussycat," one of
Henry's names in *The Dream Songs*) a familiar greeting in the
land of the dead and that no recognition could possibly equal
the fame he had hoped to achieve. Randall has left us and is at
rest; he died and his panic died with him. The self-torment of
Berryman, who is also heading toward death, cannot do
Randall any good.

In song 127 Berryman was tormented by doubt about the
causes of Jarrell's death, and depicted Jarrell in Limbo—an
uneasy soul who could not rest until the truth was known.
Randall's death was judged a suicide, and Henry felt uneasy
about his loss. He immediately sent a long letter to Randall's
widow to discover what had really happened. Song 262—
addressed to Jarrell, though his name is not mentioned—
recalled Berryman's poems on his father's suicide. Jarrell's
death had unintentionally caused Berryman, his Conradian
double or secret sharer, permanent pain and forced Berryman
to understand, identify with and perhaps follow Jarrell's
destiny—as Marlow had followed Kurtz's to the edge of the
abyss. Though Jarrell would not have wished it, Berryman
shares his friend's terror and watches the despairing spectacle
with love, pity and a kind of admiration.

In the last book of poems published during his lifetime,
Berryman obsessively returned to Jarrell. He placed him with
other sympathetic writer-friends: Lowell, Bellow and Bishop,
and—evoking the name of Jarrell's third book, his absent wife,
Mary, and his two stepdaughters—sealed their bond by

frankly declaring that he had killed himself. Randall expressed his own great theme of loss when he walked into a moving car in a North Carolina night.[29] Nobody realized the seriousness of Jarrell's illness because of his deceptively cultivated and controlled exterior. Berryman was completely surprised by the suicide of his apparently urbane and secure friend, and his poems about Jarrell reveal that Berryman had little understanding of his deeply disturbed emotional life.

4

John Berryman and Robert Lowell

I

Lowell's long and deep friendship with Jarrell was based on the shared experiences of youth, similar teachers and tradition, and respect for Jarrell's critical insight. But Lowell was temperamentally closer to Berryman and their affinity was more emotional than intellectual. Lowell was a leader who rebelled against his family traditions: a Harvard man who left Cambridge for Kenyon, a Puritan and a Protestant who converted to Catholicism, a naval officer's son who was a conscientious objector in the war. Yet Lowell remained an aristocrat and drew on his heritage to nourish his poems. Berryman was a wounded outsider who was always trying to fit in to school, college and academic life. Both poets led emotionally volcanic lives, with eruptions of drink, violence, madness and broken marriages. The passionate Berryman, who had a far greater talent than the prosaic Jarrell, was to Lowell a more serious poetic rival. Robert Fitzgerald perceptively summarized Lowell's relations with his two poet-friends: "Randall Jarrell instructed him, John Berryman rivalled him. Each was a masterly and inspired poet, but neither had quite his range over politics in the grand sense. Both were his friends, and of both he wrote with subtle penetration and affection. . . . No one has equalled in comprehension, precision and sympathy his piece on Berryman's *Dream Songs*."[1]

In his review of Maxwell Geismar's *The Last of the Provincials*, Berryman mentioned in passing that "One or two extraordinary things, like Robert Lowell's poetry, were helped into existence by some of this [modern] criticism."[2] Though he was probably thinking of the seminal influence of Ransom, Tate and Jarrell, Berryman could also claim some significant credit. He proudly remembered proposing some persuasive changes in Lowell's major poem, "The Quaker Graveyard in Nantucket"; and perhaps hinted at this by alluding to Lowell's "IS, the whited monster" in song 237: "they swam toward what may be IS." Berryman's "Boston Common" dealt with Saint-Gaudens' bronze statue of Robert Gould Shaw and his Negro militia twenty years before Lowell's "For the Union Dead." And the title of Lowell's "Tenth Muse" in that volume came from a poem by Berryman's heroine, Anne Bradstreet.

In his *Paris Review* interview Berryman also acknowledged Lowell's potent effect on his own work and suggested that his treatment of New England culture and history in *Homage to Mistress Bradstreet* (1956) was in part a response to *Lord Weary's Castle* (1946): "I see the influence of *Lord Weary's Castle* in some of the later poems in *The Dispossessed* [1948]. There's no doubt about it. In the Bradstreet poem ... I sort of seized inspiration, I think, from Lowell, rather than imitated him." Berryman also expressed his homage to Master Lowell in 1948 by attempting to write a sequence of Eclogues, including one character, Colin, "a dedicated powerful figure," based on his friend.[3] Lowell's famous "Skunk Hour" ends with the image of the mother skunk swilling the garbage pail; song 107 begins: "Three 'coons come at his garbage."

The affinity of the two poets becomes clear when comparing their poems on similar subjects: on the theme of incarceration and on Che Guevara and Rembrandt. Lowell and Berryman borrowed the title of their prison poems from Henry James' "In the Cage" (1898), a story of a romantic but alienated "cage-girl," handling the cryptic telegrams of the great world, who rescues the dashing Captain Everard from a scandal and is rewarded by his profound indifference. Lowell's "In the Cage" (1944), published in *Lord Weary's Castle* and reprinted in *Notebook*, describes his own six months' imprisonment for draft evasion in the Federal Correctional Center at Danbury, Connecticut, during 1943–44. He portrays his fellow inmates—the lifers, a colored fairy, a Bible-twisting Israelite—and notes how "Fear, / The yellow chirper, beaks its cage." (Berryman praised this line in his review of the book.) Berryman's "The Cage" (1950) refers to Pound's capture and imprisonment in the penal cage at Pisa, and describes Berryman's later visit to Pound. Trapped in a hospital for the criminally insane in Washington, Pound tediously rants about the conspiracy of "Bankers and Yids." The poem on Pound also ends with the central metaphor of the empty cage that swings in the wind.[4] Both poems portray the poet as prisoner—isolated from normal society, confined with outcasts and longing to escape.

Both poets wrote elegies on Ernesto "Che" Guevara—the Argentine revolutionary, companion of Castro and martyred hero. After failing to rouse the Andean tin miners, he was wounded, captured and executed by the Bolivian army on October 8, 1967. Lowell's "Che Guevara" unconvincingly compared the last armed prophet to King Charles I, executed by Cromwellian regicides, and sees him as a victim of capitalist corruption. He writes that Che was shot down for money as violence repaid violence. Berryman's longer and looser "Che" is less about the "obstinate, / proud to all hurrying deaths, seductive, amusing, / reckless as a pampas fire" leader (now reduced to "Bolivian molecules, dim slime") than about Berryman's somewhat incoherent response to his sacrificial death. For he refuses to praise, like or fear Guevara.[5] The poets dutifully and rather naively expressed the "revolutionary" sentiments of the sixties in these elegies. Lowell's ideas were consistent with his political beliefs during that period. Berryman's poem, perhaps a response to Lowell's, was more of a forced effort; and he did not choose to publish it in his lifetime.

Lowell's "Rembrandt" is a densely packed fourteen-line
poem that describes two of the artist's greatest paintings: *The
Jewish Bride* and *Bathsheba with David's Letter*. Lowell envied the
profound feeling expressed by the artist and tried to emulate it
in his own life and work. He identifies both with King David
and with Rembrandt; and posits an ideal of marriage that
justifies Bathsheba's commitment to David and was realized
in *The Jewish Bride*. Berryman's "Rembrandt van Rijn obit 8
October 1669" memorializes the three-hundredth anniversary
of his death (on the same day as Che Guevara's) and
emphasizes the neglect, impoverishment and sickness of the
artist at the end of his extraordinarily productive career. His
wife and children are dead, and Rembrandt lies ill in filthy,
furnished rooms in Amsterdam.[6] In April 1948 Berryman
categorically stated: "I see Lowell as my peer. No one else."
But Lowell wrote the first and more impressive poem on each
of these three subjects. Berryman later realized that his own
competitive imitations or sequels on subjects Lowell had
made worthy of poetic treatment were not nearly as powerful
and persuasive.

Lowell and Berryman also expressed similar themes in
their confessional poetry, though (to use Lowell's distinction)
his work was cooked and Berryman's raw. He transformed his
personal experience while Berryman merely transcribed it. A
major theme in *The Dream Songs* is that Henry hates the world
and cannot bear the thought of what it did to him (song 74).
There is something black in his heart (song 92), but he is not
guilty by reason of death (song 86). Berryman's characteristic
ideas are also portrayed in the posthumously published
Henry's Fate. There is guilt (he can tolerate everything but the
tears he invented and put in her eyes), anguish (he values the
wise and necessary words: *malheur* and *angst*), alcoholism (he
always returns to the bars after a week of hospital treatment
for vomiting, convulsions and delirium tremens), drugs (the
sedatives and stimulants, honey in the bloodstream, keep
Henry going, night and day, like a natural man). Lowell wrote
of similar drugs in a similar vein and called himself a

thorazined fixture in a rigid chair. But he also recognized that he could not continue to tolerate the repeated "breakage."[7]

Both Berryman and Lowell believed madness gave the poet a kind of visionary power and put him in touch with deeper truths that were beyond the reach of ordinary men. Both used the thoughts and feelings they had experienced under the influence of mania and drugs as a source for their poetry. And both felt guilty about their mental illness, which contributed to their misery and their depression. Mania also led (in Berryman's case) to his suicide.

When admitted to an elite Boston mental home in November 1962, Berryman said, with a shock of recognition: "Cal's hospital—McLean's." Both poets were given a ticket of leave from their hospitals and came in by cab from Golden Valley or McLean's to teach their classes at Minnesota or Boston University. Berryman, who publicized the hospital experience he shared with Lowell, observed when writing about "Skunk Hour" that in the modern world privacy is unobtainable and "hospital life is unspeakably public—one is available without will to doctors, nurses, even (usually) other patients."[8]

Caroline Blackwood has given a vivid description of her direct experience with Lowell's manic episodes. Though Lowell did not specifically discuss his madness before their marriage, it was understood between them that she knew about it from his friends. When he was normal, it was hard to believe he had been or would be mad. He was frighteningly like two different people. His mania erupted very quickly, sometimes within two hours, and he knew when it was coming. He would feel a deadly tingle crawling up his spine and exclaim: "stop me from going mad!"

When manic he forgot the specters of the past and moved obsessively back to his family trauma—his mother a cruel tyrant, his father a passive slave. His sudden mania, even when he was taking a full dosage of lithium, was terrifying. He would lose his identity, think he was Blackwood and even sign copies of her novels. (In "Double Vision" Lowell recalled:

"While we are talking, I am asking you, / 'Where is Caroline?' And you *are* Caroline.") He lost his sense of time and understanding of danger, and would even put his hand in the fire. He would lock Caroline in a room with him, threaten (without recognizing) her and become a danger to her children, whom she had to get out of harm's way. His behavior was almost enough to send her mad.

Lowell filled reams of paper while manic, but it came out as nonsense and was not at all interesting. He would also revise in a mad way, changing everything for no purpose and parodying his own careful method of creation. Later, when he recovered, he would write lucidly about his illness.

Lowell's doctor said that his medicine affected his heart and was a direct cause of his death. He dreaded having a pacemaker inserted in his chest, did not want to live by artificial means, felt that his life was over and kept saying he was going to die. In "Home," one of his last poems, he wrote: "Less than ever I expect to be alive / six months from now." When Lowell was well, Blackwood thought he would never become ill again. But he lacked the strength to fight his mania; and when he was ill, feared he was doomed to permanent insanity. He believed his mania had destroyed all his personal relations and felt profoundly guilty about this. "I can't make anyone happy," he said, "and am better out of it." Lowell was cruel only when manic. When well, he was charming, amusing, affectionate, cosy and easy to get on with.[9]

The difference of tone and technique in Lowell's and Berryman's shocking and self-loathing confessional poetry becomes evident when "Waking in the Blue" is compared with "The Hell Poem," "Man and Wife" with song 384. In "Waking in the Blue" Lowell wakes in depression, feels the *absence* of family and normal life, locates himself in "the house for the 'mentally ill,'" studies his fellow inmates, sees the shaky future grow familiar, fears his illness may be permanent and feels trapped in the destructive prison symbolized by the locked razor. In "The Hell Poem" Berryman, also in a mental hospital, compassionately describes the deranged inmates

who surround and terrify him, and who delay their return to
the desired but frightful outer world. The patients subjected
to electro-convulsive therapy are threatened with permanent
loss of memory. And the closely confined suicidal cases are
even worse: apathetic, terrified and hopeless behind locked
doors.[10] Berryman, experiencing nightmares of a witches'
sabbath, also feels trapped and fears he may never get well.

The opening line of "Man and Wife"—Lowell's version of
Modern Love—echoes Auden's marvellous lines "Out on the
lawn I lie in bed, / Vega conspicuous overhead." His
mother—whose bed Lowell and his wife lie on, "Tamed by
Miltown"—is a primary cause of his madness. He fainted,
drunk, at Hardwick's feet when they first met twelve years
ago. Now, while the vivid, swift-dying flowers ignite outside
their window, Lowell addresses his wife as if *she* were still his
savior:

> All night I've held your hand
> as if you had
> a fourth time faced the kingdom of the mad—
> its hackneyed speech, its homicidal eye—
> and dragged me home alive.

But she turns her back on him. Sleepless (despite the
Miltown), she regressively clasps the pillow instead of the poet
and pours out her no doubt well-earned invective that breaks
like an ocean on his head. She still cares enough about him to
tell the absolute truth, but he is left defenseless and destroyed
by his madness and his mate. Lowell invites us into his
marriage bed, where there is neither sleep nor sex, to witness
his domestic tragedy. The poem reveals the horrid gulf
between past love and present torment.

Lowell starts with sunrise and his mother, Berryman with
sunset and his father. With considerably more emotion and
anger, Berryman allows us to witness his impotent tirade at
the grave of his parent, who can still hurt him but is himself
beyond pain. He repeatedly makes the punishing pilgrimage

to spit on the dreadful banker who shot himself in the heart at dawn in Florida. Berryman can never accept his father's violent death, which was meant to punish his son, and wants to get right down under the grass until he too is buried and out of his misery. If he must live, then he wants, somehow, to get even with his father (forever separate in his escape to death), chop open the coffin and tear off the mouldering grave clothes to see how he is taking it.[11] But, as he must know, the mad wish to re-kill his father is more self-destructive than cathartic.

Both poems express the frustration, guilt and rage of a helpless victim, and create a powerful impact. But Lowell's emotions, more subtle and complex, more sublimated and controlled, show more insight and evoke more sympathy. His tone of restraint conveys more irony than self-pity as he moves from suffering to self-awareness.

Lowell changed his material into a marvellous poem, a perfect artifact, which contained skillful rhyme and meter, a vivid evocation of the two characters, a mastery of the dramatic scene and a convincing portrayal of their loving and merciless marital discord. Berryman's work, in contrast, was loose and flabby, with no real thought behind it. Berryman appealed to the reader's sense of pity and injustice; Lowell made no such appeal. These poems show that mania gave Lowell poetic power, but crippled Berryman, who expressed raw emotion but rarely succeeded in making great art out of mental illness. In this, as in many other respects, it was possible to emulate but not to equal Lowell's towering achievement.

II

Lowell and Berryman shared another unusual trait. Though both were gentiles, they identified to an extraordinary degree with Jewish culture and character: with the Bible, with intellectual idols like Marx, Freud and Einstein, and with the passionate style of argument in the *Partisan Review* circle. Recalling with vengeful zest Lowell's fixation on his nineteenth-century Jewish ancestor, Major Mordecai Myers, Jean Stafford liked to call A. J. Liebling her "first completely Jewish husband."[12]

In an interview in *Life* magazine, Lowell emphasized the Jewish influence on contemporary culture and associated himself with the spiritual qualities of the Jews: "Jewishness, and not just of the New York variety, is the theme of today's literature. . . . We're lucky to have the Jewish influence. It's what keeps New York alive; not only writers and painters but also the good bourgeois who support the arts. Consider the list of patrons and benefactors of any cultural enterprise. Do I feel left out in a Jewish age? Not at all. Fortunately, I'm one-eighth Jewish myself, which I do feel is a saving grace."

Thinking perhaps of Freud's remark: "Because I was a Jew I found myself free of many prejudices which restrict others in the use of the intellect: as a Jew I was prepared to be in the opposition and to renounce agreement with the 'compact majority,'" Elizabeth Hardwick made the same identification as Lowell. She positively associated Jews with radical thought and responsiveness to Old World culture: "[Even in Kentucky,] my aim was to be a New York Jewish intellectual. I say 'Jewish' because of their tradition of rational skepticism: and also a certain deracination appeals to me—and their openness to European culture . . . the questioning of our arrangements of society, sometimes called radicalism."[13]

Berryman's sympathetic identification with the Jews and emphasis on the Jewish aspect of his own character was even stronger than Lowell's. His second wife, and his close friends Saul Bellow and Delmore Schwartz, were Jewish. He wrote essays on Isaac Babel and Anne Frank. He once planned a long cycle of poems, called "The Black Book," about the Nazi persecution of the Jews and published four sections in *Short Poems*. He began to study Hebrew in 1954 and expressed his ambivalence about being taken for a Jew in *Recovery*: "People

often think I *look* Jewish—resentment, liking." In song 48 he
says that the resurrection, "A Greek idea, / [is] troublesome to
imaginary Jews, / like bitter Henry." And in his major story,
"The Imaginary Jew" (1954), the gentile hero is mistaken for
and symbolically identifies with persecuted and victimized
Jews in order to expiate imaginary transgressions. (Two
postwar novels, Arthur Miller's *Focus*, 1945, and Laura
Hobson's *Gentleman's Agreement*, 1947, have similar themes.)

In his Author's Notes to *Recovery*, Berryman listed his
"Jewish" qualities. He considered his study of Hebrew theo-
logical as well as literary, and wondered if it might be possible
to convert to Judaism:

> Horror of anti-semitism.
> Excitement over Babel! Buber! the Hasidim! Bloch's
>   music!. . . .
> resentment of Cal's tiny Jewish blood. . . .
> [Attraction to] Jewish girls.
> [Enjoyment of] Yiddish stories and slang.
> my Hebrew effort. . . .
> regular Old Testament study at last, this year.
> my anthology of Yiddish poetry! . . .
> unique devotion to *Job*. . . .
> *To become a Jew*—the wonder of my life—it's *possible*! Rabbi
>   Mandel is coming at 2:30.[14]

Lowell and Berryman's cultural Jewishness was a bond that
united them with each other as well as with the Jews
who—like mad poets—were outcasts and victims.

III

Lowell first met Berryman—whom he called a performer and
prima donna—at Princeton, through Allen Tate's wife
Caroline Gordon, in 1944. Eileen Simpson recalled that these
difficult men (like Jarrell and Berryman) did not hit it off well

at first: "The poets, who already knew and admired each other's work, were diffident, Cal scowling and whispering, John holding his head as if his neck [were] in traction."

Things improved considerably, however, when the Berrymans visited Lowell and Jean Stafford at their summer house in Damariscotta Mills, Maine, in July 1946. Between his release from jail in October 1944 and the break-up of his marriage at the end of the summer, Lowell "was enjoying a rare period of equilibrium. . . . Before the publication of *Lord Weary's Castle*, with the fame he had dreamed of in sight, he was still free of the demands fame brings."

Both men were myopic; Lowell affected a Southern accent, Berryman an English one; and they discovered they had similarly unhappy relations with their parents. They talked about poetry by day (the next best thing to writing it) and gossiped by night. Berryman praised Delmore Schwartz's poetry as much as Lowell praised Jarrell's. Berryman "wished that Cal and Delmore admired each other as much as he admired both, and was saddened that there had been a rift between them." Schwartz had hinted that Stafford was interested in another man (perhaps himself) and had been punched by Lowell for intriguing. The Berrymans' visit, by mutual consent, stretched from a weekend to two whole weeks.

On the first evening Berryman was ecstatic and told Eileen: "Aren't they *delicious*? Aren't you glad we came?" But he saw Lowell, who had the good looks of a matinée idol, as an amorous as well as a poetic rival; and after a few days anxiously asked his wife: "You're not falling in love with Cal, are you?" Lowell later recalled that "John was ease and light. We gossiped on the rocks of the millpond, baked things in shells on the sand, and drank, as was the appetite of our age, much less than now."[15] Stafford, whose novel *Boston Adventure* (1944) had just been a great success, brilliantly satirized all her summer visitors in her late story "An Influx of Poets."

Just after the visit, Berryman wrote enthusiastically to Lowell: "I haven't found anyone so pleasant since Delmore in

1939." And in August Lowell replied: "As for your heart, we intend to hold on to it through the formless future." The following spring, in Princeton, the translator William Arrowsmith captured an image of the poets that seemed to symbolize their competitive ascent to Parnassus: "Lowell and Berryman, both barefoot, were climbing up the big sycamore tree which shaded the small, stone Revolutionary house. Lowell was perched at the very top of the tree, on the uppermost branches. Just beneath him, trying to get higher, higher than Lowell, was Berryman. . . . In retrospect, it seemed a nice image of the intense rivalry between these two poets"—with Lowell on top and Berryman failing to reach him.

The dominant themes of Berryman's long and enthusiastic review of *Lord Weary's Castle* in *Partisan Review* (January–February 1947)—emphatically titled "Robert Lowell and Others"—were competition, ambition and the dangers of fame. In a modest and somewhat uneasy disclaimer, he thrice mentioned Jarrell's review of *Land of Unlikeness*, which had appeared in the *Partisan Review* (Winter 1945), as if Jarrell had already said everything significant and his own mopping-up operation could provide only a faint echo of his rival's ideas. And Berryman repeated his praise in a review of Jarrell's *Poetry and the Age* (1953): "*Lord Weary's Castle* was one of the stiffest books to review that has ever appeared. I have reason to know: Jarrell's [in the *Nation* of January 18, 1947] was not only superior—far—to my own attempt: it is probably the most masterly initial review of an important poetic work, either here or in England, of this century."[16]

Thinking, no doubt, of his friendship with Lowell, Berryman began his review with an unconvincing denial: "In some very serious sense there is no competition either on Parnassus or on the hard way up there." But he quickly contradicted himself and added: "Without first-rate qualities, ambition is nothing, a personal disease; but given these qualities, the difference is partly one of ambition. . . . I should say from these poems that this author's ambition is limitless.

... We have before us a genuine, formidable, various, and active poet."

Berryman also invoked the authority of Hopkins and warned that America destroyed its most successful writers: "Popularity in modern American culture proved for other authors not yet physically dead a blessing decidedly sinister. ... 'I say it deliberately and before God,'" Hopkins wrote to Bridges, "'that fame, the being known, though in itself one of the most dangerous things to men, is nevertheless the true and appointed air, element, and setting of genius and its works.'" But Berryman felt, perhaps prematurely, that "Lowell is so intense tough unreasonable that he will probably be safe."

Jarrell had concluded his review of Lowell's book by declaring: "When I reviewed Mr. Lowell's first book I finished by saying, 'Some of the best poems of the next years ought to be written by him.' The appearance of *Lord Weary's Castle* makes me feel ... like a rain-maker who predicts rain and gets a flood. ... One or two of these poems, I think, will be read as long as men remember English." Berryman dutifully echoed Jarrell and stated: "[In these poems] you will observe a talent whose ceiling is invisible."[17] Jarrell's review proudly and confidently proclaimed Lowell's genius; Berryman, more aware of the need to compete and excel as a poet, was more qualified and defensive. He could not praise Lowell without feeling he was hurting himself, and deferred to Jarrell's judgment instead of formulating his own.

Berryman was the Elliston Professor of Poetry at the University of Cincinnati in 1952 and Lowell held this chair in 1954. Between these appointments, in the spring of 1953, both poets taught at the University of Iowa. Paul Engle, director of the writers' workshop, saw the drunken, apparently aggressive Berryman easily suppressed by an older lady. When he told her: "go fuck yourself," she quickly retorted: "if you knew more about women, you'd know that was impossible."[18]

The poets' correspondence resumed after the publication of *Life Studies* in 1959 when Berryman conceded: "You are only the best poet around." When Berryman phoned Lowell

in September 1959 and told him about the break-up of his brief
second marriage, Lowell immediately wrote a sympathetic
and consoling letter (similar to the one he would send to
Jarrell after his mental breakdown in April 1965). Having
been through—and survived—the same mental and marital
problems that Berryman was now experiencing, Lowell had a
profound understanding of his comrade's dejection. He
provided some vital encouragement by praising Berryman's
poetry and by reaffirming their friendship: "I have been
thinking much about you all summer, and how we have gone
through the same troubles, visiting the bottom of the world. I
have wanted to stretch out a hand, and tell you that I have
been there too, and how it all lightens and life swims back.
And it's a sorrow to think of your being alone, seeing your son
and not being with him. I've thought of your dazzling
brilliance, so astonishing to your friends, of reading in
Chicago. . . . Then our talks in Maine, meetings in New York.
There's been so much fellow feeling between us, and for so
long now. . . . The night is now passed, and I feel certain that
your fire and loyalty, and all-outedness carry you buoyantly
on."[19]

A few months later, writing to Edward Hoagland,
Berryman expressed his gratitude for Lowell's praise of the
early Dream Songs and recalled that he had tried to
reciprocate Lowell's kindness with professional and emotional
support: "Two of the men I feel *most* grateful to, with full
reason, are Saul [Bellow] & Cal Lowell. . . . [Cal] wrote me
last week for no reason a letter *so* generous & vivid about my
poem. . . . I try to remember that I helpt him in Maine on the
proofs of *Lord Weary* fifteen years ago & helpt make his
American reputation with an endless review in *Partisan* & held
his hand many times, between marriages (his & mine) in New
York, and when he was going out, and just did a living essay
. . . on his 'Skunk Hour.' "[20]

The title of Berryman's essay, "Despondency and
Madness," came from Wordsworth's "Resolution and
Independence." Thinking of the poet Chatterton, who

poisoned himself at the age of seventeen, after failing to win poetic fame, Wordsworth wrote:

> We Poets in our youth begin in gladness,
> But thereof come in the end despondency and madness.

In the early 1940s Delmore Schwartz, troubled by his own manic depression, made this couplet even more negative:

> We poets in our youth begin in *sadness*
> Thereof in the end come despondency and madness.

Berryman used "Despondency and Madness" in 1962, and twenty years later Eileen Simpson called her memoir *Poets in Their Youth*.

Berryman's most brilliant and personal essay contained a precise New Critical explication of Lowell's masterpiece. He revealed that the poem portrays Lowell's own mental illness (his strength and his weakness), the actual process of going mad as well as the fear of recurrent madness: "Our occasion is the approach of a crisis of mental disorder for the 'I' of the poem—presumably one leading to the hospitalization, or hospitalizations, spoken of elsewhere in the volume, *Life Studies*, where it stands last. Lowell's recent poems, many of them, are as personal, autobiographical, as his earlier poems were hieratic. . . . The poet can be made helpless by what is part of his strength: his strangeness, mental and emotional; the helplessness of a man afraid of going mad. . . . You feel you're going too fast, spinning out of control; or too slow; there appears a rift, which will widen. . . . I would call it virtually certain that Lowell had in mind and at heart during this ['subtle, strong, terrible'] poem not only his own difficulties, whatever they may be or have been, but the personal disorders to which other poets of his age and place have been furiously subject."[21] In discussing Lowell's mania, Berryman described his own.

Lowell was impressed by Berryman's keen insight and

persuasive argument. In March 1962, shortly after the essay first appeared, he reiterated his belief (shared by Berryman) that the poets of his generation were marked for a generic doom: "You've made an amazing guess, more or less a bull's-eye thrust into what was going on when the poem was written— all very dazzling and disturbing. What you said about other poets of our generation is something I've brooded much on. What queer lives we've had even for poets! There seems something generic about it, and determined beyond anything we could do. You and I have had so many of the same tumbles and leaps. We must have a green old age. We have both drunk the downward drag as deeply as is perhaps bearable."

When Berryman's essay was reprinted two years later, Lowell publicly commented on the interpretation. In peeling off the layers of meaning to reveal a troubled psyche, Lowell wrote, his friend had come "too close for comfort": "John Berryman's pathological chart comes frighteningly close to the actual event. When I first read his paper, I kept saying to myself, 'Why he is naming the very things I wanted to keep out of my poem.' In the end, I had to admit that Berryman had hit a bull's-eye, and often illuminated matters more searchingly and boldly than I could have wished."[22]

In his essay on "Skunk Hour" Berryman, who again went out of his way to cite Jarrell's criticism, quoted a superb stanza that Lowell had deleted from "Beyond the Alps" and remarked: "Lowell once told the present writer that the stanza took him a hundred hours; it is worth every second of the time, and may be read, despite its author, for as long as things not formular are read." Lowell followed Berryman's advice, and thanked him in the Note to *For the Union Dead* (1964): " 'Beyond the Alps' is the poem I published in *Life Studies*, but with a stanza restored at the suggestion of John Berryman."[23] The restored stanza, as Berryman perceived, reinforced the dominant thematic polarities in the poem: Caesar–Pope, pagan–Christian, gods–Mary, ruler–poet, Ovid and Lowell as exiles from Rome and the blackness of the earth, sea and Etruscan cup.

After three important poets had died in 1963, Berryman returned to the dark fate of modern poets and the closely related theme of which survivor would be the leader. In September Berryman wrote to Lowell: "Hell of a year, isn't it? Mr. Frost, Ted [Roethke] and now Louis [MacNeice] whom I loved. Keep well, be good. The devil roams." Lowell later returned to this disturbing idea—also expressed in the opening line of song 153: "I'm cross with god who has wrecked this generation"—when he wrote in "Our Afterlife, I" that this year had killed Pound, Edmund Wilson and Auden.[24]

In his late poem "The Heroes," Berryman made a crucially important and extremely revealing statement about his attitude toward his maimed contemporaries. Partly because he lacked a father, he felt a deep-rooted need to hero-worship his fellow writers, who justified his admiration and forgiveness by their weaknesses and their suffering for art. Lowell (as well as Berryman himself, for the hero-worship was also narcissistic) fit perfectly into this familiar pattern:

I had, from my beginning, to adore heroes
& I elected that they witness to,
show forth, transfigure: life-suffering & pure heart
& hardly definable but central weaknesses
for which they were to be enthroned & forgiven by me.

In 1958, using the metaphors of business and sport, Berryman had asked the poet Howard Nemerov an obsessive rhetorical question: " 'Howard, if you ever really made it big, would you want to be the only one? Out there in front all by yourself?' " In January 1963, when Berryman heard that Frost had died, he asked: "It's *scary*. Who's number one? Who's number one? Cal is number one, isn't he?" (Yeats had asked the same question after the death of Swinburne in April 1909, but had declared himself "King of the Cats.") That same month, Berryman claimed he had accepted Lowell's dominance of the poetic arena: "I've been comfortable since [the publication of *Lord Weary's Castle* in] 1946 with the feeling

that Lowell is far my superior." But the question of rivalry
and status continued to torment him. In September 1963,
during a crisis in confidence, he exposed his real attitude
toward his superior and—thinking that he ought to be either
pre-eminent or silent—rather pathetically asked Lowell: "But
why publish verse anyway? It's all right for you to do, but why
the rest of us?"[25]

IV

Lowell played a significant role in encouraging the publication
of Berryman's major work and gave him "the saving idea that
he should publish an interim volume of Dream Songs." Lowell
was discussed in three of the poems. And he wrote an
important review of *77 Dream Songs* in the *New York Review of
Books* in May 1964 (his first piece on the poet), which helped
to establish Berryman's serious reputation.

Lowell snaked cautiously into the reckless and tortured
Dream Songs by first describing Berryman's extraordinarily
frenetic and erudite character: "one heard of his huge library,
his phonograph installed by [the music critic] Bernard
Haggin, his endless ability to quote poetry, and his work on a
conclusive [but uncompleted] text of *King Lear*. . . . He was
disciplined yet bohemian; unorthodox in the ardor of his
admirations, and yet so catholic and generous that he was
hampered in finding his own voice." After a brief discourse on
the early poetry and the influence on Berryman of Auden,
Pound, Stevens and Cummings, Lowell turned to the dis-
ordered, hallucinatory, hazardous and imperfect book. It is
worth noting that Lowell, disturbed and puzzled by the "not
quite intelligible" songs, had to correct a "foolish mistake" the
following month. Guided by Berryman, Lowell stated: "Mr.
Bones is not 'one of the main characters,' but the main
character, Henry."[26] Still later he regretfully admitted:
"I misjudged them, and was rattled by their mannerisms."
Though Lowell was unable to contribute to the *Harvard*

Advocate issue on Berryman in 1969, he sent a brief letter that called the "*Dream Songs*, now completed, one of the glories of the age, the single most heroic work in English poetry since the War, since Ezra Pound's *The Pisan Cantos*."[27]

After his review had appeared in 1964, Lowell confirmed his admiration in a letter to the poet William Meredith: "In this book, he really is a new poet, one whose humor and wildness make other new poets seem tame. I read him with uncertainty and distress and quite likely envy, which is a kind of tribute." But to Berryman qualified praise, especially from Lowell, was no praise at all: "Supreme my holdings, greater yet my need" (song 64). He was disappointed by Lowell's remarks on his mannerism and incoherence ("Henry's queer baby talk was at first insufferable to me") and by his failure to see that Henry and Mr. Bones were the same character. In 1966 Berryman explained the reasons for Lowell's confusion to an interviewer: "In his review in New York, Lowell took Mr. Bones to be a different character [from Henry], and in fact he made all kinds of mistakes. He wrote the review hurriedly and I was in hospital and didn't correct him until it was too late to get into print. Well, he's apologized in print, but nobody ever sees the apology. All they see is the original version."[28] Lowell's mistake and correction (not "apology") prompted Berryman to include a useful explanation of his hero–victim in a Note to the complete *Dream Songs* (1969): "The poem . . . is essentially about an imaginary character (not the poet, not me) named Henry, a white American in early middle age sometimes in blackface, who had suffered an irreversible loss and talks about himself sometimes in the first person, sometimes even in the second; he has a friend, never named, who addresses him as Mr. Bones."

Berryman consoled himself by publishing in one of his own essays Lowell's praise of *Homage to Mistress Bradstreet* (in the review of *77 Dream Songs*): "it was with interest that I found Robert Lowell pronouncing it lately, in *The New York Review*, 'the most resourceful historical poem in our literature.'" He was also pleased by Lowell's letter expressing admiration for songs 78–91: "The Opus posth. poems seem to me the crown of your wonderful work, witty, heart-breaking, all of a piece. Somehow one believes you on this huge matter of looking at death and your whole life."[29] The great trouble, Berryman felt, was that Lowell was more enthusiastic in private than in print.

Berryman dedicated song 287 to Lowell. He wrote in song 188: "Cal has always manifested a most surprising affection / for Matthew Arnold," which may be a sly allusion to the fact that Lyndon Johnson, in a speech of August 1965, attributed to Lowell a famous line from Arnold's "Dover Beach." In his "wrecked generation" song (no. 153), Berryman wondered why he had been (temporarily) spared and noted that, by some divine dispensation, "Lowell he did not touch." In song 218 Berryman proudly listed "the Bostonian, / rugged & grand & sorrowful," among the greatest "expression kings" he had known: Yeats, Thomas, Eliot, Pound and Frost. In the *Harvard Advocate* issue (Spring 1969) that celebrated the publication of the complete *Dream Songs*, Berryman (in marked contrast to Lowell's praise of *Mistress Bradstreet*) gratuitously criticized Lowell's third book of poems: "my friends, poets, can't write narrative poems. They just can't do it—and some of them have tried. Lowell tried it in *Mills of the Kavanaughs*—and that's a bad failure." But he included Lowell, with Pound and Auden, as "the three best poets working in our language."[30] By incorporating Lowell in his pantheon of victims and heroes, Berryman judges, accepts and (by implication) equals his rival.

The form of the 385 short poems in *The Dream Songs* was a major influence on the 373 short poems in Lowell's *Notebook* (1969, revised 1970). Berryman thought *Notebook* "was an attempt to rival or catch some of the play" of his book. In 1969 Lowell acknowledged this influence, said they had the same kind of readers and minimized the possibility of jealousy: "I think I am in your debt—at least I say so in my preface. I've just completed a long poem, *Notebook of a Year. . . .* I think anyone who cared for your book would for mine. Anyway, we're accomplished beyond jealousy. Without you, I would find writing more puzzling."[31]

After the death of Jarrell in October 1965, wrote Ian Hamilton, Lowell looked "towards Berryman as the only truly formidable talent of around his own age. . . . Berryman could never have Jarrell's 'senior' role in Lowell's life, but it *was* possible for him to be thought of as an endangered, brilliant equal." Jarrell's death made Berryman seem all the more vulnerable and precious. In March 1966 Lowell wrote with grave concern: "This is really to say that I love you and wonder at you, and want you to take care. . . . Let me beg you to take care of yourself. You must be physically fragile. If anything happened to you, I'd feel the heart of the scene had gone."[32]

The nagging question of competition and status recurred twice more toward the end of Berryman's life. When the *Paris Review* interviewer asked him in July 1970 to rank his American contemporaries, Berryman (unlike Lowell, at least in private) was reluctant to do so. Instead, he tactfully replied: "Most of these characters are personal friends of mine, and you just don't sit around ranking your friends. . . . My love of such poets as . . . Roethke, and Lowell, *Lord Weary's Castle*, is very great. I would love to be in their company, and I feel convinced that I am, but I don't want to do any ranking."

After Hayden Carruth had written an extremely hostile review of *Love & Fame* in the *Nation* (November 1970), Berryman, defending himself in a letter, expressed delight that his work had been compared to that of his friends. Transforming the kind of acrimonious review that poisoned the friendships of the poets into a generous statement of praise for his colleagues, Berryman, in a surprising tactic, accepted Carruth's judgment of his peers: "It would not surprise me a bit to learn (in Heaven) that Lowell, Roethke, Schwartz, Jarrell, Miss Bishop and [Richard] Wilbur 'have produced individual poems finer in poetic integrity and formal congruency than anything in the works of Berryman.' The company is positively bracing! My pals! Does this bastard really after all think me comparable with them (though of course inferior)? The fact is, I think at least four of them have done exactly what he says, and I am happy to think so because I love their finest poems better than my short poems so far. (Only as of long poems might I be interested in claiming parity.)" Gary Arpin noted that *Love & Fame* "elicited not simply negative appraisals, but frequently hostile and mocking comments. The most hostile critics spoke of being 'disgusted' by the subject matter; friendly critics worried that Berryman had lost his talent."[33] The critics' scornful response to *Love & Fame*, like the damning response to Jarrell's *The Lost World*, intensified his depression and pushed him toward suicide. He read proof of *Delusions, Etc*, but could not face the reviews and killed himself before the book appeared.

Increasingly insecure as his poetry deteriorated toward the end of his life, Berryman took comfort in quoting Lowell's much-valued puff to local reporters who came for an interview: "I've just had a very fine letter from my old friend Robert Lowell." He thinks *Love & Fame* is "one of the great poems of the age. A puzzle and triumph for anyone who wants to write a personal devotional poem. Along with your [Opus] posthumous poems, in my mind the crown of your work." When they met for the last time in New York in December 1970, Berryman addressed Lowell "with an awareness of his dignity, as if he were Ezra Pound at St. Elizabeth's."[34] Then, expressing his fear of impending death, which Lowell mistook for a personal rejection, Berryman exclaimed that they would never meet again.

V

Berryman's last, naked-nerved poems were a series of suicide notes. His fate (like Hemingway's) had seemed to him predestined since his father's suicide in 1926. Berryman had expressed his themes of guilt and death as early as "The Possessed." His sins made him feel that the figure of death would not leave him. A quick thrust of a knife would penetrate his heart and extinguish his guilt. In the more prosaic "Of Suicide," he was again "possessed," connected his father's fate to his own, rejected his mother's help and gave specific reasons—alcoholism, the break-up of his third marriage—to explain his desire for self-immolation.

In his last book, *Day by Day* (1977), Lowell also wrote a poem on suicide. The thought of self-destruction came to him in nightmarish imaginings of future horrors. And he wondered if he had restrained himself for noble or base reasons—if he deserved credit for not attempting suicide or blame for fearing that he would blunder during that "exotic act."[35]

The theme of self-extinction, which Lowell compared to the flash of a burnt-out bulb, continued in Berryman's two posthumous volumes. An untitled poem in *Henry's Fate* described a self-slain young gifted girl, his protégée, whose desperate letter arrived with the news of her death. In despair, he imagined the clods on her coffin and her shuddering soul wandering underground, and dubiously concluded that he expects the welcome greeting of a fellow Catholic when he too commits suicide. In "Henry's Understanding" (which Lowell quoted at the conclusion of his obituary essay), Berryman recalled with nightmarish precision the suicidal impulses he managed to suppress while visiting the inhospitable Richard Blackmur in Hartington, Maine, just before his stay with Lowell in the summer of 1946. He wanted to strip off his clothes, walk across the lawn, descend the bluff and drown himself in the "terrible water" that stretched out to the island.[36]

Finally, in an astonishing, last, terror-filled yet strangely objective poem, written on January 5, 1972, less than forty-eight hours before his suicide, Berryman made a direct connection between mania and poetry, and predicted that if his wife did not confine him or the police hold him for observation, he would leap to an icy death from the high bridge over the Mississippi River in Minneapolis:

Sharp the Spanish blade
to gash my throat after I'd climbed across
the high railing of the bridge
to tilt out, with the knife in my right hand
to slash me knocked or fainting till I'd fall
unable to keep my skull down but fearless

Jarrell, always fascinated by sports cars and car racing, threw himself into a passing car. Berryman—more daring and extreme—leaped from a bridge and (like Icarus) plunged toward the water to his death. On January 7, only six months after the birth of his daughter Sarah, his resources exhausted and mind in despair, he finally completed what he had started on the railroad tracks at school and on the ledge with Eileen. Though he did not first cut his throat, "'he jumped up on the railing, sat down and quickly leaned forward. He never looked back at all.' . . . He fell about 100 feet, landing near the second pier of the municipal coal docks and rolling 15 to 20 feet down the embankment. . . . According to his death certificate, he died at the scene of 'multiple traumatic injuries.'" Auden is supposed to have invented a malicious joke in which Berryman left a note that read: "Your move, Cal."[37]

VI

Lowell turned white when, while living in England, he received a telephone call from New York with the news that Berryman was dead. The following month he wrote an obituary article and phoned it in to the *New York Review of Books*. His memoir of Berryman, less tender and more tortured than his 1964 review of *77 Dream Songs*, followed the pattern of his tribute to Jarrell. Lowell noted that both men "had the same marvelous and maddening characteristic: they were self-centered and unselfish." Lowell recalled their first meeting in 1944, the long visit to Damariscotta Mills in July 1946, Lowell and Jarrell's disastrous dinner with the Berrymans in

September of that year, their visit to Pound at St. Elizabeth's, and their last sad encounter. He described Berryman's poetic persona as "poignant, abrasive, anguished, humorous." Alluding to Swift's bitter epitaph on himself, Lowell said: "An indignant spirit was born in him; his life was a cruel fight to set it free." Lowell characteristically considered the death of "*extremist poets*, as we are named in prefunerary tributes," and (echoing the cut-throat image in Berryman's last poem) observed: "I feel the jagged gash with which my contemporaries died, with which we were to die." He rhetorically asked: "Were they killed . . . by our corrupted society? Was their success an aspect of their destruction?"[38] And he concluded that the work was indeed worth the suffering. Throughout the memoir Lowell assumed the carefully constructed persona of the exasperated fatherly helper, reflecting on his tragic generation of poets.

Lowell wrote three poems about Berryman: the first, when Berryman was still alive, in the late 1960s; the second (published with a revised version of the first) just after Berryman's death, in January 1972; and the third, less compressed and more discursive, after re-reading *The Dream Songs* in the mid-1970s. All three poems combine literary allusions with Lowell's sympathetic memories of Berryman. Lowell began the first poem by emphasizing that they have been through the same experiences and truly understand each other, that poets pay the penalty for the power of words by liberating a monster that devours them. Alluding to Wordsworth's "violet by a mossy stone" and Milton's "Fame is the spur," Lowell insisted there could be no escape to pastoral privacy and that fame could indeed destroy the heart. He evoked three writers who died in their forties—George Herbert, Henry Thoreau, Blaise Pascal—and compared them to the aged patriarch Abraham, beloved of God and his own people, who roamed through the world with less hope of fame than the dead writers or the modern poets. The fourteen-line blank-verse poem, though somewhat forced, was congenial and compassionate.

The second fourteen-line poem to Berryman (like Auden's elegy of Yeats, who also died in January) opened with a wintry setting—a contrast between Minneapolis–Boston and still-green England, where Lowell was then living—and with a menacing echo of John 9:4: "The night cometh when no man can work." Lowell then remembered their last, disturbing exchange of words during December 1970 in New York (also mentioned in Lowell's obituary notice), when he asked, "When will I see you, John?" and Berryman, sensing his imminent death, replied: "I was thinking through dinner, I'll never see you again." He then described Berryman's shaggy appearance and volatile character (Berryman was insecure, but surely not gay or tough) and placed him in threatening conjunction with one of their patron saints, Dylan Thomas, who actually had died in St. Vincent's Hospital. Lowell mentioned Joyce (who represents a fanatical dedication to art), recalled Berryman's schoolboy anecdote of sacrificial sports and (alluding to the Declaration of Independence) ironically called suicide "the inalienable right of man."

The longer third poem (like the obituary) suggested that Lowell's affection for Berryman diminished after the fame that followed *The Dream Songs* had intensified his egoism and self-absorption. In recent years they had met only when the elated Berryman was reading his Dream Songs on the poetry circuit. He spoke loudly but was deaf to Lowell; isolated, then as now, in his own unreachable world. Lowell included Berryman and himself among the *poètes maudits* (a phrase invented by Verlaine). He then recalled their common history as students and teachers, on fellowships, traveling in Europe, veterans of the Cold War, and finally admitted they had become as obsessed with alcohol as they once had been with writing. (Ford called himself "an old man mad about words.") While grieving, Lowell remembered their enthusiastic discussions, during Berryman's visit to Maine in 1946, of the broken syntax in Shakespeare's late plays. Lowell thought the last Dream Song ("Fall comes to me as a prize / to rouse us toward our fate") seemed to mock Berryman's catlike escape from family and students in order to leap to his death.[39] But Lowell (as in his obituary essay) seemed to feel the achievement was worth the sacrifice. Lowell's three poems and obituary on Berryman expressed his ambivalent admiration for and exasperation with the friend whose fate seemed a warning to the endangered survivors.

VII

While on a visiting professorship at All Souls, Oxford, in the spring of 1970 (when Berryman was writing his suicidal poems), Lowell met the beautiful Guinness heiress, Lady Caroline Blackwood. She has been the Lou Salomé of our time and attracted men of genius. She first married the painter Lucian Freud, then the composer Israel Citkowitz, with whom she had three children. She became pregnant by Lowell early in 1971: had a son, Sheridan, in September; married the poet in Santo Domingo in October 1972; and has lived with and described his mental illness.

Like Jean Stafford and Elizabeth Hardwick, Blackwood portrayed Lowell in her fiction. In *The Step-Daughter*, he appears as Arnold, a lean, elegant, well-dressed, clever and cruel husband. He dumps his hefty damaged daughter, who has survived the debris of two former marriages, with his third wife. He then announces he is leaving her, but makes no arrangements to remove the unwanted child: "Arnold had always chosen to remove himself from all painful human situations in order to pretend they do not exist. . . . He himself wants to re-marry, and he prefers to make me remain single so that he can always feel that I am alone and still waiting for him, if ever at some future date he might need me available."[40] His model for the poet with a devoted wife and mistress was Ezra Pound.

Lowell had apparently left Blackwood in September 1977 and was returning to Hardwick (who also was "still waiting for him, if ever at some future date he might need" her) when he had a fatal heart attack in the taxi that carried him from the airport into Manhattan. Lowell's painful disengagement

from Hardwick, the manic periods that frightened and
exhausted his new wife, and Caroline's acute nervous depression, were the subjects of the poems in *The Dolphin*, which
he wrote while living through the emotional chaos. Just as
Scott Fitzgerald had used Zelda's correspondence in *Tender is
the Night*, so Lowell used Hardwick's intensely private letters
in his work—though he knew they would tear her apart.
In the modern period, suffering women novelists—from
Katherine Mansfield, Jean Rhys and Elizabeth Smart to Jean
Stafford, Elizabeth Hardwick and Caroline Blackwood—have
been dominated and victimized by selfish and manic male
writers.

5

Theodore Roethke and Jarrell, Berryman, Lowell

Theodore Roethke, an attractive and appealing person, was also the odd man out. He came from German rather than British stock, and was less intellectual and sophisticated than the others. His poetry was also very different from theirs. Neither cerebral nor allusive, it was rooted in natural imagery and the pastoral tradition, joyous and affirmative rather than negative and despairing. A follower of the melodious and mystical tradition of Smart, Blake and Clare, of Lawrence, Williams and Dylan Thomas, Roethke had a pure lyric talent.

Though his personal life was also marred by alcoholism and mental breakdowns, his emotional instability did not lead to the gloom of the Lowell circle. For Roethke's religious vision enabled him to use his manic periods to perceive deeper truths and heighten his poetry. While the others made poetry out of their personal experiences, Roethke's art grew out of his intuitive response to the natural world. Unlike the others, Roethke continued to develop his talent and perfect his art, and wrote his best work at the end of his career. Lowell and Berryman, by contrast, had already done their best work by 1970, and Jarrell had come to the end of his creative life before his suicide. Roethke and Lowell were the only ones to exert an important influence on the younger generation. Roethke had a clear impact on James Dickey, Robert Bly, Ted Hughes and Sylvia Plath as well as on his pupils James Wright, Richard Hugo, Carolyn Kizer and David Wagoner.

All four poets had lost their fathers and were lost sons. The
fathers of Berryman, Jarrell and Lowell were weak failures.
But Otto Roethke was a powerful and successful man, who left
his son the Prussian rage for order (in his art, if not his life)
and the great poetic legacy of garden and greenhouse—his
"symbol for the whole of life, a womb, a heaven-on-earth."
Otto's death from cancer in 1923, when Ted was fifteen, was a
shattering experience. Roethke's widow believed it was the
key to his mental illness.[1]

Roethke's feelings for his father were a complex and
disturbing mixture of fear and love. In poems like "My Papa's
Waltz" and "Otto" he celebrated, from a child's point of view,
Otto's high spirits, manly courage and miraculous ability to
create living things. In "The Saginaw Song" he portrayed
his father's commanding presence (a striking contrast to
Commander Lowell, who was struck down by his son). Otto,
a typical Prussian, slapped young Ted with his stern hand and
evoked respect by his severity. And in "The Rose" Ted
described his father—godlike in the midst of his creations—
representing in his impressive character and work, in the
love and loyalty he inspired, a kind of earthly perfection. Otto
would straddle the benches and lift Ted over the high-
stemmed flowers that seemed to flow toward him and beckon
him out of himself. There was no need for heaven with that
divine father and those paradisical roses.[2]

Roethke was a big, bearish man—he stood six feet, two
inches tall and weighed 220 pounds—with the same frame and
form as Wallace Stevens and James Dickey. Born and raised
in Saginaw, Michigan, an ugly Midwestern town about eighty
miles northwest of Detroit, he graduated from the University
of Michigan in 1929, studied law for a term at Michigan and
did a year of graduate work in English at Harvard,[3] before
beginning his academic career as teacher and tennis coach at
Lafayette College in Pennsylvania. He was deeply attached to
Saginaw and often returned to stay with his mother and
younger sister, who waited on him and typed his poems.

Like Berryman and Lowell, Roethke had fantasies of sex
and power. He boasted to James Dickey "of having an 'in'

with the Detroit 'Purple Gang,' of having all kinds of high-powered business interests and hundreds of women in love with him." Though gross when drunk (and he drank heavily), he could when sober be touchingly noble and extremely funny. According to his close friend at the University of Washington, Robert Heilman (who wrote the most vivid memoir of the poet), Roethke "was frank, unpretentious, even rather innocent; stratagems and calculations [though he would sometimes attempt them] were beyond him."[4]

Roethke showed the sensitive, despairing and over-whelming side of his personality during his love affair in June 1935 with the poet and *New Yorker* critic Louise Bogan. Bogan (twelve years older than Roethke) conveyed the atmosphere of their brief, high-spirited and passionate moment, and of his great size, appetite and humor, by comparing him to a Saint Bernard (the dog, not the monk): "I, myself, have been made to bloom like a Persian rose-bush, by the enormous love-making of a cross between a Brandenburger and a Pomeranian, one Theodore Roethke by name. He is very, very large . . . and he writes very, very small lyrics. 26 years old and a frightful tank. We have poured rivers of liquor down our throats, these last three days, and, in between, have indulged in such bearish and St. Bernardish antics as I have never before experienced."

When the affair and excitement had ended, Bogan, with more objectivity, analyzed the manifest faults in his character: neurosis, alcoholism, vanity, provinciality, self-ignorance and despair: "'If he could shake off that neurotic seeking for bottle-made oblivion and grow up out of the peacocking town-bullishness bred in him, no doubt, by the fine normal womanhood of Ann Arbor, Mich., he'd be quite a person.' Ultimately, she warned, he would have to fight: against his depressions, his self-indulgences, his temperament, his family, his ambition." Torn between ambition and self-doubt, and deeply insecure, Roethke expressed characteristic sympathy with all vulnerable victims, with all innocent, hapless and forsaken things.[5]

Roethke's burden of guilt and fear (guilt about surviving

his father, fear that he could not survive without him) derived
from childhood and led to a childish but desperate desire for
praise and approval. A friend wrote that "he needed adulation
badly, but [like Berryman and Jarrell] no amount of it could
counteract his fears." Roethke felt that he needed more than
talent and genius to succeed to the crown of American poetry.
Recalling his gangster fantasies, he wished to emulate the
subtle yet successful self-promotion in "Yeats' career, in part
so managed, so stagey, a kind of gentleman racketeer."
Intensely aware of the prizes and honors that brought
privilege and status, he felt he deserved all the help he could
get and (as Bogan said, with some exaggeration) "made a
point of knowing all the right people *everywhere*, since the start
of his career."[6] But his close friends were minor poets—Bogan,
Rolfe Humphries, Stanley Kunitz—and he was not, like
Lowell, closely connected to the centers of power.

Roethke felt his maneuvers were necessary because the
competition was tough. Isolated and often stranded in the
American Northwest, he had to work hard for the contacts
and commendations that came quite naturally to the Eastern
and Southern literary cartels. As Conrad Aiken (that seasoned
veteran and enemy of Jarrell) said of the New Critics in 1941,
the year Roethke published his first book: "I think the
Tate-to-Blackmur-to Winters-to Brooks (Cleanth)-to-Ransom
roundelay is becoming a menace, and with widening rings,
and ought to be dealt with, but they're tough babies."
Evoking his favorite gangland metaphor, Roethke told his
future biographer, Allan Seager, that they ought to consolidate
their power: "I still say we could function more efficiently as a
Michigan mob . . . as those Southerners do. Boy, do they stick
together." And when writing to Dylan Thomas about his
tribute to the Welshman's *In Country Sleep*, he contrasted his
highly charged rhetorical work to that of his rivals: "At least it
will be a change from the patty-cake Lowell and Jarrell play in
print."[7]

Roethke was well aware that literary reputations were
measured by the acclaim received from the centers of power:

from the journals in New York and from the leading academic critics. Lowell had cultivated Ransom, Tate and Warren, who were prominent and influential poet–critics. Influenced by Eliot, they worked within a Southern literary tradition, practiced and advocated a rational Augustan classicism, a civilized expression of ideas, archaism and wit, harmonious and regular verse forms. (A comparison of Ransom's "Bells for John Whiteside's Daughter" with Thomas' "A Refusal to Mourn" or Roethke's "Elegy for Jane" will immediately illustrate the contrasting traditions.) So when Roethke talked about the "Michigan mob," he knew he was talking in vain because there was no such thing as local poetry. To be successful, poets had to have recognition and rewards from the reigning kings.

The poet Louis Simpson claimed that Roethke followed the prevailing fashion, "was always very conscious of what was in and what was out, and trimmed his sails accordingly." But there is substantial evidence to suggest that Roethke maintained his individualistic and idiosyncratic principles at a time when Eliot and Auden were the most influential poets. Roethke rejected classical models, intellectual constructs, learned allusions, urban settings, urbane tone, impersonal subjects and a literary rather than a personal approach to mystical experience. He believed that the poet, in order to be true to himself, must search for a universal vision through direct apprehension of the natural world. "I do think the conceptual boys are too much in the saddle," he told his kindred spirit, William Carlos Williams; "anything observed or simple or sensuous or personal is suspect right now." And he nobly added: "There is a deep and abiding energy in all living things which can aid our human strength and contribute to our destiny."[8]

In 1944 he complained to Williams (who also lacked recognition at that time) that his most characteristic work, "All those greenhouse ones and the nutty suburban ones, came back from Ransom" at the *Kenyon Review*. But three years later, when Ransom finally saw the light and accepted his poems, he sent a new piece (typed by Lowell, when they were at Yaddo) and wittily remarked: "Regarding your *becoming* a convert to my work: I console myself that those slow of faith are, in the end, the firmest."[9]

Roethke did not name Jarrell, Berryman and Lowell among the dozen contemporary poets who had helped him. He never wrote about them (though they all wrote about him), and declared he did not expect the kind of detachment and love from contemporaries that Lowell had received from Jarrell and Berryman. Instead, the man who sardonically referred to himself, only a few years before his death, as "the oldest younger poet in the U. S. A.," entered the literary arena like Hemingway and committed himself to the struggle for recognition.

Fellow poets, disciples and colleagues agreed that his crude and competitive drive was probably his worst and certainly most obvious fault. James Dickey suggested that Roethke's egoistic yet anguished aggression was based (like Berryman's) on a lack of self-confidence. And he rhetorically asked: "Why all this insistence on being the best, the acknowledged best, the *written-up* best? . . . And why the really appalling pettiness about other writers, like Lowell, who were not poets to him, but rivals merely? . . . His broad, boyish face had an expression of constant bewilderment and betrayal, a continuing agony of doubt. He seemed to cringe and brace himself at the same time."[10]

Richard Hugo, who had been Roethke's pupil at Washington, agreed that "he was far too competitive for his own good. . . . Roethke's love of prizes, rave reviews, and applause would sometimes prevent him from emphasizing to the student the real reward of writing." And Robert Heilman revealed how Roethke felt about Berryman and Lowell: "Ted did feel enormously competitive vis-à-vis other poets, jealous of the recognitions that came to them, and a little inclined to disparage them and think their work not up to his. . . . I'm fairly certain he thought Berryman belonged in a lower drawer. . . . Lowell was of course the big rival—the principal competitor for awards, honors, etc. Ted respected him, but wanted to think him a lesser figure."[11]

While the other poets feared and tried to avoid manic episodes, Roethke—who came to believe that manic power was essential to great writing—deliberately tried to induce his derangement. He was less afraid of madness than of failure to realize his poetic gifts and actually wished "for an illness—for something to come to grips with, a break from reality." He cultivated physical exhaustion and emotional extremes—which would push him over the edge—by means of starvation, sleeplessness, frenetic activity, drunken binges, overdoses of drugs and exposure to intensely cold weather. He referred to the insane German poet (much admired by Berryman) and asked: "What would you rather be—happy or Hölderlin?" And he devoutly believed: "In a dark time, the eye begins to see."[12]

Richard Hugo observed that few "great artists, including Yeats, could be credited with risking their very being for their work." Roethke, who knew the terrible cost, continued to take the risks and pay the penalties. "Once you become too hyperactive and lose too much sleep," he explained in a typically offhand manner, "you'll cross a threshold where chaos (and fever) ensues. And believe me, chum, it's always a chancey thing whether you get back or not. . . . I've been crawling in and out of hospitals the last three weeks. For two weeks I was in the Albany Hospital taking some electric treatments"— though he feared they would "turn his brain to jelly." Like Lowell, he was pacified by the dangerous electro-convulsive therapy. Alluding to the savage writer who became senile at the end of his life, Roethke wrote with terrifying brevity:

Swift's servant beat him.
Now they use
A current flowing
From a fuse.[13]

In an interview of January 1963, the last year of his life,

Roethke vividly recalled his deliberate and catastrophic derangement of the senses in East Lansing, Michigan, on November 18, 1935. Referring to Rimbaud's letter of 1871, Roethke's long, disjointed, stream-of-consciousness description resembled the narration of a dream to a psychiatrist:

I played the Rimbaud business of really driving myself, seeing . . . [if] you could really derange the senses, and it can be done, and let me tell you, I did it. . . . I got in this real strange state. I got in the woods and started a circular kind of dance. . . . I kept going around and just shedding clothes. . . . I understood intuitively what the frenzy is. That is, you go way beyond yourself, and . . . this is not sheer exhaustion, but this strange sort of a . . . not illumination . . . but a sense of being again a part of the whole universe. . . . It was one of the deepest and most profound experiences I ever had. And accompanying it was a real sexual excitement also . . . and this tremendous feeling of actual power.

You have this curious sense that you're actually being transformed literally into an animal. You start getting fantasies—I mean, of power, lion-like power. . . . Of course, this was madness, you see, but the relationship between the ecstasy and madness is . . . one of the things that the headshrinkers know. . . . I woke up on the morning . . . with very little sleep, and decided I wanted to get to [the Dean's] office. I took a little walk on the edge of the city. There I got so cold I lay down and took off a shoe, and there I had . . . this is again real loony, and goes beyond—there was a curious crabhole, and I lay there and started whistling to this thing, as if you were really trying to call it out of the earth. . . . Then I got scared; it started getting cold; it was November, and I started to run with only one shoe on. . . . I was barefoot . . . well, symbolically, yet. I got into a gas station. There was a guy . . . I just associated him with my father. I was out on my feet, see, just punchy from . . . you know, I hadn't slept for five nights, and I said, "Can . . . get me, drive me." . . . He drove me to the campus, and I came in, you know, just like someone who had been beaten for five rounds. . . . The trouble in these high states of consciousness is that *everything* gets heightened. . . .

The *real* point is that this business of the dance accompanies exaltation of the highest, the human thing, and it also goes into the Dionysian frenzy, which in modern life hardly anyone even *speaks* of anymore. . . . This is exactly what [the dervishes] felt when they were rolling in the circular, you know, frenzy thing. And your perceptions, as I say, both in sight and particularly in sound *and* smell [are heightened and] . . . you get the transfer of senses. . . . You feel one way that you are eternal, or immortal, and it doesn't seem to be a cheap thing either. And furthermore, death becomes, as it were, an absurdity, of no consequence. And also the notion, conception, of time is completely subjective.

The essential elements of Roethke's manic or mystical experience are the same as those in his poetry: the Dionysian dance, feeling of cosmic connection, sense of transcendent power, evocation of the creatures of the earth, heightened perception of the natural world and illusion of immortality. And the poetry inspired by his mania transcended ordinary reality, exalted men's affinity with the natural cycle and *seemed* (in retrospect) to give a certain validity to his interpretation.

Neal Bowers has argued that Roethke's walk in the cold night went beyond madness to ecstasy. What Roethke saw and felt (or what he thought he saw and felt) during his manic flight "was transcendent truth, a reality beyond what we normally regard as real."[14] But it would be more accurate to say, if we analyze rather than merely accept Roethke's point of view, that he tended to enjoy his mania ("it was a real sexual excitement") and tried to rationalize his mental breakdowns (long after the event) by embellishing and elevating them to the kind of mystical experiences described by the seventeenth-

century poets, Thomas Traherne and Henry Vaughan.
Though these poets may also have heightened their consciousness by lack of food and sleep, they achieved a feeling of
religious transcendence without going mad. It is quite likely
that Roethke mistook incoherence for omnipotence, and that
part of his illness was his inability to recognize that he was
seriously sick.

II

Roethke's transcendent and musical poetry provided a striking
contrast to Jarrell's rational and prosaic verse. Roethke and
Jarrell were not close friends and their contacts were fairly
superficial. But he sought and finally won Jarrell's much-
desired though somewhat qualified praise. Both poets expressed a similar pathos when describing the "lost world" of
their childhoods ("I'd stand upon my bed, a sleepless child /
Watching the waking of my father's world.— / O world so far
away! O my lost world!"). But Roethke told Stanley Kunitz
that he disliked Jarrell's poetry, probably because it seemed
forced and intellectual rather than spontaneous and fluent.
They met in Seattle in the fall of 1956, when Jarrell
read from *Poetry and the Age*. Roethke wrote a disparaging
limerick on Jarrell, but later changed his mind about Jarrell's
character and came to respect him as a critic. Though Jarrell
lived in North Carolina, Roethke saw him as a political ally of
Lowell and exclaimed: "What a set-up the Eastern poets
had!"[15]

In 1958, when he published *Words for the Wind*, Roethke
told Lowell: "I thought I'd have Doubleday send [Randall] a
book, though I despair of his ever reading anything of mine
except 'My Papa's Waltz'"—which had appeared ten
years previously. In an interview of 1961, Jarrell justly called
Roethke "one of the best-known, and best, lyric poets." And in
his compendium review, which appeared a month after
Roethke's sudden death, the rational Jarrell squeamishly

commented on Roethke's attraction to the primordial ooze. He praised Roethke's delicacy, force and originality, but ended by emphasizing the intellectual limitations of his poems: "he is a powerful Donatello baby who has love affairs, and whose marsh-like unconscious is continually celebrating its marriage with the whole wet dark underside of things. He is a thoroughly individual but surprisingly varied poet. . . . Instead of conquering and living in one country, Roethke has led expeditions into several and won notable victories in each. . . . But do they mean enough? Are not parts . . . better than the whole? Don't such poems tend to have impressive 'positive' endings of a certain rhetorical insincerity?"[16] Like Berryman and Lowell, Jarrell refused to see beyond the literal meaning of Roethke's work (lest he become a more formidable rival than he seemed) and to realize that his world of marshy plants and dark animals put him in touch with the cycles of nature, that his affirmations celebrated the organic structure of the universe.

III

Berryman held the power during his first contact with Roethke. In January 1939 (before either of them had published a book) Berryman, recently returned from his studies at Cambridge, was the poetry editor of the *Nation*. Roethke, teaching at Penn State, sent in four poems; and though Berryman politely praised "Highway, Michigan," he rejected them. A decade later, when Berryman was still drifting around the academic world and Roethke had a permanent position at the University of Washington, the former replaced the latter for a term during Roethke's mental breakdown.

They first met during Edmund Wilson's Christmas party at Princeton in December 1952. The pudgy but formidable Wilson had asked Berryman: "This man Roethke—is he any good?" and when Berryman replied: "He's brilliant," Wilson invited him to the party. Wearing pinstripe trousers and a pyjama cord, Roethke entered the room like a fighter coming into the ring and greeted Berryman as if he had never heard of him. Apparently sober, Roethke sat next to his host on the sofa, grabbed Wilson's jowl and asked: "What's this? Blubber?"[17]—an abysmally poor way to cultivate influential critics. When introduced to a doctor at the same party, Roethke, fearing he was about to be committed, suddenly knocked the doctor down. As the madcap poet was quietly hustled away, the guests were assured he was not usually so dangerous.

In January 1953 Roethke married the young and beautiful Beatrice O'Connell, who had been his student at Bennington. Beatrice Roethke and Eileen Berryman, who disliked each other's husbands, both recalled their meetings in Rome and London in the summer of 1953, when the poets were on what Lowell called "our fifties' fellowships / to Paris, Rome and Florence." Beatrice got off to a bad start with Berryman. She thought he resembled a rabbit or rat, with a long space (later masked by a beard) between his nose and lip. She was irritated by his complaints that he had received neither enough recognition as a poet nor sufficient social invitations— though he often failed to appear when he was invited to parties. She tried to ignore Berryman; and when he turned nasty, she told Roethke: "You ought to punch him in the nose." But Roethke was a genial drunk who admired *Mistress Bradstreet* and was on friendly terms with Berryman. He did not follow her advice, and merely said: "Berryman's crazy, but in a boring way." The poets met again in London when Berryman gave a party at the flat of John Davenport—a "character," critic and friend of Dylan Thomas. Beatrice also went to the National Gallery with Berryman, who spent a long half hour, in a manner she found affected, looking at the angels with lutes in Piero's *Nativity*.[18]

Eileen's recollections of the summer of 1953 reveal the undercurrent of tension whenever the high-strung poets came together and the swirling tides of suspicion beneath the surface of their friendship. "John was somewhat calmer than he had been," she wrote of Rome in her memoir, "or at least was less driven to declaim his stanzas to the world. Ted would not have been attracted to such monomania because he was having difficulties of his own. Though sweet-tempered and not at all combative as he had been in Princeton, he was high, if not manic, as we guessed the night he insisted that a group of us who had had dinner together go with him to a German restaurant to have another meal. . . . The suspiciousness he felt toward John (based, I think, on John's having replaced him at the University of Washington when he was in the hospital—i.e., John's having taken over his classes behind his back), gradually diminished."

In Eileen's novel, *The Maze*, Roethke appeared as Will Hendy, just married to a lovely bride. He sends Roxana greenhouse flowers when she is in a London hospital with a back injury and tries to justify his bizarre social behavior by explaining: "You know, Canary, I'm wild about that girl, but I warned her before we married that I wasn't housebroken. She wouldn't listen." None of Will's acquaintances can understand the gross disparity between the man and his work or believe, as one character says, that "that big slob could write such delicate lyrics."[19]

One of Berryman's students at Iowa in the fall of 1954 remembered him "speaking with great delicacy and warmth of Roethke—in particular of the poems of *The Lost Son* and *Praise to the End!*," which were so different from his own work: "'Why, Ted Roethke,' he would say, 'Ted Roethke is the only man who . . . *thinks* like a flower!'" In the *American Scholar* (Summer 1959), Berryman was less enthusiastic about *Words for the Wind*. He mentioned Roethke's unusual tenderness and said *The Lost Son* proved "that all previous poets' attention to plants had been casual. Flowers and weeds alike writhed and lived on the page as they never had before." He stressed (as Jarrell liked to do in his reviews of Berryman) the influence of Whitman and Yeats, noted Roethke's lack of development and expressed some serious doubts about his future: "Few critical readers will feel that his new self-reformation is as yet either at all complete or satisfying. The channel is unclear. One can only express gratitude and wish luck." Roethke, insatiably hungry for acclaim, was irritated by Berryman's urbane condescension and patronizing comment on his "plants." But W. D. Snodgrass showed a deeper understanding of Roethke's achievement and wrote that in *Words for the Wind* he "seems to have accomplished . . . a language which many of the best poets of his age and younger, among them Lowell and Berryman, have been dreaming about and working toward."

A decade later, and seven years after Roethke's death, Berryman could afford to be more generous. The egoistic author of *Love & Fame* recalled their rivalry in Rome and Roethke's infantile demand for attention (which was shared by Berryman): "Roethke? A marvelous poet. We had a long session one time in Rome. He wanted me to read his recent poems, and I wanted him to read *Mistress Bradstreet*. However, he didn't keep his part of the bargain. He no more cared about my work than a hole in the head. It was impossible not to like him, but difficult to make him a real friend, in both cases because he was so childish. He was interested in love and money: and if he had found a combination of them in something else, he would have dedicated himself to it instead of poetry."[20] Berryman's hostile and gratuitous remark revealed more about himself than about his friend and seriously misjudged Roethke's passionate commitment to his art.

Berryman elegized the older poet, as he had so many of his dead friends, in Dream Song 18, "A Strut for Roethke." Berryman's dance, in a sad jazz rhythm, celebrated Roethke's voracious personality; referred to the place where he had died while swimming (Bainbridge Island, across Puget Sound from Seattle); mentioned his greenhouse theme, his lyric voice and the high cost the alcoholic, sick, mad poet had paid for his work. He hits a low note to mourn the lost roarer who staggered on and sang of flowers. The only consolation was that Roethke would never again have to face sterility, failure and the pain of creation: "No more daily, trying to hit the head on the nail." He now lies within his familiar earth: "The Garden Master's gone."

In January 1966 Berryman sent the poem to Beatrice with what he called "a letter pseudo-consoling: (1) he went thro' 3 phases, & was in at least the 2nd a daring & true & beautiful poet, (2) he cannot suffer any more." Roethke's last interview, seven months before his death, provided his premature but positive epitaph for Berryman: "I've often thought sometimes that [when] the suicidal leaps from the window, when he hits that pavement and is just a blob, who knows, maybe he explodes into a million universes and he is happy."[21]

IV

Berryman began his review of Roethke's work with a long, perceptive contrast between the minds and methods of Roethke and Lowell, the most powerful and original talents of the last fifteen years. Berryman noted their geographical as well as intellectual and temperamental opposition, defined their essential qualities and remarked on the fundamental difference in their personalities:

> The contrast is so deep that one would almost be justified in adopting the terms "Eastern" and "Western" style, without much reference to the fact that Lowell is from Boston and lives there, Roethke from Michigan, living in Seattle. Lowell's work is Latinate, formal, rhetorical, massive, historical, religious, impersonal; Roethke's Teutonic, irregular, colloquial, delicate, botanical, and psychological, irreligious, personal. It is hardly an exaggeration to say that Lowell is a poet of completed states, Roethke a poet of process. Both are witty, savage, and willing to astonish, but the fundamental unlikeness is great. If both are authoritative, the nature of their

authorities differs, Lowell's being a traditional authority, Roethke's an experiential one. Lowell is formidable, Roethke endearing.

During an interview of 1966, Berryman repeated many of these ideas but also mentioned the points they had in common: "a feeling for human fate, both extremely serious, both absolutely first-class (one now dead to us)."[22]

A comparison of their poems on similar themes—the sale of a family home after the owner's death and hydrotherapy for mental illness—shows significant similarities in the two essentially different poets. Roethke's "Sale," in his first volume, *Open House* (1941), catalogues in five precise and polished quatrains, each with its own repeated rhyme, the contents of an aristocratic mansion, which might have belonged to Lowell's forebears. The last line of each quatrain revealed the secret but omnipresent atmosphere of evil and decay: an attic of horrors, a closet of fears, grandfather's sinister hands, the watery eyes in an ancestral portrait by John Singleton Copley "And the taint in a blood that was running too thin."

Roethke's poem expressed the viewpoint of an outsider, impervious to the fatal legacy of the sinister house. Lowell's "For Sale," in *Life Studies* (1959), described, from the insider's view, the sale of his father's retirement cottage at Beverly Farms, northeast of Boston. A sheepish plaything, lived in just a year, it "was on the market [in August 1950,] the month he died." Its contents seemed waiting for the mover who followed on the heels of the mortician. The last relic of the house, Charlotte Lowell, feared loneliness and mooned about the place as if she had stayed on a suburban train "one stop past her destination."[23] Roethke's satire on moral decay and the desolation of death is sharply observed and technically skilled. Lowell's is more personal and poignant.

Roethke's "Meditation in Hydrotherapy," which did not appear in book form during his lifetime, is based on his treatment at Mercywood Sanitarium outside Ann Arbor after his mental breakdown in November 1935. The meditation is connected to the image in "The Meadow Mouse" of "The paralytic stunned in the tub, and the water rising." The old-fashioned and ineffective therapy is meant to cure his will to die and refit him "for the true and good" life. But he is overcome by emotional numbness, unable to discard his depressing thought and destructive impulse. As he sees his dreary past sliding down the drain, he cannot believe he soon will be himself again.

Lowell's "Hydrotherapy," in *Notebook* (1970), also portrays himself meditating (like Archimedes or Marat) in a tub. Soaking in a stark setting but surrounded by familiar objects, he is denied alcohol and "dry" for the first time in his adult life. Contemplating his cure, Roethke says: "The flesh is willing to repent." Lowell characteristically transforms the rows of tubs into church pews, reflects on original sin ("Adam's gums still leave blood on the apple"[24]) and vainly tries to summon the insight that would help cure his illness. Both poems—hopeless, ironic, bitter—suggest the futility of this somatic treatment.

V

Both Roethke and Lowell adopted a bear persona and a shambling bearish gait. Roethke wrote: "I'll sing and whistle romping with the bears . . . This animal remembering to be gay," and for a time Lowell addressed his letters to "Dear Bear." In February 1949, just before his first major break-down, Lowell suspended Tate outside an apartment window and recited the "Ode to the Confederate Dead" in a bear's voice. Both Roethke and Lowell were diagnosed as manic-depressive; and their deepest bond, though they never saw each other ill, was the connection between their madness and their poetry.

Lowell flaunted and exposed his illness while Roethke (more vulnerable in academic life) was ashamed of and concealed it. When sent to a mental hospital, he told close friends he was going on vacation. But after Lowell had published *Life Studies*, Roethke portrayed himself more openly as a mad poet and freely discussed his mania in a late interview. As Stanley Kunitz observed: "The onset of his best work coincided with his discovery that he need not feel guilty about his illness; that it was a condition he could explore and use; that it was, in fact, convertible into daemonic energy, the driving power of imagination."[25]

Caroline Blackwood has revealed that Lowell was completely incapacitated by his mania. But Roethke did not stop writing during his illness: "He worked continually and many of his poems were written in hospitals." Roethke yearned for manic episodes as "breaks with reality." "Lowell never romanticized his illnesses," writes James Breslin, "but [afterwards] he was able to make creative use of the collapse of his personal life and of the self-examination encouraged by his treatment."[26]

Since Roethke used the manic episodes to heighten the perceptions he already had, his chaotic inner life and unresolved neuroses were a source of creativity. He was able to enrich his metaphysical poetry with mad thoughts in language that blended naturally with his humor and slangy expressions. Lowell's involuntary and uncontrollable madness, by contrast, condemned him to hurt others and yet survive to write about his illness. Lowell needed his manic episodes to give him poetic material. The record of the suffering he caused, so different from the progressive illumination in Roethke's "In a Dark Time," was expressed in agonizing poems like "Man and Wife."

Roethke first met Lowell at the writers' conference at Olivet, Michigan, in July 1937. The younger poet arrived with Ford and Tate and, Roethke later said (as Berryman had said of Roethke), "never lost an opportunity to recite his latest poems."[27] A more significant meeting took place at Yaddo, the writers' colony near Saratoga Springs, New York, in June 1947. Lowell, not terribly impressed, found Roethke "a ponderous, coarse, fattish, fortyish man—well read, likes the same things as I do, and is quite a competent poet." (Roethke, who cultivated a tough, Germanic persona, admitted: "I may look like a beer salesman but I'm a poet.") They spent a great deal of time drinking, fishing, playing croquet and tennis. Roethke re-read Lowell, became more charitable and conceded there was certainly a raw power in his best work. But he also described Lowell as one of those "tough characters not always in sympathy with my kind of thing."[28]

At the end of the summer Roethke told the critic Kenneth Burke, who had been his colleague and mentor at Bennington, about the development of the friendship and their travels together. He felt Lowell's principal weakness was his own greatest strength and commented on Jarrell's inflation of Lowell's poems: "Robt. Lowell I liked very much: we did a lot of fishing and reading and beer-drinking; went up together to Breadloaf and read to the School of English; went to see some fancy friends of his at Ipswich, Mass. etc. I don't think his ear (Lowell's) is especially subtle, and some areas of experience he doesn't seem to understand. Not very much intuitive perception; too much influence of A. Tate and too much concern and respect for formal (stanza-form) order . . . but the best of his stuff has a rough power, I think. It's not all that R. Jarrell says it is, but so what."

The fine novelist J. F. Powers, who (along with Elizabeth Hardwick and Mary McCarthy) was also at Yaddo that summer, gave an extremely perceptive account of the relations of the high-strung antagonists: "My feeling is that Ted felt that Cal was too successful with (rather than in) his work—this was 1947, and *Lord Weary's Castle* was big. Ted also took the view, and when Cal was present too, that he (Cal) was rather out of it, abstracted, dotty, and liked the line he made up about Cal, frequently quoting it, 'Ratttleass from Boston, Mass.' In much the same way, Cal was amused by Ted, in and out of his presence, there being no difference as there was, some, where Ted's attitude toward Cal was concerned in and out of his presence—Ted growled and shook his head over Cal's success in the later case. But Ted was very ambitious, not up to disguising it—like his appetite for food and drink, it just came out."[29] Lowell could disguise his competitive spirit under a suave manner. And Roethke— incapable of masking his feelings, even if he wanted to—deeply resented his demeanor.

The friendship at Yaddo led to mutual visits and readings in Seattle and Boston, compassionate letters from Lowell about Roethke's illness (and his own) and, finally, Lowell's elegy on Roethke. Writing to J. F. Powers in February and June 1948, Lowell pronounced a premature judgment on the limitations of Roethke's work. (Both poets tended to stress the other's weakness.) When *The Lost Son* appeared, Lowell adopted the condescending tone of Jarrell and Berryman, who felt that Roethke's poems lacked intellectual depth and high seriousness, that flowers, plants and the "wet dark underside of things" were not worth writing about. Lowell also explained why he had decided not to review the book: "My final judgment on his poetry is pretty complicated—a fairly small thing done, at its best, with remarkable clarity and freshness. But this wouldn't please him or sell his book like hot cakes. If somehow he could forget about renown and arriving and all that. . . . Since I wrote Ted about his book, I've heard nothing, though I was honest and enthusiastic. I don't think I could have written a review that would have satisfied him."[30]

The poets seem to have drifted apart during the next decade, when Roethke published *Praise to the End!* and Lowell *The Mills of the Kavanaughs* (both 1951). After Lowell's chubby, bald and round-faced daughter Harriet was born, he affectionately said that she looked "like the great Ted Roethke." In 1956 Lowell told J. F. Powers that Roethke had been as "growly as ever" when Jarrell was reading his work in Seattle. The following year, Lowell followed Jarrell to the University of Washington and sent Powers a lively account of his frenetic visit and of the tragic and horribly familiar letter he had received from Roethke: "Did I tell you about my reading in Seattle last spring and staying with Ted. He has a lovely

young (early thirties) Bennington student wife. Much prettier
and more mature and frailer than Ted. She was in a strange
barbed wire hospital for TB, and Ted was on the town. He
serves only whiskey to his students. After four days, I was all
but dead: eating, reciting poetry, hearing Roethke poetry,
losing at bowls, inspecting fifty thousand dollar modern house
with Irish Victorian furniture that Ted, feeling that he was
Von Hindenburg, wished to buy from the painter Morris
Graves. It was really great fun. When June came Ted's wife
returned to him and he bought a much simpler house, then
late this September I had a wild letter: 'Well, it's happened
again! Same old routine: 4 or 5 city police (as the boogs say)
dragging me off to the same old nut-bin.'"[31]

In the spring of 1958, when Roethke had regained his
sanity and Lowell was recovering from his almost annual
manic episode, Lowell wrote three moving letters—from one
wounded veteran to another—about the mental and marital
troubles that were their bond. He believed the poet's agonies
helped him to create. And he had a desperate need to talk to a
fellow sufferer who also would extend the sympathy and
understanding of a psychiatrist:

> I feel great kinship with you. We are at times almost one
> another's shadows passing through the same jungle. . . . I,
> too, am just getting over a manic attack. Everything
> seemed to be going swimmingly, then suddenly I was in
> the hospital—thorazine, windy utterances, domestic
> chaos. . . . When you come we can spill out to each
> other. . . .
>
> Agitated depression! I know only too well and fre-
> quently how you must feel. I hope the agitation at least
> animates and lessens that awful feeling of lowness and
> idleness that comes after our dizzy explosions. I keep
> thinking of Housman's phrase for Meredith, "a galvanized
> corpse." . . .
>
> I heard somewhere that you and Beatrice had separ-
> ated. I hope this won't be final. She seems such a beautiful

person and wise wife. To my grief, I too tried to break away from Elizabeth. It was all part of my mania and nonsense. . . . You mustn't feel you have done anything irreparable. All that was lost is returned. We even bring back certain treasure from our visits to the bottom.[32]

Berryman's unpublished letters to Lowell were deferential in tone; but Roethke's (sometimes sent from a mental hospital) were humorous, agitated, exasperating, egoistic and demanding. Pushed beyond the point of tolerance, Lowell tersely replied to one of them: "P. S. Stop complaining!" In September 1958 Roethke returned to their opposition of intuition and intellect, which he had mentioned in the letter to Kenneth Burke, and told Lowell, with unusual modesty: "I don't 'know' anything, in the formal sense and have to play by ear and instinct; whereas you have a mind and a real education behind you. Hence your 'chatting' [in class] is probably far better than my bellowing and prancing."[33]

When they met and drank together their conflicts and criticism—muted in the letters—were openly and aggressively expressed. Stanley Kunitz said that their meetings in the early 1960s, as their competition intensified, were not particularly happy occasions. At one meeting Lowell got drunk, offensively baited Roethke and attacked his poetry. Confident that his poetic line was more melodic, Roethke roared back: "You, with your tin ear, dare say that to me!" Kunitz commented that "Cal tried to pass the incident off as a piece of drunken foolery, but I know the charge rankled, for he recalled it to me years later, after Ted had died." Yet Roethke also realized that he could not rely entirely on music and that his poems lacked intellectual substance. In his notebooks he recorded: "All ear and no brain / Make Teddy inane."[34]

Ian Hamilton stated that Lowell was "never wholly converted to Roethke's work, although he would politely name him in any list of his favorite contemporaries. . . . His praise for Roethke's actual poems never quite rings true." Yet Lowell's comments in letters to Roethke and other friends, after *Words for the Wind* had appeared in 1958, reveal that he was more positive about Roethke than Hamilton suggests. Lowell knew that Roethke had precisely the talents that he himself lacked. In February 1959 Lowell (always shrewd about the politics of poetry) told Roethke he had correctly predicted "the National Book [Award] would go to you, when I saw the list of the judges, and could have picked up quite a little money if I had bet on you against the favored but not much admired John Berryman." After intensifying the competition, he ambiguously added: "I am glad we are not rivals." The following year Lowell wrote, with disingenuous deference: "You are certainly a master, our only one except Auden."[35]

In April 1960, three years after Lowell's visit to Seattle, Roethke stayed with Lowell in Boston and gave readings at Wellesley and Harvard.[36] Philip Booth acknowledged the poets' rivalry, but gave an idealized version of Lowell's self-effacement on this occasion: "Competitive as Cal can be in . . . conversation, his generosity to poets he values is without competitive edge. Several springs ago, when Roethke was reading around Boston, Cal gathered every known poet east of the Hudson for an evening party on Marlborough Street: that they might meet Ted, that Ted might meet them. . . . Ted had up-stage center, deferred to nobody, and revelled in it. Cal let him, happily." But Elizabeth Hardwick, the hostess at Marlborough Street, gave a more realistic account of the collision of the two great egos, noting that they competed in illness as in art: "I think Cal admired Roethke's work, but no room could contain the two of them at the same time. They were competitors in symptoms. I remember that Cal told me that he and Roethke were someplace around Boston, traveling in and out of the city by train. And Cal said, 'Would you believe it, he expected *me* to get the tickets, *me* to make all the arrangements.'"[37]

In October 1960 Lowell told J. F. Powers that he had received two sad notes from Roethke, who had been hospitalized (for the fifth time) in an Irish sanitarium. That same

month, Roethke published "Some Remarks on Rhythm" in
Poetry, placed Lowell in some rather odd company and praised
the versification in the innovative *Life Studies*: "The breath
unit [the natural pause, is] the language that is natural to the
immediate thing, the particular emotion. Think of what we'd
have missed in Lawrence, in Whitman, in Charlotte Mew, or,
more lately, in Robert Lowell, if we denied this kind of poem."
In his *Paris Review* interview the following year, Lowell noted
their emotional affinity, mentioned the striking contrast in
their poetry and stressed the disorderly element in Roethke's
work, though it was often more technically skilled than his
own: "We've read to each other and argued, and may be
rather alike in temperament actually, but he wants a very
musical poem and always would quarrel with my ear as I'd
quarrel with his eye. He has love poems and childhood poems
and startling surrealistic poems, rather simple experience
done with a blaze of power. He rejoices in the rhetoric and the
metrics, but there's something very disorderly working there.
Sometimes it will smash a poem and sometimes it will make it.
The things he knows about I feel I know nothing about,
flowers and so on. What we share, I think, is the exultant
moment, the blazing out. Whenever I've tried to do anything
like his poems, I've felt helpless and realized his mastery."[38]
Neither Roethke nor Lowell could combine the ear and eye as
Yeats and Auden did.

Lowell's critical remarks incited the hypersensitive
Roethke (for whom too much praise was just enough) to try to
overtake Lowell in the homestretch of their careers. Roethke
(like Jarrell on the Princeton visit to the Berrymans) had
mocked Lowell's dynastic poetry. Referring in August 1961 to
Lowell's prose autobiography "91 Revere Street," he declared
that his own poems were a reaction against "Cal's We-love-
ourselves us Yankee prose." In February 1963, when he was
completing the poems in *The Far Field*, published posthumously
in 1964, Roethke claimed, with unusual confidence: "I've got
old Cal beat, but really." And speaking in his final interview
of "In a Dark Time," his most ambitious poem on madness

and mysticism, he wildly exclaimed: "I had the sense that this is one of the great poems of our time. I mean, I just knew it. . . . [I sent it to] Cal Lowell, 'cuz I thought, 'Cal, ha, ha, think you know something about religious experience; get a load of this.' "[39] Roethke's philistine language revealed that Lowell, in a peculiar sort of way, had provoked the poem that was meant to surpass the religious works in *Lord Weary's Castle*.

Roethke was naturally considered the leading poet in his home territory. After Thomas Kinsella's reading at the University of Washington in July 1963, with Roethke seated prominently in the front row, someone provocatively asked the Irish poet: "who do you consider the greatest living American poet?" and Kinsella immediately replied: "Robert Lowell." Roethke, despite his boasts about beating Lowell, was still quite insecure. During the party for Kinsella, he became furious and shouted: "That bastard, damn him. Did you hear what he said?"[40]

In the spring of 1963, while in a turbulent mood, Roethke wrote a devastatingly honest letter to Lowell, an infantile and unintentionally comical self-exposure that expressed his deep-rooted resentment of Lowell's overwhelming advantages—his casual manner, superior education, distinguished lineage, private income, prominent reputation, confident translations, literary dictatorship and powerful connections:

> I had been very depressed by our meetings in New York—perhaps childishly: enraged, (almost) that you just have me sitting around while you were off to the headshrinkers. I just felt you were being cavalier. . . .
>
> I have had perhaps the boring presumptuousness to think of you as a younger brother, better educated, having more "advantages"—the old love-hate business. . . .
>
> Let me make a confession about "Otto." I deliberately wrote it in a form you use (superbly) about *my* old man because I was tired of reading about your damned relations. . . . My bloodline is a damned good one. . . .
>
> I've always been jealous of that private income which

protects you, as I've never been protected. And I'm
jealous of the fact that the PR boys practically faint when
your name is mentioned. And I sneer, only to myself,
about your "Imitations" (*Imitations?*—You mean Des-
ecrations?) probably because anything I'd try of that sort
would be inept and idiotic. . . . And I do think you should
resist the role of literary dictator, even though the role is
being thrust on you. . . .

I was enormously flattered, slobbering egomaniac that
I am, by your reference to me . . . in the *Paris Review*. . . .

Oh yes, one more thing. I'm jealous of the fact that you
know Eliot and he likes and values you; while I have really
been given the brush.[41]

Lowell's last long letter of July 10, 1963, three weeks
before Roethke's sudden heart attack in Washington, gently
answered Roethke's hysterical outburst. He finally admitted
that there *was* a dangerous rivalry in poetry. Despite this, he
reaffirmed his friendship with Roethke, praised his talents,
confirmed their common bonds and noted their disastrous
lives. And he wisely prophesied that one day a book would be
written about them all:

About the rest, with all your comparisons of our careers,
backgrounds, etc. . . . I remember Edwin Muir arguing
with me that there is no rivalry in poetry. Well, there is.
No matter what one has done or hasn't done (this sounds
like a prayer) one feels each blow, each turning of the
wind, each up and down grading of the critics. . . .

It does make me happier that you exist, and can do
many big things that I have no gift for. We couldn't be
more different, and yet how weirdly our lives have often
gone the same way. . . .

There's a strange fact about the poets of roughly our
age, and one that doesn't exactly seem to have always been
true. It's this, that to write we seem to have to go at it with
such single-minded intensity that we are always on the
point of drowning. . . .

There must be a kind of glory to it all that people coming later will wonder at. I can see us all being written up in some huge book of the age. But under what title?[42]

When Lowell, whom Roethke had coupled with Whitman, finally read *The Far Field* in July 1964, he found it was derivative and rather limited. "Cal is reading new Roethke," Philip Booth reported from Castine, Maine, "marking the margins of passages he particularly likes. . . . [But he] says it feels slack when you think of the Whitman it comes from. . . . 'But Ted's just *aw*fully good at things like this. . . . *No*body can do that better.'"

Lowell's last comments on Roethke, in an interview of 1971, once again recalled their competition (which always came to mind when he thought of Roethke), condemned Hemingway's famous metaphor of boxing literary giants to win the championship and concluded that the self-absorbed Roethke—like the egoistic Berryman—had a good ear but did not listen to other people: "I think we have a famine for greatness. . . . Roethke fevered to be the best poet, and perhaps strained for the gift. . . . I dislike the law of the boxing ring for the arts. . . . Roethke, the fine craftsman, had the innocence and deafness of a child."[43]

Lowell survived his poet-friends and wrote elegies for Roethke, Jarrell and Berryman. One of the seven original poems in *Near the Ocean* (1967) was the four-stanza "For Theodore Roethke: 1908–1963." He revised and lengthened this into a fourteen-line poem in *Notebook* (1970) and reprinted it in *History* (1973). The final, superior version of the elegy began with the water metaphor that pervades the poem (for Roethke had died while swimming) and with a trivial anecdote about Roethke sharing a bathroom with a woman painter at Yaddo. Sixteen years later, during a summer in Maine, Lowell dreamed ambivalently of his dead friend. But the next morning, Roethke had disappeared into the cold, cloudy, seabird-filled sky and merged with the maternal ocean. When Lowell addressed his subject directly, the lines were curiously vague and bland:

You honored nature, helpless, elemental
creature, and touched the waters of the offing;
you left them quickened with your name: Ted Roethke.[44]

Lowell's portrayal of the sea was not nearly as effective as
Roethke's "Meditation at Oyster River" or "The Long
Waters." His elegy was oddly disjointed, for the lines on
Yaddo, so different in tone, were later added to the *Notebook*
version; and the sea metaphor did not have the same thematic
significance in the terrestrial context of *Notebook* as it had in
Near the Ocean. The poem suggested that Lowell had not been
able to resolve his ambivalence or overcome his hostility. He
wrote as if he had no deep feeling for Roethke, nothing
significant to say about him, and were merely performing a
funereal duty. Lowell's several elegies on Jarrell and Berryman
were more deeply felt; and the exciting and exasperating
Roethke lived and died more vividly in Berryman's poem than
in Lowell's.

6

Epilogue: Sylvia Plath

I

Sylvia Plath was significantly influenced by Roethke and Lowell; elegized by Lowell and Berryman. Her poetry also derived its power from madness. Their example encouraged her to develop the expression of mental anguish and had a dramatic effect on the next generation of American poets. Her life and work show some striking similarities to the four poets discussed in this book. Plath's father, who died when she was a child, was a significant figure in her poetry. Though nourished and stimulated by marriage to a fellow writer, she was intensely competitive and ambitious, and (toward the end of her life) felt victimized by her poet-husband. In search of a poetic style, she came under the magnetic influence of Dylan Thomas. She identified with the Jews as archetypes of suffering. She endured periods of madness, believed that mania could deepen awareness and inspire great art. She saw the poet as a sacrificial figure and committed suicide. Her posthumous fame was far greater than her reputation during her lifetime.

Though Plath never met Jarrell nor discussed his poetry, certain aspects of her life and personality resembled his. They were brilliant students and showed great poetic promise while still in their teens. They were fascinated by German culture and history. They venomously portrayed colleagues and friends in their idiosyncratic novels. They were conventional, domestic, puritanical and repressed. They had a rigid, all-or-nothing personality that could shatter in times of crisis. They attempted suicide and finally succeeded.

Like Berryman, Plath did graduate work at Cambridge University, had a self-lacerating black humor, mourned and execrated her dead father, predicted her suicide in her poetry and left young children to suffer a parent's death, which had blighted her own life. *Recovery* portrayed Berryman's alcoholism, *The Bell Jar* described Plath's madness. Though a generation younger than Berryman, Plath had a certain influence on his work. Song 92, a hospital poem with symbolic flowers, is "a conscious variation on Sylvia Plath's 'Tulips.'"[1]

The theme of the witty song 187—"Them lady poets must not marry, pal"—echoes James' "The Lesson of the Master" and Yeats' "The Choice": "The intellect of man is forced to choose, / Perfection of the life or of the work." Most modern poets tried for perfection of the work and were forced, by creative anguish, to sacrifice the life. Berryman suggests that it is nearly impossible for a married woman—responsible, through her children, for "perfection of the life"—to be a poet. When Plath failed to resolve the conflict between life and art, she poured out her last poems and abandoned her children. Berryman uses Plath to represent his own condition by contrasting her marriage to the solitary life of literary lesbians and spinsters—Sappho, the Brontës, Emily Dickinson, Marianne Moore and Elizabeth Bishop. Plath has handed in her credentials and left the two surviving infants and a widower to make what they could of her death. He compares Plath's short life to the longevity of Moore and Bishop and describes her violent death as if she had merely resigned from life. He emphasizes the effect of her suicide on her infants (both less than three years old) and stresses the ineradicable guilt of the husband who betrayed and survived her.

In the crucial song 153, Berryman places Plath among the poetic casualties of the "wrecked generation": Roethke, Blackmur, Jarrell, Schwartz. But Plath, not part of this generation by birth (Blackmur was twenty-eight years older than Plath), was linked to it by her tragic fate. Since she died, by her own hand, *before* any of the other poets, her death became, for Berryman, both a symbol of the artist's sacrifice and a prediction of his own fate.

Berryman's formal elegy (song 172), like those on Roethke and Jarrell, compresses the essence of Plath's life into eighteen lines. Concentrating on her suicide, he stares at the geography of grief that marks her brooding photograph and speaks of the torrent of poetry (inspired by the break-up of her marriage) as well as of the deep depression that made "the oven seem the proper place for you." He imagines the screams of her orphaned children and offers a conventional consolation. Since she died at thirty, after two suicide attempts, her "torment here was brief." A lonely and guilty survivor, Berryman wonders why he alone is left and whether he should continue to bear the pain of life. In a late interview Berryman tried to suggest grandiose reasons for Plath's emblematic suicide: "From public officials we expect lies, and we get them in profusion. . . . Perhaps Sylvia Plath did the necessary thing by putting her head in the oven, not having to live with those lies."[2] But Berryman's rationalization was absurd (nobody ever killed himself because politicians lie) and he was actually using Plath's death as a model or excuse for his own.

Plath knew Roethke and Lowell personally and apprenticed herself to their work. Plath, who believed in signs and omens, would have been struck by the similarities between Roethke's life and her own. Their fathers, Otto Roethke and Otto Plath, were born in Pomeranian towns (Pasewalk and Grabow) less than one hundred miles from each other and came to America as children. Otto Plath's father, like Otto Roethke's son, was named Theodore; Plath's husband was called Ted. Plath's father earned a Master's degree at the University of Washington, where Ted Roethke spent most of his academic career. The death of their fathers during their childhood was the most traumatic event in the lives of Roethke and Plath. Both felt guilt as well as loss, suffered mental breakdowns and endured electric shock treatments. Both portrayed their fathers as God-like figures and absorbed the symbols of their fathers' work—the greenhouse and the beehive—into their poetic vision.

Ted Hughes has pointed out that Sylvia Plath began her close and sympathetic study of Roethke when isolated at Yaddo in 1959. She plundered him directly at first, but in "Poem for a Birthday" transformed his work into her own distinct style: "She had always responded strongly to Theodore Roethke's poems, but it was only at Yaddo, in October, that she realized how he could help her. This sequence began as a deliberate Roethke pastiche, a series of exercises which would be light and throwaway to begin with, but might lead to something else. . . . The result was a series of pieces, each a monologue of some character in an underground, primitive dream. STONES was the last of them, and the only one not obviously influenced by Roethke. It is full of specific details of her experience in a mental hospital."[3]

Plath's *Journals* confirm Hughes' statement about Roethke's influence. Just before her birthday, on October 27, she adopted Roethke's greenhouse imagery and began to write a sequence of seven poems—on her breakdown, suicide attempt and confinement in a mental institution—which expressed, for the first time, the distinct voice of *Ariel*: "Ambitious seeds of a long poem made up of separate sections: Poem on [her] birthday. To be a dwelling on madhouse, nature: meanings of tools, greenhouses, florists' shops, tunnels, vivid and disjointed. An adventure. Never over. Developing. Rebirth. Despair. Old women. . . . That greenhouse is a mine of subjects. . . . Yesterday: an exercise begun, in grimness, turning into a fine, new thing: first of a series of madhouse poems. October in the toolshed. Roethke's influence, yet mine."[4]

Plath adopted Roethke's short lines, bumpy cadence and fragmented language as well as his plant imagery and his concern for creatures victimized by the cruelty of nature. Quoting D. H. Lawrence in "Some Remarks on Rhythm," Roethke wrote: "'It all depends on the pause, the natural pause.' In other words, the breath unit, the language that is natural to the immediate thing, the particular emotion." Plath repeated this idea about rhythm in an interview of 1962. Using Lowell and Roethke to exemplify craftsmanship, she declared: "The poets I delight in are possessed by their poems as by the rhythms of their own breathing. Their finest poems seem born all-of-a-piece, not put together by hand: certain poems in Robert Lowell's *Life Studies*, for instance; Theodore Roethke's greenhouse poems."[5] In 1959, then, Lowell's *Life Studies* and Roethke's *Words for the Wind* propelled Plath in the direction of her greatest work.

Marjorie Perloff has demonstrated, with parallel passages, how in "Poem for a Birthday" Plath "perfectly assumes [Roethke's] voice, his image patterns, his aphorisms," but does not share his attitude toward the "lovely diminutives" of nature. Margaret Uroff has noted Roethke's influence on two other Plath poems written at Yaddo: "Mushrooms" and "The Burnt-Out Spa," with its Roethkean image—"little weeds insinuate / Soft suede tongues." And she concludes that Roethke had a technical and thematic impact on a poet whose temperament was quite different and response to nature more guarded: "His association of the human and natural world, his search for his own identity through this association, the uncertainty and vulnerability he admits, as well as his poetic confrontation of his own insanity—all these attitudes and interests find expression in Plath's poem. . . . She took from Roethke's poetry certain images, rhythms, and a general idea of how she might handle madness as a subject for poems; but 'Poem for a Birthday' shares neither Roethke's participation in nature nor his driving sincerity and openness."[6]

Roethke's influence on Plath's last poem, which Hughes did not mention, has not been noticed. In "In A Dark Time," his greatest poem on nature, Roethke refers to his tense balance on the abyss and states: "The edge is what I have." In "Edge," Plath predicts her own death as clearly as Berryman did in his final poem. She imagines herself laid out as a corpse, surrounded by her dead children, coiled near the empty pitchers of milk.[7] In Plath, the Roethkean flowers stiffen and the odors bleed. She is ready for death.

Fellow poets were quick to notice the new influence on her poetry. Anne Sexton, a friend whose work was often linked with Plath's, said: "I remember writing to Sylvia in England after *The Colossus* came out [in 1960] and saying something like . . . 'if you're not careful, Sylvia, you will out-Roethke Roethke,' and she replied that I had guessed accurately and that he had been a strong influence on her work. . . . Not that her lines reminded me of Roethke—but the openness to metaphor, the way they both have (and Sylvia even more so in her last work) of jumping straight into their own image and then believing it. No doubt of it—at the end, Sylvia burst from her cage and came riding straight out with the image-ridden darer, Roethke."

Another extremist poet, W. D. Snodgrass, who had been a student of both Lowell and Jarrell, suggested that Roethke's influence may also have reached Plath indirectly, through Hughes: "It seems to me to be very interesting that she would take Roethke's voice, because I think very much of her work was determined by her hatred of her husband, by her detestation of the man who is the greatest living English poet, an incredibly powerful man, and one who often takes much the same subject matter that Roethke takes, but is better at it."[8]

On February 1, 1961, just before her miscarriage and appendectomy, Plath met Roethke in London. In a letter to her mother, she praised his work, acknowledged his influence and admired his character: "Ted and I went to a little party last night to meet the American poet I admire next to Robert Lowell—Ted (for Theodore) Roethke. I've always wanted to meet him, as I find he is my influence. . . . He's a big, blond, Swedish-looking man, much younger-seeming that his 52 years. . . . Ted and I got on well with him and hope to see him again."

In early March, Eric White, of the Poetry Book Society, told Roethke about the desperate plight of Plath and Hughes, and the older poet responded generously: "Hughes did not keep accounts and at that time was nearly destitute—Sylvia Plath was in a hospital for an operation and Hughes was trying to keep house with their year-old child. . . . Ted, who admired the work of both Hughes and Sylvia Plath, was immediately concerned and wanted to send her flowers, but, he said, he was leaving England and would not have the time, so he gave White some money and asked him to do it for him. Later, he tried to get Ted Hughes a job at Washington."[9] It is just possible that Roethke sent the tulips that inspired Plath's hospital poem and influenced Berryman's Dream Song.

II

Plath's connection with Lowell, as with Roethke, was personal and literary. Both came from Boston and were inspired by the dolorous greys of the Massachusetts coastline. Both were married to successful writers. They knew each other socially; and Plath audited Lowell's poetry-writing class at Boston University in the spring of 1959. Lowell wrote an introduction to *Ariel* and an elegy on Plath, and discussed her life and work in several interviews, articles and letters. Both struggled against the forces of disintegration, suffered cyclical break-downs (Lowell every year or two, Plath every decade) and were hospitalized in McLean's. Elizabeth Hardwick's description of Plath's mental illness and suicidal urges was clearly based on her experiences with Lowell: "Persons suffering [from mental illness] in this way simply do not have room in their heads for the anguish of others—and later may seem to survive their own torments only by an erasing detachment. . . . We think of these self-destructive actions as more or less sudden or as the culmination of an unbearable depression, one that brings with it a feeling of unworthiness and hopelessness, a despair that cannot imagine recovery."

Plath first met Lowell in June 1958, shortly after his release from McLean's, when she was teaching at Smith College. She knew about and identified with his mania, though she described it with ironic humor. As a Bostonian, she found his ancestry as impressive as his art. Though she was teaching at Smith and living in Northampton, he appropriated her home territory, assumed his kingly stance and persuaded her to search for his forebears: "We met the mad and very nice poet Robert Lowell (the only one, 40-ish, whom we both admire, who comes from the Boston Lowells and is periodically carted off as a manic depressive). . . . He is quiet, soft-spoken, and we liked him very much. I drove him around Northampton, looking for relics of his ancestors, and to the Historical Society and the graveyard."[10]

The atmosphere in the spring of 1959—when Plath audited Lowell's course with Anne Sexton and George Starbuck and then repaired to the Ritz to discuss their suicides—was extremely clinical. Plath had given up her teaching position and moved to Boston. She worked as a secretary in Massachusetts General hospital and typed up the psychiatric case histories she described in her story, "Johnny Panic and the Bible of Dreams." She began to see her old psychiatrist, Ruth Beuscher, who had treated her after the suicide attempt of August 1953. Her visit to her father's grave in Winthrop, in March, inspired one of her most personal poems, "Electra on Azalea Path." Lowell, once again a patient at McLean's during April–June 1959, was temporarily released from the hospital in order to teach his classes at Boston University. In May 1959 he published *Life Studies*, his first book in eight years, which he had been reading to his students. It was a major breakthrough in style and theme, and described his confinements in McLean's.

Plath's journals of February, March and May 1959 (in contrast to her chirpy letter to her mother the previous June) expressed increasing disillusionment with Lowell's teaching and character—though she still valued his criticism of her work: "Lowell's class yesterday a great disappointment: I said a few mealymouthed things. . . . Lowell good in his mildly feminine ineffectual fashion. Felt a regression. The main thing is hearing the other students' poems & his reaction to mine. . . . Criticism of 4 of my poems in Lowell's class:

criticism of rhetoric. He sets me up with Anne Sexton, an honor, I suppose. Well, about time. . . . How few of my superiors do I respect the opinions of anyhow? Lowell a case in point." Sexton reported that Lowell was impressed by Plath's work and "felt her poems got right to the point."[11]

Plath responded more favorably to Lowell's poetry than to his teaching. In May 1958, a month before she met him in Northampton, she had been excited by his work and compared it to the poetry of Ted Hughes: "read some of his poems last night and had oddly a similar reaction (excitement, joy, admiration, curiosity to meet and praise) as when I first read Ted's poems in *St. Botolph's* [in 1956]: taste the phrases: tough, knotty, blazing with color and fury, most eminently sayable." In an interview of October 30, 1962, she recalled her reaction to the extraordinary revelations of *Life Studies*: "I've been very excited by what I feel is the new breakthrough that came with, say, Robert Lowell's *Life Studies*, this intense breakthrough into very serious, very personal, emotional experience which I feel has been partly taboo. Robert Lowell's poems about his experience in a mental hospital, for example, interested me very much." And in a review of Donald Hall's anthology, *Contemporary American Poetry*, a month before her death, she again praised Lowell's "tightrope walks of a naked psyche."[12]

Hughes noted that Lowell had enabled Plath to transcend the formal constraints of her first book, *The Colossus*: "Reading Lowell in 1958 had really set her off to break through whatever blocks there were. . . . She had tried for a way out through Robert Lowell's early manner of writing (as in 'Point Shirley')."[13] Following Hughes' hint, critics have detected Lowell's influence in several poems by Plath. Ian Hamilton noticed that "You are a bastard, Michael, aren't you! *Nein*" in "Thanksgiving's Over" (*The Mills of the Kavanaughs*) found its way into the conclusion of Plath's most famous poem: "Daddy, daddy, you bastard, I'm through." Katha Pollitt called Plath's "The Babysitters," about a summer with the rich on the north shore of Massachusetts, a "Lowellian

exercise"—in the manner of "My Last Afternoon with Uncle
Devereux Winslow" (*Life Studies*). And Jerome Mazzaro wrote
of "Memories of West Street and Lepke" (*Life Studies*): "As
that poem had seen his own breakdown, shock treatment, and
recovery in terms of the electrocution of Czar Louis Lepke of
Murder Incorporated, Plath's heroine [in *The Bell Jar*] sets her
own breakdown, shock treatment, and recovery against the
electrocution of Ethel and Julius Rosenberg."[14]

Lowell also left his mark on a number of other poems. The
surging rhythm and alteration of long and short lines in "The
Quaker Graveyard in Nantucket" (*Lord Weary's Castle*)
appears in the topographical "Point Shirley" (the extreme tip
of Winthrop) just as the oceanic and religious imagery of
Lowell's poem appears in Plath's "Finisterre" (the western-
most tip of Brittany). Lowell's identification with tyrants—
Napoleon and Hitler—recurs in Plath's "The Swarm" and
"Daddy." His poems about mental hospitals, like "Waking in
the Blue" (*Life Studies*), freed Plath to write about her own
similar experiences in "The Jailer." In at least one instance
Plath seems to have influenced Lowell. Her lines "The blood
jet is poetry, / There is no stopping it" in "Kindness"
(published February 17, 1963) reappears in Lowell's "The
Severed Head" (*For the Union Dead*, October 1964) when the
writer's pen drips "a red ink dribble on us, as he pressed / the
little strip of plastic tubing clipped / to feed it from his
heart."[15]

After Plath's death, Lowell placed her in the manic
tradition and praised her combination of authenticity and
technique: "She was truly driven, but with the mercy of great
opportunities. . . . Maybe, it's an irrelevant accident that she
actually carried out the death she predicted . . . but somehow
her death is part of the imaginative risk. In the best poems one
is torn by saying, 'This is so true and lived that most other
poetry seems like an exercise,' and then one can back off and
admire the dazzling technique and invention. Perfect control,
like the control of a skier who avoids every death-trap until
reaching the final drop."

Lowell developed these ideas in an essay that first appeared in the *New York Review of Books* (May 12, 1966) and was reprinted as a Foreword to the American edition of *Ariel* (1966). He recalled Plath (whom most men found attractive) as "willowy, long-waisted, sharp-elbowed, nervous, giggly, gracious—a brilliant tense presence embarrassed by restraint. Her humility and willingness to accept what was admired seemed at times to give her an air of maddening docility that hid her unfashionable patience and boldness." Lowell listed her horror-show themes and (with hindsight) said they led directly to her death: "These poems are playing Russian roulette with six cartridges in the cylinder. . . . Her art's immortality is life's disintegration." Unlike Berryman's poems, which (Lowell felt) justified his personal suffering, the poems of Plath—who died so young and at the height of her astonishing powers—"tell that life, even when disciplined, is simply *not* worth it."[16]

In an interview of 1971, after *Ariel* had established her posthumous reputation, Ian Hamilton asked Lowell's opinion of Plath. Lowell praised her corrosive style and (like Berryman) placed her with the greatest women poets:

> I glory in her. I don't know whether she writes like me. In an extreme Life-and-Death style, she is as good as Sir Walter Raleigh; no, she's not as good, but no poetry has a more acid sting. Few women write major poetry. Can I make this generalization? Only four stand with our best men: Emily Dickinson, Marianne Moore, Elizabeth Bishop and Sylvia Plath. It's a rough road. Sylvia is not the most enchanting, she's perhaps my least favourite, but she belongs to the group, and has her half dozen supreme, extreme poems. Years ago, Sylvia and Anne Sexton audited my poetry class. Anne was more herself, and knew less. I thought they might rub off on each other. Sylvia learned from Anne.

The following year, in his obituary of Berryman, Lowell,

with grim irony, criticized the tendency to link the extremist poets with death. He insisted that Plath, who died at an early age, was an exception: "I must say something of death and the *extremist poets*, as we are named in often prefunerary tributes. Except for Weldon Kees [1914–55] and Sylvia Plath, they lived as long as Shakespeare, outlived Wyatt, Baudelaire and Hopkins, and long outlived the forever Romantics, those who really died young."[17]

Lowell's poem "Sylvia Plath" (1971) precedes the elegies on Jarrell and Roethke in *History*. But he adopts a sharper and more didactic tone to dissociate himself from the feminist view of Plath, which made her into a poetic victim—snuffed out by male oppression. Lowell begins with three statements in the form of questions. The first quotes John Bayley's comment on Plath—"A miniature mad talent"—which recognizes the real if limited scope of her manic poetry; the second—"rising in the saddle to slash at Auschwitz"—alludes to her horse Ariel and her poem "Daddy"; the third describes the conflict between her career and family. He resents Plath's being used to justify feminist attacks on marriage and babies, mentions the unexplained fact of 60,000 American infant deaths a year and implies that our society cannot afford to continue its irrational hostility to reproduction.

Lowell's weak poem on Plath was convincingly attacked in Clive James' *The Metropolitan Critic* (1971) and in John Carey's review of James' book. Both critics felt the use of Auschwitz by poets who had never experienced the horrors of the extermination camps reduced the tragedy of history to the level of bad taste. James stated that the "sheer shrieking inadequacy" of the lines look pitiful to anyone with a knowledge of the Nazis. Carey, with a characteristic sneer, condemned Lowell and Plath's habit of commandeering the disasters of history "as if they were upsets in their own little psyches." In an angry letter to the *New Review*, Lowell praised Plath in ambiguous tones and weakly defended himself on technical rather than ideological grounds: "I wasn't trying to refute John Bayley's witty and imaginative, 'Plath, a *miniature mad talent*'. . . . I was parodying and gibing when I wrote with inflation, 'rising in the saddle to lash [*sic*] at Auschwitz,' and '*I am a woman*'. . . . Sylvia was a rash writer, but not as Carey implies 'brandishing.' It's hard to write now of her posthumous royal shadow, her honest cruelty, her insolent rightness. My critic's confusion comes perhaps from my trying to mix high poetic style with a lower, quicker style that talked to the character of the person with love, mockery and awe."[18]

Lowell, who had encouraged Plath's poetry by his example and his art, was disturbed about his responsibility for its suicidal direction and cultish influence. Berryman, who mentioned Plath's infants (instead of statistical infant deaths) and followed the same destructive impulse as Plath, responded more sympathetically than Lowell to her character and work.

III

Plath experienced three major crises in her life: the death of her father, a week after her eighth birthday, in November 1940; her suicide attempt in August 1953; the break-up of her marriage in the summer of 1962. The rest of her life was a series of intellectual, academic, literary, social, emotional and maternal triumphs.

Sylvia's father, Otto Emil Plath, was born in north Germany on April 13, 1885. His father, a blacksmith, had emigrated to North Dakota, and Otto arrived in New York at the age of sixteen. He worked in his uncle's food and liquor store, put himself through grade school in a year, learned English perfectly and spoke it without a trace of an accent. He graduated from Northwestern College in Minneapolis in 1910, but was rejected by his family when he renounced his plans for the Lutheran ministry. He earned a Master of Arts degree at the University of Washington in 1912; and then vanished into obscurity during the war years, when conditions became difficult for German immigrants. In 1915 he married his first wife, Lydia, but soon separated from her. In "Little Fugue"

Sylvia says that Otto worked in a California delicatessen during the Great War.[19]

Otto was a tall, erect, handsome man with blue eyes, ruddy complexion, high parted hair, neat brush moustache and cleft chin. He emerged in Boston after the war and, sixteen years after his Master's degree, earned a Doctor of Science in applied biology at Harvard. Friends who knew him in the 1920s said Otto was aware of his diabetic condition, but continued to indulge his sweet tooth and devour rich foods. (His interest in bees first developed in boyhood when he searched for honey to satisfy his appetite.) In 1929 he met Aurelia Schober, the American-born daughter of Austrian immigrants, who was a high-school teacher and a graduate student in his Middle High German class at Boston University. Otto went to Reno to obtain a divorce and married Aurelia in Carson City on January 4, 1932.

Otto was four years younger than Aurelia's father and twenty-one years older than his wife (born in 1906). He had learned nothing about flexibility and compromise from his first marriage; and by age, education, rigidity and authoritarian temperament (colleagues noted "he gets what he wants when he wants it"), he naturally dominated his second wife. In an effort to make up for lost time in the academic world, Otto devoted himself, with Prussian single-mindedness, first to the expansion of his doctoral thesis into *Bumblebees and Their Ways* (1934) and then to a chapter on insect societies in *A Handbook of Social Psychology* (1935). None of his papers and books on the dining-room table could ever be moved. (When Plath and Hughes bought a house in Devon, she told Aurelia that she wanted her husband to have a study where he would no longer have to move his papers.) Otto and Aurelia had almost no social life, and she had "to become more submissive, although it was not in [her] nature to be so." Sylvia was born in Jamaica Plain, a south Boston suburb, on October 27, 1932, during their first year of marriage. Her brother Warren appeared, exactly as planned, two and a half years later.

After only four years of marriage that had been dedicated

to work, Otto became seriously ill at the age of fifty-one. He spent the next four years, like Tolstoy's Ivan Ilych, slowly and resentfully dying. Aurelia wrote that he suffered from loss of weight, chronic cough and sinusitis, and was always exhausted, anxious and easily upset. He mistakenly believed that he had lung cancer, and refused to consider surgery. She was heartbroken to see the once-strong, powerful and handsome man lose his strength and deteriorate emotionally and physically. The scientist refused to consult a doctor and would explode with rage when urged to seek medical advice. After four years of deterioration, in mid-August 1940, Otto accidentally stubbed his toe and Aurelia discovered his foot was black with gangrene. His disease was finally diagnosed as advanced diabetes mellitus, which could have been controlled, if treated in time, with diet and insulin. Otto irrationally exclaimed: "God knows, why have I been so cussed!" Aurelia, confused and distressed by Otto's death wish, as she later would be by Sylvia's, thought: "All this needn't have happened; it needn't have happened." Their doctor wondered: "How could such a brilliant man be so stupid."

Otto, who would "never submit to surgery," had his toe cut off. But the gangrene continued to spread, and on October 12, 1940 his left leg was amputated at the thigh. Neither operation saved him; and he died in the hospital of an embolus of the lung on November 5. Aurelia, who had tried to shield the children from their father's illness, did not take them to the funeral. When she told Sylvia that her father had died, the child reacted as if the deity had committed a social gaffe, exclaimed: "I'll never speak to God again!"—and decided to go to school. That afternoon, Sylvia insisted her mother sign a handwritten document that said: "I PROMISE NEVER TO MARRY AGAIN."[20] After four years of emotional stress and partial neglect, Sylvia demanded her mother's devotion. Aurelia faithfully kept her promise and (unlike Berryman's mother) did not expose her children to the traumatic adjustment of a second marriage. At Otto's insistence, Aurelia had resigned her teaching position to become a wife and mother, and given up her friends to devote herself to his work. In return, she got a domestic tyrant at the beginning of her marriage and a hopeless invalid at the end. Only the extraordinary success of her children could compensate for her suffering and sacrifice. Six months after Otto's death, Sylvia published her first poem in the *Boston Sunday Herald.*

Plath sometimes dismissed Otto as "a sort of fuddy-duddy professor who dealt with bugs down in Boston" and idealized his life and death in her early story, "Among the Bumblebees." But her memory darkened as she grew older. In her novel *The Bell Jar* (1963), Esther Greenwood's German-speaking father, associated with the dark forests of the Teutonic unconscious, "came from some manic-depressive hamlet in the black heart of Prussia." Her enraged, guilt-wracked mother secretly hated her secretarial job "and hated him for dying and leaving me no money because he didn't trust life insurance salesmen."

In her more nakedly expressive journals of the mid-1950s, Plath raged against the death of her father and held her parents responsible for her misfortune. She blamed Otto for virtually taking his own life in order to escape from his wife and children; and hated Aurelia for marrying an old tyrant who had died before giving her a father's love: "I have never known [him]; even his mind, his heart, his face, as a boy of 17 [the year after he came to America] I love terribly. I would have loved him; and he is gone. . . . I never knew the love of a father, the love of a steady blood-related man after the age of eight. . . . She came in one morning with tears . . . in her eyes and told me he was gone for good. I hate her for that. He was an ogre. But I miss him. He was old, but she married an old man to be my father. It was her fault. . . . I have lost a father and his love early; feel angry at her because of this."[21]

Plath expressed her love–hate attitude toward her parents in one of her most revealing poems, "Electra on Azalea Path," written in March 1959 when she was trying to come to terms with her psychic wound, typing psychological records at Massachusetts General, seeing her psychiatrist and auditing Lowell's course at Boston University—where her father had taught and her mother was then teaching. Plath has left three versions of her visit to her father's grave: in her journal, her novel and her poem.

On March 9, 1959 Plath gave a detailed description of her morbid pilgrimage to the ugly, shabby and depressing cemetery in the north Boston suburb where her family had once lived: "Went to my father's grave, a very depressing sight. The graveyards separated by streets, all made within the last 50 years or so, ugly crude black stones, headstones together, as if the dead were sleeping head to head in a poorhouse.... I found the flat stone, 'Otto E. Plath, 1885–1940,' right beside the path, where it would be walked over. Felt cheated. My temptation to dig him up. To prove he existed and really was dead. How far gone would he be?" Plath's necrophilic desire to examine the decomposed remains of her father's body—as if to prove he had wanted to die and did not care if he destroyed her life by giving up his own—has a strikingly macabre resemblance to Berryman's penultimate Dream Song, which described *his* desire to hack open his father's casket and tear off the mouldering grave clothes "to see just how he's taking it." In both cases the survivor wants to punish the father for having turned his child into a permanent victim.

In *The Bell Jar*, after her shock treatment and just before her suicide attempt, Esther Greenwood ambivalently wishes "to pay [her] father back" (rather than "repay her father"). She visits the cemetery where he is buried, picks and arranges flowers at his grave, and experiences a moment of catharsis that has been delayed for thirteen years:

He had died in the hospital, so the graveyard and even his death had always seemed unreal to me.

I had a great yearning, lately, to pay my father back for all the years of neglect, and start tending his grave. I had always been my father's favorite, and it seemed fitting I should take on a mourning my mother had never bothered with. . . .

   At the foot of the stone I arranged the rainy armful of
azaleas I had picked from a bush at the gateway of the
graveyard. Then my legs folded under me, and I sat down
in the sopping grass. I couldn't understand why I was
crying so hard.
   Then I remembered that I had never cried for my
father's death.[22]

The title of "Electra on Azalea Path" (completed on March
20, 1959) has four different meanings. Electra is the sister of
Iphigenia and Orestes, the daughter of Agamemnon and
Clytemnestra (who murdered her husband), and the subject
of a play by Sophocles. Her name also refers to the complex
described by Freud in which the daughter has an unnaturally
strong sexual attachment to the father. Azalea Path in
Winthrop Cemetery leads to the grave of her father. And—
marked by the absence of the definite article that would
normally appear in the title and by the capitalized words that
unmistakably echo the name of her mother—the title suggests
Sylvia's judgment on Aurelia Plath. Sylvia expresses the
meaning of the poem through the voice of the mythical and
psychological Electra, who stands as close as she can get to
her dead father.
   The opening stanza describes Plath's reaction to her
father's death. She retreated into the lightless hibernaculum of
Otto's subjects, the bees, just as she would later retreat into
the dark cellar of the family house when she tried to kill
herself. Denying her biological father, she claims to be "God-
fathered into the world from my mother's belly"—like the
divine Athena, born full-blown from the head of Zeus. After
Otto's death had freed Aurelia, Sylvia "wormed back under
[her] mother's heart." Nobody died in her dream of her
father's epic achievement, but she woke in the cemetery and
found his name, gravestone and bones in the "cramped
necropolis."
   Plath then describes the path to his poorhouse plot, the
cheap plastic evergreens on the neighboring grave and (using

a German word) the "ersatz petals" dripping red, like blood. In the fourth stanza, the italicized words recall the sacrifice of Iphigenia, which raised the winds that carried the Greeks to Troy, and Clytemnestra's red carpet, which led Agamemnon to his bloody death when he returned from the wars. Plath remembers that just after her birthday on October 27, 1940 an ominous scorpion (the symbol of her mother) announced her father's death.

Continuing the metaphor of classical tragedy in the final stanza, Plath—in a devastating mixture of exorcism and excoriation—specifies the gangrene that destroyed her father's leg and caused the maimed colossus to collapse, mentions her inability to accept the reality of his death, calls Otto "an infamous suicide," blames him for her own suicide attempt (the cut-throat razor rusting in her neck), begs forgiveness for sniffing out his grave and concludes that her self-destructive love has nearly killed both of them—for she is only half alive:

> I am the ghost of an infamous suicide,
> My own blue razor rusting in my throat.
> O pardon the one who knocks for pardon at
> Your gate, father—your hound-bitch, daughter, friend.
> It was my love that did us both to death.

Like the relatives of all terminal patients, Aurelia and Sylvia must sometimes have wished, if only unconsciously, for Otto's death. It would have finally freed them from the physical burden and emotional anxiety of his illness. It would have allowed them to reconstruct their own lives and focus their attention on one another. Plath (armed with psycho-analytic insight) admitted this when defining the source of her guilt. Speaking for herself as well as for her mother, she told a friend: "I adored and despised him, and I probably wished many times that he were dead. When he obliged me and died, I imagined that I had killed him."[23]

After Otto's death, Aurelia, who had developed a bleeding ulcer, moved from Winthrop to Wellesley, a more prosperous

suburb west of Boston. She assumed her husband's responsibilities, and supported Sylvia and Warren by teaching
secretarial studies at Boston University. She also maintained
the atmosphere of Germanic rigor and intellectual competition
engendered by Otto. And she taught her exceptionally bright,
ambitious, scholarship-winning children that it was important
to develop a strong inner life and strive toward idealistic goals.
Aurelia provided a "strong" framework, but ignored Sylvia's
inner wound—a source of her poetry—which emerged later
on.

There were two profound problems between mother and
daughter. Aurelia alive eventually became as much of a
burden as Otto dead. First, was Sylvia's overwhelming sense
of obligation for her mother's sacrificial efforts. To compensate
for the loss of the father, Aurelia gave her daughter all the
moral and material advantages of an American childhood.
Sylvia told Warren, with typically morbid diction, three
months before her suicide attempt, in May 1953, that Aurelia
would actually "kill herself" for her children if they calmly
accepted everything she wanted to do for them. Since she was
unusually altruistic, they had to oppose her selflessness as
they would oppose a dangerous disease. Second, was the need
to reject her mother's values—from the Unitarian Church and
the Girl Scouts to sexual purity and financial success—which
had formed a superficial carapace around Sylvia's molten
core. Though Aurelia was tough on the surface, one of Sylvia's
friends observed that "Mrs. Plath over-reacted to everything.
. . . She gushed all over the place, everything was sweet and
dear and touching, tears in her eyes all the time."[24] Only
after Sylvia had destroyed the part of the mother in herself,
rejected Aurelia's concepts of work, love, marriage, home and
family, and exhausted her feelings of gratitude, could she
finally express her hatred of her parents in the *Ariel* poems.

The six-hundred-page volume of Plath's letters to her
mother, written from the time she entered Smith College on a
scholarship in September 1950 to her death in February 1963,
reveals an utterly conventional and conformist character—the

epitome of the American college girl of the Eisenhower fifties. She had to wear the right clothes, be bright and sparkling, hide her intellectual brilliance, worship her teachers, fill her correspondence with clichés, write formula stories for ladies' magazines, fulfill her numerous obligations, maintain a rigorous schedule, excel in all her activities, plan for the future and "catch" a tall handsome man from a good Eastern college.

At once guarded and open, always writing what her mother wanted to hear, Plath never lowered her confident mask until another mask had been prepared. After her first year in college she wrote, in the language of sentimental romance, that it was overwhelmingly pleasurable to return from her experiences in the adult world and to sleep in blissful peace and security in her own family home. After her marriage and during her second year as a Fulbright student at Newnham College, Cambridge, the relentlessly effervescent and strenuously cheerful coed promised to get rid of her knee socks forever and become an adult. But the latter-day Daisy Miller never quite managed to do so. As late as May 1962, less than a year before her death, Plath said she no longer had the energy to attempt the "exotic" recipes in her beloved *Ladies' Home Journal.*[25]

In October 1954, during her last year at Smith, Plath admitted: "I am really regrettably unoriginal, conventional, and puritanical basically, but I needed to practice a certain healthy bohemianism for a while to swing away from the gray-clad, basically-dressed, brown-haired, clock-regulated, responsible, salad-eating, water-drinking, bed-going, economical, practical girl I had become." But her idea of "healthy bohemianism" was acting frivolous over coffee and bridge, creating casseroles and conversations, taking "blazing jaunts in yellow convertibles to exquisite restaurants." Her college roommate, Nancy Hunter, observed that Plath actively disliked the little band of rebels in the dormitory and "except for the penetrating intelligence and the extraordinary poetic talent she could have been an airline stewardess or the ingenuous heroine of a B movie."[26] Yet the extremely competitive Plath was outraged ("a rank travesty") when her friend George Starbuck won the Yale Younger Poets award in 1959 and vowed that her main poetic rivals—May Swenson, Isabella Gardner and Adrienne Rich—would soon be eclipsed by her achievement.

Plath's two extraordinary deviations from convention (hidden from her mother until the moment of disaster) were sexual adventures and suicidal impulses. In the fall of 1950 she admitted that she desperately needed to feel physically desirable at all times. But when an older college student suggested sex, she responded in the most frigid tone and quite forcibly told him that she would never consent to his desire for sexual intercourse. In 1954, after her suicide attempt and release from McLean's, her psychiatrist provided her with a diaphragm. She encouraged Plath to break away from her mother's influence, accept her sexual desires and free herself from the burden of virginity. Plath eagerly responded to this advice, surprised and seduced her old boyfriend Philip McCurdy in January 1954 and went to bed with Richard Sassoon (grandson of the poet Siegfried) in May.

Her strangest sexual experience, at once voracious and clinical, took place in the summer of 1954 when she was sharing a flat with Nancy Hunter in Cambridge, Massachusetts. Plath fictionalized the event in *The Bell Jar* when the virgin Esther Greenwood hemorrhages horribly after submitting to Irwin's painful and unsatisfactory defloration. Edwin (called Irwin in the novel) was a tall, emaciated, balding, myopic, repellently ugly and intellectually brilliant biology professor at a local college. Though she told Nancy that Edwin had raped her, Plath went on a picnic with him the next day and continued to see him. As Plath's reckless accidents in skiing, horse riding and driving proved, she "enjoyed" (to use one of her favorite words) dangerous situations, but could rarely escape their consequences. After achieving her sexual freedom, Plath proudly recorded that she had lost her puritanical inhibitions: "Never felt guilty for bedding with one, losing virginity and going to the Emergency Ward in a spurt of blood."[27]

IV

The second major crisis in Plath's life was the suicide attempt, at the age of twenty, in Wellesley on August 24, 1953. Apart from her father's death in 1940, Plath's life had been a triumphant success: perfect behavior at home, perfect grades at school, scholarships, awards, honors, prizes and publication in popular magazines, *Seventeen* and *Mademoiselle*. She felt superstitious about her unbroken streak of good luck and told her mother that the gods might soon destroy her smooth and placid life.

Disturbed by the example of Otto's passive suicide, Plath was fascinated by the possibility of killing herself. In November 1950, when she was dateless and depressed, the sudden appearance of a boyfriend changed her mood and prompted her to rant on about *never* committing suicide, because an unexpected event could suddenly change your mood. Two years later, while having trouble with a science course that might ruin her perfect grades, she recognized her neurotic feelings and stated, with considerable exaggeration, that she frantically thought of killing herself to get out of the course, that small difficulties seemed like insurmountable obstacles and that the core of her life had fallen apart.[28] That same month she asked why brilliant women writers like Sara Teasdale or Virginia Woolf killed themselves; and later admitted that she had been "reduplicating" Woolf's suicide by attempting to drown herself in July 1953.

The first serious sign of mental instability appeared during an academic and emotional crisis at Smith in November 1952. Her carapace suddenly shattered and she gave vent to her repressed rage: "I felt the mask crumble, the great poisonous store of corrosive ashes begin to spew out of my mouth. I have been needing, more than anything, to talk to somebody, to spill out all the tight, jealous, envious, apprehensive neurotic tensions in me." The following month, she walked past the state mental hospital in Northampton, listening to the inmates screaming and wondering why people cross the borderline into insanity.

After winning a national competition among college students, Plath spent June 1953 as one of the twelve guest-editors of *Mademoiselle* in New York. She was paid a salary and expenses, went to fashion shows and parties, interviewed well-known writers like Elizabeth Bowen and Marianne Moore. After achieving success in this glossy world, she was horrified to discover that she hated it. She returned to Wellesley in July, exhausted and depressed, to learn that she had been rejected for Frank O'Connor's creative-writing class at Harvard Summer School and that her maternal grandmother was close to death. When Aurelia noticed some partially healed razor gashes on her daughter's legs, Sylvia exclaimed: "I just wanted to see if I had the guts. . . . Oh, Mother, the world is so rotten! I want to die! *Let's die together!*"[29]

Plath was subjected to an unsuccessful series of electro-convulsive shocks, which she described with black humor and gruesome imagery in *The Bell Jar*: "Dr. Gordon was fitting two metal plates on either side of my head. He buckled them into place with a strap that dented my forehead, and gave me a wire to bite. . . . Then something bent down and took hold of me and shook me like the end of the world. Whee-ee-ee-ee-ee, it shrilled, through an air crackling with blue light, and with each flash a great jolt drubbed me till I thought my bones would break and the sap fly out of me like a split plant. I wondered what terrible thing it was that I had done."

Plath's novel suggests some of the reasons for her mental breakdown. She felt guilty about desiring the death of her father and feeling unnatural hostility toward her mother, and later realized she had transferred her murderous impulses toward her mother onto herself. She also experienced disil-lusionment and uncertainty, felt unworthy of the benefits she had received, could not meet her own exalted standards, was unable to write and succumbed to the pressure of external events. Finally, Plath's shock treatments (like Hemingway's) intensified instead of relieving her depression and made her fear (like Lowell and Berryman) that she would end up in a straitjacket—permanently insane. After the horrible shock treatments, she told a friend, "the only doubt in my mind was the precise time and method of committing suicide. The only alternative I could see was an eternity of hell for the rest of my life in a mental hospital, and I was going to make use of my last ounce of free choice and choose a quick clean ending."[30]

But her attempt was neither quick nor clean nor conclusive. On August 24, when her mother was out of the house, she broke open a steel case, took a bottle of forty sleeping pills and left an unconvincing note: "Have gone for a long walk. Will be home tomorrow." Taking a glass of water and a blanket, she entered the crawl space in the basement, replaced the pile of wood that had covered the opening and swallowed the pills. "At first nothing happened," she wrote in *The Bell Jar*, "but as I approached the bottom of the bottle, red and blue lights began to flash before my eyes. The bottle slid from my fingers and I lay down. The silence drew off, baring the pebbles and shells and all the tatty wreckage of my life. Then, at the rim of vision, it gathered itself, and in one sweeping tide, rushed me to sleep."

But Plath, so efficient in everything else, botched her suicide. She took too many pills, vomited them up and lapsed into unconsciousness. Three days later—while family and friends, Boy Scouts and police searched frantically for her—Lady Lazarus came back to life. She banged her head on the rough rocks of the low cellar and instinctively called for help. Her brother heard her moans and rescued her from the premature grave: "maggots had been scraped 'like sticky pearls' off her flesh when she was first freed from the crawl space; and her face was a swollen mass of multicolored bruises under a mop of dirt-clotted hair. A scar ravaged her distended right cheek; and two ugly sores punctuated the corners of her cracked lips."

She spent five months under the care of Dr. Ruth Beuscher[31] at McLean's, and had successful shock therapy. After her recovery, Plath—like Berryman, Roethke and Lowell—believed the terrible suffering she had endured during this period had provided the subject matter of her greatest poetry and had been an extremely valuable experience. In January 1954, patched up and almost as good as new, she returned for the spring semester at Smith.

V

During her first year in Cambridge, England, Plath met the poet Ted Hughes at a literary party. The youngest of three children, Hughes was born in 1930 in a gloomy valley of the Yorkshire Pennines, near Brontë country. His father, a carpenter who had fought in the Gallipoli campaign of 1915, moved to southern Yorkshire in 1937 and kept a newsagent's shop. Hughes served in the RAF during 1948–50, won a scholarship to Pembroke College, Cambridge, in 1951 and read archeology and anthropology. After taking his degree in 1954, he worked briefly as a gardener, night watchman, zoo attendant, teacher, reader for Rank films, and began to publish his cruel and original poetry. *Hawk in the Rain* immediately established his reputation in 1957.

Plath had read Hughes' work and was instantly attracted to his rugged features and rebellious character. They began as they ended, passionately and violently. On February 26, the day after their first meeting, she recorded in her journals (later published by Hughes in a censored version): "then he kissed me bang smash on the mouth [omission]. . . . And when he kissed my neck I bit him long and hard on the cheek, and when we came out of the room, blood was running down his face. [Omission.] And I screamed in myself, thinking: oh, to give myself crashing, fighting to you. . . . I would like to try just this once, my force against his." She had found a man whose might and talent were even greater than her own. She constantly praised the tremendous strength of her new-found colossus, but feared it might one day be used against her: "I have fallen terribly in love, which can only lead to great hurt. I met the strongest man in the world . . . a large, hulking, healthy Adam . . . with a voice like the thunder of God."[32]

Both Plath and Hughes had come from humble back-grounds and won scholarships to Cambridge. Though the cheerful coed did not seem the type to attract the rough outsider, she was an exotic contrast to her reserved and studious English classmates. Physically attractive, sexually responsive, intelligent, capable and talented, Plath was dedicated to poetry, convinced of Hughes' genius and fiercely loyal to the man and his art. Shortly after her death, Hughes noted the startling impression she had on English friends and praised the qualities that made him want to marry her: "People who met her were alarmed or exhilarated by the intensity of her spirits. Her affections were absolute. Once she had set her mind to it, nothing was too much trouble for her. The lovely firm complexity of design, the cleanly uncompromising thoroughness that shows in her language, showed in everything she did. And in spite of the prevailing doom evident in her poems, it is impossible that anybody could have been more in love with life, or more capable of happiness, than she was."

Hughes and Plath were the Heathcliff and Catherine, the Lowell and Stafford of their time. They inspired and sustained each other's work, but carried the seeds of destruction in their idealistic love. In "The Other Two" she wrote: "We dreamed how we were perfect, and we were." But she also wrote, with the mechanical force she had used to grind out women's stories, of "bringing each other to full capacity and production."[33]

Plath married Hughes, breaking the college rules, four months after they had met, on June 16, 1956. They spent July and August in the Spanish fishing village of Benidorm, on the Mediterranean coast near Alicante. In letters to her mother soon after their marriage, Plath continued to praise the perfection of her husband and to identify herself with him in a dangerous way:

> I can't for a minute think of him as someone "other" than the male counterpart of myself, always just that many steps ahead of me intellectually and creatively so that I feel very feminine and admiring.   (September 1956)

> He is better than any teacher, even fills somehow that huge, sad hole I felt in having no father.   (November 1956)[34]

During the next three years Plath completed her second year at Cambridge, taught for a year at Smith, worked in Boston, attended Lowell's class and wrote at Yaddo, before returning to England in December 1959. Her journals during the Benidorm period have not been published. But her entries during 1957–59 expressed a more realistic awareness of their intense attachment, her dependence on Hughes and the dangers of their suffocating intimacy:

> I think I must live in his heat and presence, for his smells and words—as if all my senses fed involuntarily on him, and deprived for more than a few hours, I languish, wither, die to the world.   (May 1958)

> Dangerous to be so close to Ted day in day out. I have no life separate from his, am likely to become a mere accessory.   (November 1959)

On April 1, 1960 Plath's daughter, Frieda, was born in London, and in October her first volume of poems, *The Colossus*, was respectfully received. In February 1961 (just after meeting Roethke) she had a miscarriage and in March an appendectomy. Plath and Hughes moved to Devon in August, and their son, Nicholas, was born on January 17, 1962. Three days later, Plath told Aurelia that the children reflected the temperamental contrast of their parents: "[Frieda] is almost hysterically impatient, [Nicholas] is calm and steady, with his big dark eyes and a ruddy complexion."[35]

On June 7, 1962 Plath—either deliberately deceiving her mother (as she often did) or completely unaware of Hughes' affair with another woman—told Aurelia: "This is the richest and happiest time of my life. The babies are so beautiful." When Aurelia came to Devon two weeks later—which could only have increased the emotional conflicts—she noted that Sylvia was extremely jealous of Ted's affair and that the atmosphere was tense and anxious.

Hughes' affair with Assia Gutman began in the spring of 1962 when she visited their home in Devon with her Canadian poet-husband. The daughter of a Russian-Jewish doctor and a German-gentile mother, Assia was born in Berlin in the 1930s, when the Nazis rose to power. She was a beautiful woman, with long black hair, dark skin and long-lashed grey eyes. After Plath's death, she gassed herself and her young daughter. Hughes' *Crow* (1971) is dedicated to the "Memory of Assia and Shura."

Since Hughes has never explained the reasons for his unhappiness, his love affair or his departure from Devon, the dissolution of their marriage has been seen only from Plath's point of view. Her biographer has suggested the problems that developed from their different backgrounds and temperaments (expressed in Hughes' "You Hated Spain"), the struggle between two artistic egos, the conflict between her literary career and maternal responsibilities, the normal decline of sexual passion, the male desire for freedom and the affair with Assia. Hugh Kenner has cynically asked if Hughes suddenly tired "of being trapped in a *Seventeen* story." Whatever the reasons, they were clearly unhappy and might have destroyed each other if they had remained together for the sake of the children. The disillusionment, violence and hatred of her possessiveness, expressed in Hughes' Baudelairean "Lovesong," suggest he had to leave the succubus—to save her as well as himself:

His promises were the surgeon's gag
Her promises took off the top of his skull
She would get a brooch made of it
His vows pulled out all her sinews
He showed her how to make a love-knot
Her vows put his eyes in formalin
At the back of her secret drawer
Their screams stuck in the wall.[36]

Though Plath's whole thought had been to please him, she had failed to do so. His departure was even worse than his death, for it meant that she had lost his love. In August 1962, when Assia called Hughes, Plath tore the telephone out of the wall and drove off to see her friends, the Comptons, in another village. On the way, she went "off the road, deliberately, seriously, wanting to die," but ran onto an old airfield without hurting herself. That day Plath, whose "affections were absolute," told Elizabeth Compton: "When you give your heart to somebody, you can't take it back. If they don't want it, it's gone."[37]

It is not clear whether Hughes was merely having an affair and would return if forgiven or if he intended to leave Plath for Assia. Plath condemned the intransigent attitude of the wounded wife in her review of Malcolm Elwin's *Lord Byron's Wife*, which appeared in the *New Statesman* in December 1962: "Annabella's refusal to grant her spouse an interview . . . let alone try to make a go of it, seems due to . . . a consistency fixed by the ego-screws of pride and a need to be forever, like Milton's God, tediously in the right." But her own stance remained resolutely rigid. Writing to her mother on August 27, she announced her separation from Hughes in the language of a soap opera: "I simply cannot go on living the degraded and agonized life I have been living, which has stopped my writing and just about ruined my sleep and my health." Plath expressed resentment of the success he had achieved while she sacrificed her art for her family, but reaffirmed her admiration for his poetry in words that seemed to echo Hughes' justification of his infidelity: "I know he is a genius, and for a genius there are no bonds and no bounds."

After Hughes left Devon in early October, Plath, who had absorbed his interest in supernatural powers and black magic, expressed her hatred in a ritualistic exorcism of his "heat and presence": "when the moon was at a certain stage, she skimmed from his desk 'Ted's scum,' microscopic bits of fingernail parings, dandruff, dead skin, hair, and then, with a random handful of papers collected from the desk and wastebasket, she had made a sort of pyre in the garden and around this she drew a circle. She stepped back to a prescribed point, lit the fire with a long stick of a torch and paced around, incanting some hocus-pocus."[38]

Plath had said: "I have no life separate from his." Like many abandoned wives, she pretended she was much happier without her husband. "Living apart from Ted is wonderful," she told her mother, "I am no longer in his shadow, and it is heaven to be liked for myself alone." But her pride was shattered and she also confessed to her mother: "The horror of what you saw and what I saw you see last summer is between us and I cannot face you again until I have a new life."[39]

VI

Plath's literary reputation is based on the poems written during the last two months of her life and published posthumously in *Ariel*. Her creative spurt, analogous to the last glorious year of Keats' life, was compressed into an even shorter span and inspired by the certain knowledge of death. In October, wrote Hughes, "when she and her husband began to live apart, every detail of the antagonist seemed to come into focus, and she started writing at top speed, producing twenty-six quite lengthy poems in that month." On December 2, the flow stopped abruptly; and on January 28 she began to write again. "Kindness," "Words," "Confusion," "Balloons" and "Edge" were composed during the last week of her life.

When discussing the demonic plumage and Mephistophelian music of *Ariel*, Hughes observed that in her later poems "there is a strange muse, bald, white and wild, in her 'hood of bone,' floating over a landscape like that of the Primitive Painters, a burningly luminous vision of a Paradise. A Paradise which is at the same time eerily frightening, an unalterably spot-lit vision of death."[40]

Plath had spent most of her life studying for examinations, suppressing her individuality, acting conventionally and writing formulaic stories. She bitterly resented her father's death, her mother's sacrifice, her husband's success. His betrayal hurt her into poetry and suffering finally enabled her to reach and reveal her deepest feelings. Her extremist poetry—emotion recollected in emotion—was more extreme than any of her predecessors'. It forced the confessional mode to the edge of exhibitionism and hysteria. Renouncing her former mode of writing and her mother's *Weltanschauung*, she justified her final poems by alluding to the Nazis and telling Aurelia: "What the person out of Belsen—physical or psychological—wants is nobody saying the birdies still go tweet-tweet, but the full knowledge that somebody else has been there and knows the *worst*, just what it is like." ("The worst is not," says Edgar in *King Lear*, "So long as we can say 'This is the worst.'") And in "Three Women" she declared that it is a terrible thing to reveal yourself, to expose your heart and let it walk out in the world.[41]

Lyric and dramatic poets have traditionally transformed their experience into formal structures that can both distance the event and heighten it. Byron and Keats, Eliot and Lowell, intellectualized personal suffering. But Plath tried to make the horror and pain more immediate and intense by employing a tone and diction that picked open the scab of her wound instead of sublimating the sensation. The Nazi imagery and identification with the Jews in "Daddy," "Lady Lazarus" and "Death & Co." clearly reveal her unique contribution to modern poetry as well as her suicidal impulse.

Like Lowell and Berryman, Plath was an imaginary Jew.

While in college, she told her mother that she was, in many ways, close to Jewish beliefs. And the deracinated daughter of a gentile immigrant—a girl who had a number of Jewish boyfriends and lovers—explained to a Jewish friend why she identified with that culture: "Everybody today seems so rootless. I know I do. Only the Jews seem to be part of something, to belong to something definite and rooted. I'd like to have that feeling. Maybe I'll marry one someday and give birth at a plow in Israel." Dorothea Krook, her Jewish tutor at Newnham, struck by Plath's intellectual intensity, wondered if she were Jewish and noted her unusually "passionate feeling for Jews and her sense of belonging with them."[42]

Plath's early story, "The Perfect Setup," published in *Seventeen* in October 1952, described the withdrawal of a WASP family from Jewish neighbors. *The Bell Jar* opens with a reference to the electrocution in June 1953 of the convicted spies, Julius and Ethel Rosenberg, which foreshadows Esther's disastrous shock treatments ("something leapt out of the lamp in a blue flash and shook me till my teeth rattled"). Her major work on the Jewish theme is her shocking poem "Daddy" (October 1962). During a reading on BBC radio, Plath linked "Daddy" with the Electra of her "Azalea Path" poem and explained that the speaker's father was a Nazi tyrant, her mother a Jewish slave: "Here is a poem spoken by a girl with an Electra complex. Her father died while she thought he was God. Her case is complicated by the fact that her father was also a Nazi and her mother very possibly part Jewish. In the daughter the two strains marry and paralyze each other—she has to act out the awful little allegory once over before she is free of it." Joyce Carol Oates has mistakenly claimed that "like many who are persecuted, [Plath] identified in a perverse way with her own persecutors, and not with those who, along with her, were victims."[43] Though Plath should, by background, have identified with her German father, she sympathized instead with the Jewish victims.

The cruel catharsis of "Daddy" reverses the elegiac tone of "On the Decline of Oracles" ("My father died, and when he

died / He willed his books and shell away"), absorbs the
barbarous Gothic imagery of "Little Fugue" ("You had one
leg, and a Prussian mind") and adopts the brutal Orwellian
image of "The boot in the face" (O'Brien's picture of the
future is "a boot stamping on a human face—forever"), which
had also appeared in "Ode for Ted," "The Beekeeper's
Daughter" and "Berck-Plage."

The poem opens with the Plath-speaker exclaiming that
she will no longer allow her father, who betrayed her by dying,
to oppress her. For thirty years she has lived like a foot
enclosed in his black shoe (Otto's foot was amputated),
scarcely daring to breathe or sneeze. (The "Achoo" comes
directly from the infantile reversal of cause and effect
portrayed on the first page of Joyce's *A Portrait of the Artist as a
Young Man*: "Dante gave him a cachou every time he brought
her a piece of tissue paper.")

Plath and Berryman share a perverse desire to free
themselves by killing their God-like fathers. But Otto died
before she could kill him. She remembers swimming with him
off Nauset, on Cape Cod, where Plath tried to drown herself in
July 1953. Unlike the Jews, she lacks roots and cannot speak
to her father in his harsh and obscene language. (In *The Bell
Jar*, Esther says: "each time I picked up a German dictionary
or a German book, the very sight of those dense, black,
barbed-wire [Gothic] letters made my mind shut like a
clam.")

In "Daddy" Plath associates herself with the Jewish
victims—Kafkaesque symbols of alienation and suffering, who
affirmed a mode of survival against tremendous odds. The
Jews are being shipped to extermination camps by her Aryan,
Fascist, Luftwaffe, Panzer, Meinkampf, swastika'd, rack-and-
screw father. A steam engine drags her off like a Jew to
Dachau, Belsen, Auschwitz. She speaks like a Jew and may
actually be a Jew. She makes the connection between her
father's death, which (like a vampire) bit her "pretty red heart
in two," and her suicide attempt—to "get back, back, back to
you." After she has been rescued from death, she makes a

voodoo model of her father (as she did of Hughes) and uses it to destroy him.

In the fourteenth stanza, the white flame of hatred suddenly but subtly shifts from Otto Plath to Ted Hughes (the "Daddy" of her children) as the two villains merge into a single figure. "And I said I do, I do" alludes to her marriage vows, puns on the familiar pronoun *du* and connects to the negatives of the opening line: "You do not do, you do not do." She is now through with her daddy–husband. She refers to her rage when she heard Assia calling for Hughes and tore the telephone out of the wall. She now wants to kill both her father and her husband, for Hughes has also tormented her. She wants to drive a stake into the hearts of the demonically possessed and unspeakably cruel betrayers who divided her heart in two. Alluding to the Devon village, the folklorish rites and the manifest guilt of her husband, she repeats the incantation of the incriminating "you" and is finally released from his evil powers:

> They are dancing and stamping on you.
> They always *knew* it was you.
> Daddy, daddy, you bastard, I'm through.[44]

Plath's poem has been subject to devastating criticism that reveals serious flaws in her work. James Dickey takes a tough, no-nonsense approach to mental illness and dismisses the pretentious exploitation of self-pity and "suicide chic": "'Daddy' is ridiculously bad; it's embarrassing. . . . She's the Judy Garland of American poetry. If you want to kill yourself, you don't make an *attempt*; you do it. You make sure that the thing comes off. Suicide *attempts*, and then writing *poems* about your suicide attempts, is just pure bullshit!" George Steiner, more seriously, considers the propriety of the Nazi imagery. He believes that Plath has no moral nor aesthetic right to compare her personal unhappiness to the mass extermination of an entire race, that she commits "a subtle larceny when [she] invokes the echoes and trappings of Auschwitz and appropriates the enormity of ready emotion to [her] own private design."[45] But the validity of this criticism does not diminish the power of the poem. Its brilliant technique, complex themes, unique voice and desperate agony—which become much clearer in the context of Plath's biography—transcend its limitations and achieve a tremendous impact. Plath's deliberately shocking use of Nazi imagery (only her *distance* from the Nazi experience enabled her to write about it in such an excruciating yet detached manner) was a bold and successful attempt to enlarge—in the modern mode—poetic experience and poetic diction.

In February 1956, a week before she met Hughes, Plath recorded: "I feel like Lazarus: that story had such a fascination. Being dead, I rose up again, and even resort to the mere sensation value of being suicidal, of getting so close, of coming out of the grave [on the third day!] with scars and the marring mark on my cheek." During her BBC reading, Plath alluded to the Nietzschean idea that "One pays dearly for immortality: one has to die several times while still alive," and said: "The speaker is a woman who has the great and terrible gift of being reborn. The only trouble is, she has to die first."

In "Lady Lazarus," Plath—who had just survived the Devon car crash in August 1962—feels condemned to a ten-year cycle of suicide attempts. Like Kafka's Hunger Artist, she is an exhibition and public spectacle, and the peanut-crunching crowd shoves in to see her unwrapped from her shroud. She compares the "calling" of suicide and poetry; and though she has failed twice, is ironically proud of her past record. Dying is also an art and she has learned to do it very well. Playing on three meanings of "charge" (fee, electric current and thrill), she imagines herself dismembered and distributed like the relics of a saint or melted down in a Nazi oven to "A cake of soap, / A wedding ring, / A gold filling." Yet even the final solution is not final. The poem ends with the vindictive threat of a red-haired she-devil who devours fathers and husbands as naturally as other women breathe.[46]

Plath said that "Death & Co." "is about the double or

schizophrenic nature of death—the marmoreal coldness of Blake's death mask, say, hand in glove with the fearful softness of worms, water and other catabolists [which break down organisms]. I imagine these two aspects of death as two men, two business friends, who have come to call." "Death & Co.," impersonal as a business establishment, includes everyone in company with death because everyone is dying from birth. But the particular menace of this poem occurs when Plath portrays her own sweet-looking infants, their little feet protruding from the toga-shrouds, laid out in the icebox of the morgue. After confronting the two morbid messengers, she eerily imagines her own death and hears the tolling of the funereal bell that signals: "Somebody's done for."

Like many poets, Plath felt compelled to write in order to impose structure and meaning on the chaos of her life. In an interview at the end of her miraculous month, October 1962, she spoke of the satisfactions of her art: "I don't think I could live without it. . . . I find myself absolutely fulfilled when I have written a poem, when I'm writing one. . . . I think the actual experience of writing a poem is a magnificent one."[47] This is, of course, a healthy and natural attitude, for writers usually become depressed during periods of sterility. Jarrell killed himself when he felt he could not write any more, Berryman when he faced the decline of his poetic powers. But it is extremely unusual for writers to commit suicide at the very peak of their genius. Plath may have set a suicide date, written frantically, kept her promise to herself and authenticated her agony by her death. The long tradition of manic and suicidal poets—merging in Plath like a cataract narrowing at the ledge—poured on to her all its downward and destructive motion. Her destiny was clear and she fulfilled it.[48]

VII

In December 1962, between her two spurts of poetry, Plath and her children moved from Devon to London and she rented a flat in Primrose Hill which Yeats had lived in as a child. Hughes, who had helped her find the flat, visited the children once a week. On December 21, desperately attempting to hold her mask in place, she wrote her mother (as she had written before the break-up of her marriage): "I have never been so happy in my life." But when the poetry critic Al Alvarez visited her on Christmas Eve, the cracks in her life had turned into fissures: "[Her hair] hung straight to her waist like a tent, giving her pale face and gaunt figure a curiously desolate, rapt air. . . . [It] gave off a strong smell, sharp as an animal's."[49]

It is difficult to find rational reasons for irrational behavior, for the suicide who has lost the ability to see some light beyond the darkest moment. Plath was deeply wounded by the betrayal—the worst since her father's death—of the man she had idolized and adored. And the conditions during the last weeks and days of her life were grim. The deep snow and frozen streets during the coldest English winter in a century and a half kept her confined to the flat with two small infants. The pipes froze, the roof leaked, filthy water backed up in the bathtub, power cuts made the rooms icy and sometimes dark. The infants had 'flu; and she suffered from chronic sinusitis, physical exhaustion, loss of weight and lack of sleep. Isolated and lonely—for most of their English friends remained loyal to Hughes—she had lost her German *au pair* and was waiting for a replacement. She felt guilty toward her mother and friends, whom she had savaged in *The Bell Jar*, when the novel was published under a pseudonym on January 23. She now drank the black milk of despair. She feared another breakdown, more shock treatments and permanent insanity. And she was unable to find a psychiatrist or get a hospital room. Plath could have dealt with many of these problems, but the total effect was overwhelming.

Letters from her psychiatrist, support from her family, hope for reconciliation with her husband, even the absolute fulfillment of her poetry and the love of her children could not sustain her. Elizabeth Compton remarked: "Her children were central, nothing in their lives should be touched, not out of ego but fear, and she could be savage as a leopard in defending her offspring." Yet her despair was so deep that she was willing to sacrifice them in an even crueler way than she had been sacrificed by her father.

In July 1958, after her year of teaching at Smith, Plath and Hughes had been unable to save a bird they had tried to nurse back to life: 'we figured it would be a mercy to put it out of its misery, so we gassed it in a little box. . . . Five minutes later [Ted] brought it to me, composed, perfect and beautiful in death."[50] Plath, who had identified with Jewish victims in extermination camps, gassed herself on Monday February 11, 1963. Alvarez has reconstructed and described the scene: "Around six o'clock that morning, she went up to the children's room and left a plate of bread and butter and two mugs of milk, in case they should wake hungry before the *au pair* girl arrived. Then she went back down to the kitchen, sealed the door and windows as best she could with towels, opened the oven, laid her head in it and turned on the gas."

Alvarez mentioned that the elderly painter in the flat below was knocked unconscious by the seeping gas and that the new Australian *au pair* girl (Butscher says she was an English nurse) expected at 9 a.m. could not get into the house. And he speculated that Plath did not expect to die: "It was 'a cry for help' which fatally misfired." But Alvarez did not tell the whole story and his theory has radical flaws. He did not explain what the children—who were clearly in some danger from the gas that knocked out the painter—did or discovered between 8 a.m. (when they usually woke up) and 11 a.m., when the girl finally got into the flat. He did not explain why Plath insisted on returning from a weekend visit to friends who had urged her to stay with them on Sunday night. And—most importantly—he did not explain how she could have survived with her head in the gas oven from 6 to 9 a.m. In a devastating letter of November 1971, when Alvarez's chapter was first serialized in the *Observer*, Hughes declared: "The sweepingly speculative theories, which he bases on his 'facts,' and which he presents in such a positive official tone, about our marriage and her death, are from beginning to end, to my knowledge, inaccurate . . . [and go] against the findings of the coroner."[51]

As Plath intended, her suicide left Hughes with an intolerable burden of guilt and increased her literary reputation. She left Hughes her torment, her children, her manuscripts and her poems. Apart from "The Howling of Wolves" and "Song of a Rat," in which he confronts pain and death with stoic acceptance, Hughes wrote no poetry for three years after her suicide. In his Foreword to her *Journals* he stated: "I regarded forgetfulness as an essential part of survival."[52] Since Plath left no will, Hughes inherited her literary estate and decided which of her works would be published. His triple authority as husband, poet and critic— expressed in fourteen essays, introductions, notes and letters about Plath—has had a profound influence on our understanding of her life and art.[53]

Plath's short life and violent death catapulted her into literary history and transformed her (like Dylan Thomas) into a cult figure. Between February and October 1963, Hughes published thirty-nine of her poems in the *Observer*, *London Magazine*, *Atlantic Monthly*, *New Yorker*, *Encounter* and *Review*. *Ariel*, a cultural time bomb that exploded two years after her death, and expressed the rebellious spirit of the sixties, had a powerful impact in England and America. In addition to the small private-press editions, *The Bell Jar* was reprinted in 1966, *Crossing the Water* and *Winter Trees* (both edited by Hughes, though he was not mentioned on the title page) appeared in 1971, *Letters Home* in 1975, *Johnny Panic* in 1979, *Collected Poems* (which won the Pulitzer Prize) in 1981 and *Journals* in 1982. Far more of Plath's work was published after her death than during her lifetime.

Our age is obsessed by its own capacity for self-destruction: by pollution, drugs, AIDS, poison gas, radiation, terrorism, genocide, death camps and nuclear war. The manic poets, who enriched our lives as they ruined their own, symbolize individual examples of this destructive impulse. We are fascinated by their suffering and see it as a vicarious substitute for our own. Jarrell spoke for all the poets when he observed with stark honesty: "Pain comes from the darkness / And we call it wisdom. It is pain."[54] The most impressive characteristics of the manic poets were their passionate commitment to art and their considerable courage in the face of overwhelming catastrophe.

Notes

Chapter One: The Dynamics of Destruction

1. Robert Lowell, "91 Revere Street," *Life Studies and For the Union Dead* (New York, 1967), p. 24.
2. Interview with Gertrude Buckman, London, August 15, 1985.
3. Quoted in Jeffrey Meyers, *A Reader's Guide to George Orwell* (London, 1975), p. 20; John Dos Passos, *The Best Times* (New York, 1966), p. 210.
4. Robert Lowell, "Unwanted," *Day by Day* (New York, 1977), p. 121; Lowell, "Grandparents," *Life Studies and For the Union Dead*, p. 69.
5. John Berryman, *The Dream Songs* (New York, 1969), song 235.
6. Randall Jarrell, *Letters*, ed. Mary Jarrell (Boston, 1985), p. 219.
7. W. H. Auden, "On the Circuit," *Selected Poems*, ed. Edward Mendelson (New York, 1979), p. 248.
8. Percy Bysshe Shelley, *A Defence of Poetry*, ed. John Jordan (Indianapolis, 1965), p. 80; Allen Tate, "Postscript," *T. S. Eliot: The Man and His Work*, ed. Allen Tate (New York, 1966), p. 389.
9. Plato, *The Republic*, trans. and ed. Francis Cornford (Oxford, 1941), p. 329.
10. Irv Broughton, "An Interview with Allen Tate," *Western Humanities Review*, 32 (1978), 319.

11. Quoted in Allan Seager, *The Glass House: The Life of Theodore Roethke* (New York, 1968), p. 132.

12. Robert Lowell, "Visiting the Tates," *Sewanee Review*, 67 (1959), 557–559; Robert Lowell, "For Michael Tate: August 1967–July 1968," *Notebook*, revised edition (New York, 1970), p. 251.

13. Randall Jarrell, "Tate versus History," *Kipling, Auden & Co.* (New York, 1980), p. 65; Jarrell, *Letters*, p. 132.

14. Quoted in John Haffenden, *The Life of John Berryman* (London, 1982), p. 394. (Jarrell's judgment of Tate appears in "Fifty Years of American Poetry," *The Third Book of Criticism*, New York, 1965, p. 322.) Broughton, "Interview with Allen Tate," *Western Humanities Review*, p. 319.

15. Quoted in Geoffrey Moore, "Dylan Thomas," *Kenyon Review*, 17 (1955), 261.

16. Karl Shapiro, "Dylan Thomas," *In Defense of Ignorance* (New York, 1955), pp. 172–173, 182; Elizabeth Hardwick, "America and Dylan Thomas," *A View of My Own* (New York, 1962), pp. 103–104, 110–111.

17. Robert Lowell, "The World I Breathe," *Hika*, 6 (March 1940), 22; Jarrell, "Poetry in a Dry Season," *Kipling, Auden & Co.*, p. 36; John Berryman, "Dylan Thomas: The Loud Hill of Wales," *The Freedom of the Poet* (New York, 1976), p. 285.

18. Jarrell, *Letters*, pp. 336–337. See Robert Lowell, "Thomas, Bishop, and Williams," *Sewanee Review*, 55 (1947), 493–496; Jarrell, *Kipling, Auden & Co.*, pp. 217–218, 242–243; Berryman, *Freedom of the Poet*, pp. 282–285, 292–293.

19. Theodore Roethke, "Dylan Thomas: Elegy," *On the Poet and His Craft*, ed. Ralph Mills, Jr. (Seattle, 1965), pp. 90, 92; Theodore Roethke, "Elegy," *Collected Poems* (Garden City, New York, 1975), p. 138.

20. John Berryman, "The Art of Poetry," *Writers at Work: The "Paris Review" Interviews*, Fourth Series, ed. George Plimpton (New York, 1977), p. 303; John Berryman, "In

Memoriam (1914–1953)," *Delusions, Etc.*, (New York, 1972), pp. 28–29.

21. Winfield Scott, "Our Saddest Stories Are Biographies," *New Republic*, 145 (November 30, 1961), 18; Russell Fraser, *A Mingled Yarn: The Life of R. P. Blackmur* (New York, 1981), p. 173; Ernest Hemingway, *Green Hills of Africa* (New York, 1935), p. 28.

22. Quoted in Ian Hamilton, *Robert Lowell: A Biography* (New York, 1982), p. 351; Lowell, "For John Berryman," *Day by Day*, p. 27.

23. Berryman, *Dream Songs*, song 153; John Berryman, "A Point of Age," *Short Poems* (New York, 1967), p. 9.

24. T. S. Eliot, "*Ulysses*, Order and Myth," *Dial*, 75 (November 1923), 483; Richard Kostelanetz, "Conversation with Berryman," *Massachusetts Review*, 11 (1970), 344.

25. Berryman, *The Dream Songs*, song 152; Saul Bellow, Foreword to John Berryman, *Recovery* (New York, 1973), p. xiv.

26. Søren Kierkegaard, *Journals*, trans. and ed. Alexander Dru (New York, 1959), p. 153; Martin Berg, "An Interview with John Berryman," *Minneapolis Daily*, January 20, 1971, p. 10.

27. Thomas De Quincey, *Recollections of the Lakes and the Lake Poets*, ed. David Wright (London, 1970), p. 75; William Heyen, "John Berryman: A Memoir and an Interview," *Ohio Review*, 15 (1974), 59, 64. There were actually seven American Nobel laureates before 1972; Pearl Buck (repressed by Berryman) and T. S. Eliot were the sober ones.

28. Quoted in Jay Martin, "Grief and Nothingness: Loss and Mourning in Robert Lowell's Poetry," *Psychoanalytic Inquiry*, 3 (1983), 478.

29. Friedrich Nietzsche, *Thus Spake Zarathustra*, *The Portable Nietzsche*, trans. Walter Kaufmann (New York, 1954), p. 129.

30. Roethke, "In a Dark Time," *Collected Poems*, p. 231.

31. Berryman, "A Winter-Piece to a Friend Away," *Short Poems*, p. 88; Heyen, "John Berryman," *Ohio Review*, p. 64.

32. Plato, *Ion*, *Five Dialogues*, trans. Percy Bysshe Shelley (London, 1924), pp. 6–7; Plato, *Phaedrus*, trans, Walter Hamilton (London, 1973), p. 46; E. R. Dodds, *The Greeks and the Irrational* (Berkeley, 1951), p. 80.

33. Søren Kierkegaard, *Either/Or*, trans. David Swenson (Princeton, 1959), I.19.

34. Fyodor Dostoyevsky, *Notes From Underground*, trans. Andrew MacAndrew (New York, 1961), p. 93; Lowell, "Home," *Day by Day*, p. 114.

35. Arthur Rimbaud, letter of May 15, 1871, *Complete Works*, trans. Paul Schmidt (New York, 1975), pp. 102–103; John Updike, *Hugging the Shore* (New York, 1984), pp. 555–556; Jean-Paul Sartre, *The War Diaries*, trans. Quintin Hoare (New York, 1985), p. 29.

36. Quoted in Neal Bowers, *The Journey from I to Otherwise* (Columbia, Missouri, 1982), pp. 10, 12. (In "The Retreat," misquoted by Roethke, Vaughan wrote: "But felt through all this fleshly dress / Bright shoots of everlastingness.") Berryman, "The Art of Poetry," *Writers at Work*, p. 322.

37. Nietzsche, *Twilight of the Idols*, *The Portable Nietzsche*, p. 549; Friedrich Nietzsche, *The Will to Power*, trans. Walter Kaufmann (New York, 1968), pp. 30–31.

38. Randall Jarrell, "Deutsch Durch Freud," *The Complete Poems* (New York, 1969), p. 267; Berryman, *The Dream Songs*, song 327; Robert Lowell, "Freud," *The Dolphin* (New York, 1973), p. 46.

39. T. S. Eliot, "Tradition and the Individual Talent," *Selected Essays, 1917–1932* (New York, 1932), pp. 7, 9, 10, 4.

40. David Heymann, *American Aristocracy: The Life and Times of James Russell, Amy and Robert Lowell* (New York, 1980), pp. 78–79.

41. Anton Chekhov, *Lady with Lapdog*, trans. David

Magarshack (London, 1964), p. 279; Leslie Fiedler, "The New Mutants," *Partisan Review*, 32 (1965), 524.

42. John Bayley, *Selected Essays* (New York, 1984), pp. 8, 48.
43. Ian Hamilton, "A Conversation with Robert Lowell," *The Review*, 26 (1971), 26; quoted in Derek Mahon, "I'd like them to say I was heartbreaking," *Listener*, 112 (December 6, 1984), 10.
44. Quoted in Hamilton, *Robert Lowell*, p. 314.
45. Anne Sexton, "Classroom at Boston University," *Harvard Advocate*, 145 (November 1961), 13; Kathleen Spivack, "Lear in Boston: Robert Lowell as Teacher and Friend," *Ironwood*, 13 (1985), 88, 86.
46. Anne Sexton, "The Barfly Ought to Sing," *The Art of Sylvia Plath*, ed. Charles Newman (Bloomington, Indiana, 1970), p. 175.
47. George Painter, *Marcel Proust: A Biography* (London, 1959), p. 52; Elizabeth Hardwick, *Bartleby in Manhattan* (New York, 1984), p. 181.
48. Robert Lowell, letter to J. F. Powers, November 17, 1947, courtesy of Professor Powers; Lowell, "Middle Age," *For the Union Dead*, p. 7; Lowell, "The Dolphin," *The Dolphin*, p. 78; Lowell, "Les Mots," *Notebook*, p. 38.
49. Quoted in Thomas Beer, *Stephen Crane* (New York, 1923), p. 233; quoted in Berryman, "The Poetry of Ezra Pound," *Freedom of the Poet*, p. 254; Theodore Roethke, *Selected Letters*, ed. Ralph Mills, Jr. (Seattle, 1968), p. 169; Selden Rodman, "Robert Frost," *Tongues of Fallen Angels* (New York, 1974), p. 45.
50. Lillian Ross, *Portrait of Hemingway* (New York, 1961), p. 35.
51. Quoted in Frank MacShane, *Into Eternity: The Life of James Jones* (Boston, 1985), p. 146; quoted in Peter Manso, *Mailer: His Life and Times* (New York, 1985), p. 239.
52. Tate, "Postscript," *T. S. Eliot: The Man and His Work*, p. 392.
53. Seamus Heaney, "Robert Lowell," *Agenda*, 18 (Autumn 1980), 23–24.

54. Hayden Carruth, "A Meaning of Robert Lowell," *Robert Lowell: A Portrait of the Artist in His Time*, ed. Michael London and Robert Boyers (New York, 1970), p. 226; Robert Bly, "Robert Lowell's *For the Union Dead*," *Lowell: A Portrait of the Artist in His Time*, p. 73.

55. Louis Simpson, "Robert Lowell's Indissoluble Bride," *A Revolution in Taste* (New York, 1978), p. 140; Interview with Stanley Kunitz, New York, December 22, 1982.

56. Stanley Kunitz, "The Sense of a Life," *New York Times Book Review*, October 16, 1977, pp. 3, 34; Alan Williamson, "A Reminiscence," *Harvard Advocate*, 133 (November 1979), 38.

57. Hamilton, "A Conversation with Robert Lowell," *The Review*, 26, p. 10.

Chapter Two: Robert Lowell and Randall Jarrell

1. John Crowe Ransom, *Selected Letters*, ed. Thomas Young and George Core (Baton Rouge, 1985), p. 226.

2. Quoted in Stephen Axelrod, *Robert Lowell: Life and Art* (Princeton, 1978), p. 30; Robert Lowell, "John Crowe Ransom," *New Review*, 1 (August 1974), 4.

3. John McCormick, "Falling Asleep Over Grillparzer: An Interview with Robert Lowell," *Poetry*, 81 (January 1953), 270; Interview with Stanley Kunitz.

4. Mary Jarrell, "The Group of Two," *Randall Jarrell, 1914–1965*, ed. Robert Lowell, Peter Taylor and Robert Penn Warren (New York, 1967), p. 285.

5. *Ibid.*, pp. 285–286.

6. Quoted in "The Second Chance," *Time*, 89 (June 2, 1967), 73; Allen Tate, "Young Randall," *Randall Jarrell, 1914–1965*, p. 230.

7. Elizabeth Bishop, "An Inadequate Tribute," *Randall Jarrell, 1914–1965*, p. 20; John Berryman, "Randall Jarrell," *Randall Jarrell, 1914–1965*, p. 17; Broughton, "Interview with Allen Tate," *Western Humanities Review*, p. 318.

8. Quoted in Hamilton, *Robert Lowell*, pp. 57–58; Robert Lowell, "Randall Jarrell," *Randall Jarrell, 1914–1965*, p. 103; Interview with Robert Fitzgerald, New Haven, December 16, 1982.

9. Jarrell, *Letters*, p. 498; quoted in Hamilton, *Robert Lowell*, p. 233.

10. *Ibid.*, pp. 4–5, 386.

11. *Ibid.*, pp. 14–15, 21; Blair Clark, "On Robert Lowell," *Harvard Advocate*, 113 (November 1979), 10.

12. Quoted in Hamilton, *Robert Lowell*, p. 38; Lowell, "St. Mark's, 1933," *Day by Day*, pp. 122, 90.

13. Quoted in Eileen Simpson, *Poets in Their Youth* (New York, 1982), p. 144; quoted in Hamilton, *Robert Lowell*, pp. 183–184.

14. Jarrell, *Letters*, p. 104.

15. Quoted in Hamilton, *Robert Lowell*, pp. 75, 91.

16. Jarrell, *Letters*, p. 105.

17. Interview with James Dickey, Columbia, South Carolina, June 7, 1981; Interview with Karl Shapiro, Davis, California, March 23, 1981; Jarrell, *Kipling, Auden & Co.*, pp. 132, 134.

18. Jarrell, *Letters*, pp. 128, 136–137, 139.

19. Randall Jarrell, *Poetry and the Age* (New York, 1955), pp. 188, 195, 199. Jarrell repeated several clever sentences from his review of *Land of Unlikeness* in his notice of *Lord Weary's Castle*. Compare *Kipling, Auden & Co.*, p. 133, with *Poetry and the Age*, pp. 192, 194.

20. Robert Fitzgerald, "Robert Lowell, 1917–1977," *New Republic*, 177 (October 1, 1977), 11; Interview with Gertrude Buckman.

21. Letters from Robert Lowell to J. F. Powers, March 30 and June 21, 1948, courtesy of Professor Powers; letter from W. D. Snodgrass to Jeffrey Meyers, December 2, 1981.

22. Quoted in Hamilton, *Robert Lowell*, p. 160.

23. Lowell, "On *The Seven-League Crutches*," *Randall Jarrell, 1914–1965*, pp. 113, 115. Lowell used Jarrell's description

of his poem "The Knight, Death, and the Devil"—"a translation of Dürer's engravings" (*Letters*, p. 247)—in his review, p. 115. But the poem is based on only one engraving. The word appears in the singular in Jarrell's original letter (Houghton Library, Harvard University) and in the plural in the printed version. Many transcriptions in Jarrell's *Letters* are inaccurate.

24. Jarrell, *Letters* pp. 284–285. The words in brackets, deleted from the published version, are in the original letter in the Houghton Library.

25. Jarrell, *Poetry and the Age*, pp. 231, 234–236.

26. Quoted in Jarrell, *Letters*, p. 339.

27. Robert Lowell, *Selected Poems*, revised edition (New York, 1978), p. 41; Jarrell, *Complete Poems*, p. 21; Simpson, *Poets in Their Youth*, p. 148. Jarrell called "Falling Asleep Over the Aeneid" one of his favorite Lowell poems (*Poetry and the Age*, p. 231) just as Lowell called "A Girl in the Library" one of his favorite Jarrell poems (*Randall Jarrell, 1914–1965*, p. 116).

28. Quoted in Ronald Hayman, *Artaud and After* (London, 1977), p. 128. For a description of Hemingway's disastrous shock treatments, see Jeffrey Meyers, *Hemingway: A Biography* (New York, 1985), pp. 546–554.

29. Quoted in Hamilton, *Robert Lowell*, pp. 399, 342.

30. Jarrell, *Letters*, p. 414.

31. Ransom, *Selected Letters*, pp. 240, 394–396, 399.

32. Quoted in Hamilton, *Robert Lowell*, pp. 275, 294.

33. Robert Lowell, "The Art of Poetry," *Writers at Work: The "Paris Review" Interviews*, Second Series, intro. by Van Wyck Brooks (New York, 1965), pp. 340, 361–362; Nathan Glick, "Interview with Randall Jarrell," *Analects*, 1 (Spring 1961), 9.

34. Quoted in Jarrell, *Letters*, p. 453; Jarrell, *The Third Book of Criticism*, pp. 332–334.

35. A. Alvarez, "Robert Lowell in Conversation," *The Modern Poet*, ed. Ian Hamilton (New York, 1969), p. 188. Jarrell actually wrote, in his review of Lowell's *third* book:

"Cocteau said to poets: *Learn what you can do and then don't do it*" (*Poetry and the Age*, p. 236).

36. Quoted in Jarrell, *Letters*, p. 487; "In Bounds," *Newsweek*, 64 (October 12, 1964), 120. Lowell left money to his friend in his will, but Jarrell predeceased him.

37. Quoted in Jarrell, *Letters*, p. 496; letter from W. D. Snodgrass to Jeffrey Meyers, December 2, 1981.

38. Quoted in Philip Nobile, *Intellectual Skywriting* (New York, 1974), p. 248; Jane Howard, "Applause for a Prize Poet," *Life*, 58 (February 19, 1965), 55.

39. Berryman, "Randall Jarrell," *Randall Jarrell, 1914–1965*, p. 17; Interview with Robert Fitzgerald.

40. Lowell, "Randall Jarrell," *Randall Jarrell, 1914–1965*, p. 101; Karl Shapiro, "The Death of Randall Jarrell," *ibid.*, p. 201.

41. Eleanor Taylor, "Greensboro Days," *Randall Jarrell, 1914–1965*, p. 238; Lowell, "Randall Jarrell," *Randall Jarrell, 1914–1965*, p. 105; Broughton, "Interview with Allen Tate," *Western Humanities Review*, pp. 317–318. The greatest modern writers have frequently been neglected. Conrad, Proust, Forster, Joyce, Kafka, Lawrence, Pound, Malraux, Auden and Greene did not win the Nobel Prize.

42. Lowell, "Randall Jarrell," *Randall Jarrell, 1914–1965*, p. 112; Jarrell, *Letters*, p. 395.

43. Hamilton, *Robert Lowell*, p. 338; Interview with James Dickey; Stanley Kunitz, "Out of the Cage," *Randall Jarrell, 1914–1965*, p. 97.

44. Quoted in Jarrell, *Letters*, p. 510.

45. Lowell, "Randall Jarrell," *Randall Jarrell, 1914–1965*, pp. 101, 103–104, 111–112.

46. Randall Jarrell, *The Lost World* (New York, 1965), pp. 21–22; Jarrell, *Letters*, p. 394; Hamilton, *Robert Lowell*, p. 369.

47. Robert Fitzgerald said during our interview that Lowell and Peter Taylor were convinced of Jarrell's suicide. Robie Macauley (in an interview in Boston on July 10,

1985) agreed that Lowell thought Jarrell had killed himself.

48. Lowell, "Ten Minutes," *Day by Day*, p. 108; Lowell, "Randall Jarrell: 1914–1965" and "Randall Jarrell," *Notebook*, pp. 115–116, 50–51. In the third elegy, Jarrell asks Lowell: "What kept you, so long, / racing your cooling grindstone to ambition?"

49. Michael Billington, "Mr. Robert Lowell on T. S. Eliot and the Theatre," *Times* (London), March 8, 1967, p. 10; D. S. Carne-Ross, "Conversation with Robert Lowell," *Delos*, 1 (1968), 166, 172.

50. Donald Newlove, "Dinner at the Lowells'," *Esquire*, 72 (September 1969), 168; Ian Hamilton, "A Conversation with Robert Lowell," *The Review*, p. 17.

51. Robert Lowell, "On Hannah Arendt," *New York Review of Books*, 23 (May 13, 1976), p. 6; Stanley Kunitz, "The Sense of a Life," *New York Times Book Review*, p. 34. In the revised version of Lowell's third elegy, Jarrell tells him: "You didn't write, you rewrote" (*History*, New York, 1973, p. 135).

52. Interview with Karl Shapiro.

Chapter Three: Randall Jarrell and John Berryman

1. Simpson, *Poets in Their Youth*, p. 111; quoted in Haffenden, *John Berryman*, p. 240; Robert Lowell, "For John Berryman," *New York Review of Books*, 18 (April 6, 1972), p. 3.

2. John Berryman, *Henry's Fate* (New York, 1977), p. 44; Berryman, *The Dream Songs*, songs 145, 76; quoted in Haffenden, *John Berryman*, p. 30.

3. Quoted in Simpson, *Poets in Their Youth*, p. 61; John Berryman, *Recovery* (New York, 1973), pp. 80–81, 191. Haffenden, *John Berryman*, p. 33, includes the phrase in brackets.

4. John Berryman, *Berryman's Sonnets* (New York, 1967),

p. 69; Eileen Simpson, *The Maze* (New York, 1975), p. 127; Simpson, *Poets in Their Youth*, pp. 233–234.

5. Simpson, *Poets in Their Youth*, p. 180; quoted in Haffenden, Introduction to *Henry's Fate*, p. xiv (Berryman's reference to gangrene was probably an allusion to Edmund Wilson's use of the Philoctetes myth in *The Wound and the Bow*); Simpson, *Poets in Their Youth*, pp. 233–234.

6. Simpson, *The Maze*, pp. 109, 129; 115–116; 142; Lowell, *Life Studies and For the Union Dead*, p. 53.

7. Quoted in Haffenden, *John Berryman*, p. 200; Berryman, "The Art of Poetry," *Writers at Work*, p. 297.

8. Berryman, *Dream Songs*, song 175; quoted in Haffenden, *John Berryman*, p. 44.

9. Berryman, "Tennis in Middle Age," *Henry's Fate*, p. 22; Simpson, *Poets in Their Youth*, p. 112.

10. Quoted in Haffenden, *John Berryman*, p. 127; John Berryman and Randall Jarrell, *Five Young American Poets* (Norfolk, Conn., 1940), pp. 45, 89–90.

11. John Crowe Ransom, Review of *Five Young American Poets*, *Kenyon Review*, 3 (1941), 378, 380; *The Poetry Reviews of Allen Tate, 1922–1944*, ed. Ashley Brown and Frances Cheney (Baton Rouge, 1983), pp. 200–201.

12. Jarrell, *Letters*, p. 30; Jarrell, *Kipling, Auden & Co.*, p. 86.

13. Oscar Williams, "Five Young American Poets," *Living Age*, 359 (January 1941), 497; Jarrell, *Poetry and the Age*, pp. 157–158.

14. Jarrell, *Kipling, Auden & Co.*, p. 137; Jarrell, *Letters*, p. 169.

15. Simpson, *Poets in Their Youth*, pp. 107, 110. Haffenden, *John Berryman*, p. xi, incorrectly states that Berryman first met Jarrell in 1950.

16. The precise date of this meeting is difficult to determine. Simpson stated: "Sometime after the publication of *Lord Weary's Castle* [December 1946], and the appearance of Randall's [January 18, 1947] and John's [January–February 1947] laudatory reviews of the book, Cal called from New York to ask if he could bring Randall to

Princeton" (p. 147). Both Simpson and Lowell wrote that Berryman complimented Jarrell on his superior review of Lowell's book, which suggests that the meeting took place in the early spring of 1947. But Jarrell's letter to Berryman, dated "[September 1946]," mentioned sending him Grierson's *A Critical History of English Poetry*, which Berryman reviewed on December 21, 1946, and referred to the poisoned canapé: "Mackie was awfully sorry to miss Princeton and I was awfully sorry to be such a comically sick visitor" (p. 169). Jarrell's letter suggests that the meeting took place in September 1946 (a few months after Margaret Marshall's party) and prompted Jarrell to send Grierson's book to Berryman. If so, then Simpson is mistaken about the date and Lowell, who said that "both poet–critics had just written definitive essay–reviews of my first [i.e. second] book, *Lord Weary's Castle*," must have meant that they read each other's reviews, before publication, in September 1946.

17. John Berryman, "Randall Jarrell," *Randall Jarrell, 1914–1965*, p. 15; Lowell, "For John Berryman," *New York Review of Books*, p. 3.

18. Simpson, *Poets in Their Youth*, pp. 148–149.

19. Berryman, "Poetry Chronicle," *Freedom of the Poet*, pp. 297–303; quoted in Simpson, *Poets in Their Youth*, p. 161. In this essay, p. 298, Berryman states that "Day Lewis' influential *A Hope for Poetry* [Oxford, 1934] named Hopkins, Lawrence, and Owen as ancestors of Auden Ltd."—though Day Lewis, in fact, named Hopkins, *Eliot* and Owen.

20. Jarrell, *Kipling, Auden & Co.*, pp. 152–153; Haffenden, *John Berryman*, p. 200.

21. Jarrell, *Letters*, pp. 213, 267, 278. Jarrell's major essays on Auden had appeared in the *Southern Review* (1941) and the *Nation* (1947).

22. Jarrell, *Letters*, pp. 309, 311, 323, 349.

23. John Berryman, "On Poetry and the Age," *Randall Jarrell, 1914–1965*, pp. 10–13; quoted in John Haffenden, *John*

Berryman: A Critical Commentary (New York, 1980), p. 37.

24. Jarrell, "Reflections on Wallace Stevens," *Poetry and the Age*, p. 134; Mary Jarrell, "Ideas and Poems," *Parnassus*, 5 (1976), 216 (the quotation in this passage is from Jarrell's "Deutsch Durch Freud"); Ford Madox Hueffer, *Ford Madox Brown* (London, 1896), p. 51.

25. Hannah Arendt, "Randall Jarrell," *Randall Jarrell, 1914–1965*, p. 8; Mary Jarrell, "The Group of Two," *Randall Jarrell, 1914–1965*, p. 297.

26. Joseph Bennett, *New York Times Book Review*, April 18, 1965, p. 24; James Dickey, *American Scholar*, 34 (1965), 646, 648.

27. Berryman, "Randall Jarrell," *Randall Jarrell, 1914–1965*, p. 14; unpublished letter from John Berryman to Mary Jarrell, October 30, 1965, Berg Collection, New York Public Library; Berryman, "The Art of Poetry," *Writers at Work*, p. 303.

28. Berryman, "Randall Jarrell," *Randall Jarrell, 1914–1965*, pp. 15–17. For Jarrell's dispute with Aiken, see his "Verse Chronicle," *Nation*, 166 (May 8, 1948), 512–513, and his reply to Aiken's attack, "The 'Serious' Critic," *Nation*, 166 (June 12, 1948), 670–672.

29. John Berryman, "Relations," *Love & Fame*, 2nd edition, revised (New York, 1972), p. 56.

Chapter Four: John Berryman and Robert Lowell

1. Berryman, *The Dream Songs*, song 58; Fitzgerald, "Robert Lowell," *New Republic*, p. 10.

2. John Berryman, "Provincial," *Partisan Review*, 15 (1948), 860.

3. Berryman, "The Art of Poetry," *Writers at Work*, p. 302; Haffenden, *Berryman: A Critical Commentary*, p. 41.

4. Lowell, "In the Cage," *Lord Weary's Castle* (New York, 1951), p. 59; John Berryman, "The Cage," *Poetry*, 75 (January 1950), 188.

5. Lowell, "Che Guevara," *Notebook*, p. 53; Berryman, "Che," *Henry's Fate*, pp. 62–63.
6. Berryman, "Rembrandt van Rijn obit 8 October 1669," *Henry's Fate*, p. 41; quoted in Haffenden, *John Berryman*, p. 197.
7. Berryman, *Henry's Fate*, pp. 24, 87, 23; Lowell, "Home," *Day by Day*, p. 114.
8. Quoted in Haffenden, *John Berryman*, p. 313; Berryman, "Despondency and Madness: On 'Skunk Hour,' " *Freedom of the Poet*, p. 318.
9. Lowell, "Double Vision," *The Dolphin*, p. 22; Lowell, "Home," *Day by Day*, p. 114; Interview with Lady Caroline Blackwood Lowell, London, March 26, 1986. Blackwood also illuminated "Night Sweat" and noted that Lowell needed liquids because his medicine made him sweat and dried him out. He required an intake of nourishment while pouring out words and drank great quantities of milk while writing in bed.
10. Lowell, "Waking in the Blue," *Life Studies*, pp. 81–82; Berryman, "The Hell Poem," *Love & Fame*, pp. 66–67.
11. Lowell, "Man and Wife," *Life Studies*, p. 87; Berryman, *The Dream Songs*, song 384.
12. Quoted in Raymond Sokolov, *Wayward Reporter: The Life of A. J. Liebling* (New York, 1980), p. 277.
13. Howard, "Applause for a Prize Poet," *Life*, p. 55; Sigmund Freud, *Letters, 1873–1939*, ed. Ernst Freud, trans. Tania and James Stern (London, 1961), p. 368; Richard Locke, "Conversation on a Book," *New York Times Book Review*, April 29, 1979, p. 61.
14. Berryman, *Recovery*, pp. 74, 241.
15. Simpson, *Poets in Their Youth*, pp. 115, 135–136, 122; Lowell, "For John Berryman," *New York Review of Books*, p. 3.
16. Quoted in Haffenden, *John Berryman*, pp. 161, 173; Berryman, "On Poetry and the Age," *Randall Jarrell, 1914–1965*, pp. 11–12.
17. Berryman, "Robert Lowell and Others," *Freedom of the*

Poet, pp. 286–287, 290; Jarrell, "From the Kingdom of Necessity," *Poetry and the Age*, pp. 198–199.

18. Phone conversation with Paul Engle, Iowa City, August 23, 1985.

19. Quoted in Heymann, *American Aristocracy*, p. 470; quoted in Haffenden, *John Berryman*, p. 325.

20. Quoted in Haffenden, *John Berryman*, pp. 329–330.

21. Berryman, "Despondency and Madness: On 'Skunk Hour,'" *Freedom of the Poet*, pp. 316–317, 321–322.

22. Quoted in Haffenden, *John Berryman*, p. 302 and Hamilton, *Robert Lowell*, p. 298; Robert Lowell, "On 'Skunk Hour,'" *The Contemporary Poet as Artist and Critic*, ed. Anthony Ostroff (Boston, 1964), p. 108.

23. Berryman, "Despondency and Madness: On 'Skunk Hour,'" *Freedom of the Poet*, p. 318; Lowell, Note to *For the Union Dead*, p. 1. In "Symposium: The Writer's Situation," *New American Review*, 9 (1970), 86, Lowell again acknowledged Berryman's help and said: "I learn from my contemporaries: Elizabeth Bishop, John Berryman, and Auden."

24. Quoted in Hamilton, *Robert Lowell*, p. 308; Lowell, "Our Afterlife I," *Day by Day*, p. 21.

25. Berryman, "The Heroes," *Love & Fame*, p. 25; quoted in Haffenden, *John Berryman*, pp. 328, 319, 323. Yeats' statement was popularized by F. W. Dupee's book, *The King of the Cats* (1965).

26. Haffenden, *John Berryman*, pp. 325–326; Robert Lowell, "The Poetry of John Berryman," *New York Review of Books*, 2 (May 28, 1964), p. 3; Robert Lowell, "Correction," *New York Review of Books*, 2 (June 11, 1964), p. 23.

27. Lowell, "For John Berryman," *New York Review of Books*, p. 4; Robert Lowell, ["John Berryman,"] *Harvard Advocate*, 103 (1969), 170.

28. Quoted in Hamilton, *Robert Lowell*, p. 350; Jonathan Sisson, "My Whiskers Fly: An Interview with John Berryman," *Ivory Tower* (University of Minnesota), 14 (October 3, 1966), 34.

29. Berryman, "One Answer to a Question: Changes," *Freedom of the Poet*, p. 329; quoted in Haffenden, *John Berryman*, p. 343.

30. David McClelland et al., "An Interview with John Berryman," *Harvard Advocate*, 103 (1969), 7, 9.

31. Quoted in Haffenden, *John Berryman*, pp. 355, 2. There is no reference to Berryman in the Afterthought and Note to *Notebook*.

32. Hamilton, *Robert Lowell*, pp. 350–351.

33. Berryman, "The Art of Poetry," *Writers at Work*, p. 305; John Berryman, "Love, fame and hostility," *Nation*, 211 (November 30, 1970), 546; Gary Arpin, *The Poetry of John Berryman* (Port Washington, New York, 1978), p. 87.

34. Berg, "An Interview with John Berryman," *Minneapolis Daily*, pp. 10–11; Lowell, "For John Berryman," *New York Review of Books*, p. 3. In this memoir of Berryman, he more honestly called the *Love & Fame* poems "profane and often in bad taste" (p. 4).

35. Berryman, "The Possessed," *Short Poems*, p. 23; Berryman, "Of Suicide," *Love & Fame*, pp. 62–63; Lowell, "Suicide," *Day by Day*, pp. 15–16.

36. Berryman, *Henry's Fate*, p. 16; Berryman, *Delusions, Etc.*, p. 53.

37. Berryman, *Henry's Fate*, p. 93; Haffenden, *John Berryman*, p. 419; quoted in Hamilton, *Robert Lowell*, p. 438.

38. Telephone conversation with Lady Caroline Blackwood Lowell, London, July 31, 1985; Lowell, "For John Berryman," *New York Review of Books*, p. 3.

39. Lowell, "For John Berryman 2," *History*, p. 203; Lowell, "For John Berryman," *Day by Day*, pp. 27–28.

40. Caroline Blackwood, *The Step-Daughter* (London, 1976), pp. 19, 45. Jean Stafford wrote about her relations with Lowell in "A Country Love Story," "The Home Front" and "The Interior Castle," *Children Are Bored on Sunday* (New York, 1953) and in "An Influx of Poets," *New Yorker*, 54 (November 6, 1978), 43–60; Elizabeth Hardwick wrote of Lowell in *Sleepless Nights* (New York, 1979).

Chapter Five: Theodore Roethke and Jarrell, Berryman, Lowell

1. Roethke, *Selected Letters*, p. 141; interview with Beatrice Roethke Lushington, London, August 7, 1985.

2. Roethke, "The Saginaw Song," "The Rose," *Collected Poems*, pp. 260, 197. In "The Lost Son," p. 54, Roethke (who did not know German well) wrote: "Ordnung! ordnung! Papa is coming!" but probably meant to say: "Achtung! achtung!"

3. Twenty years later, the same height and weight as Roethke, I also graduated from Michigan, did a term of law at Harvard and completed the academic year with graduate study in English.

4. James Dickey, "The Greatest American Poet," *Atlantic Monthly*, 222 (November 1968), 57; Robert Heilman, "Theodore Roethke: Personal Notes," *Shenandoah*, 16 (1964), 64.

5. Louise Bogan, *What the Woman Lived: Selected Letters*, ed. Ruth Limmer (New York, 1973), p. 84; quoted in Elizabeth Frank, *Louise Bogan* (New York, 1985), pp. 230–231; Roethke, "The Meadow Mouse," *Collected Poems*, p. 219.

6. Quoted in Seager, *The Glass House*, pp. 241, 165; Bogan, *What the Woman Lived*, p. 287.

7. Conrad Aiken, *Selected Letters*, ed. Joseph Killorin (New Haven, 1978), p. 253; Roethke, *Selected Letters*, pp. 132, 182.

8. Louis Simpson, *A Revolution in Taste*, p. 38; Roethke, *Selected Letters*, pp. 111, 97.

9. Roethke, *Selected Letters*, pp. 111, 131.

10. Stanley Kunitz, "Remembering Roethke" (1963), *A Kind of Order, A Kind of Folly* (Boston, 1975), p. 78; Dickey, "The Greatest American Poet," *Atlantic Monthly*, p. 55.

11. Richard Hugo, "Stray Thoughts on Roethke and Teaching," *The Triggering Town* (New York, 1979), p. 35; letter from Robert Heilman to Jeffrey Meyers, December 6, 1985.

12. Theodore Roethke, *Straw for the Fire: Notebooks, 1943–63*, ed. David Wagoner (Seattle, 1980), pp. 153, 208; Roethke, "In a Dark Time," *Collected Poems*, p. 231.

13. Hugo, "Stray Thoughts on Roethke and Teaching," *The Triggering Town*, p. 34; Roethke, *Selected Letters*, pp. 220, 117; quoted in Seager, *The Glass House*, pp. 147, 183.

14. Quoted in Bowers, *Theodore Roethke*, pp. 8–11.

15. Roethke, "Otto," *Collected Poems*, p. 217; Interview with Stanley Kunitz; Interview with Beatrice Roethke Lushington.

16. Letter from Theodore Roethke to Robert Lowell, September 24, 1958, Houghton Library, Harvard University; Glick, "An Interview with Randall Jarrell," *Analects*, 9; Jarrell, "Fifty Years of American Poetry," *Third Book of Criticism*, pp. 326–327.

17. Quoted in Seager, *The Glass House*, p. 206; quoted in Simpson, *Poets in Their Youth*, p. 221.

18. Interview with Beatrice Roethke Lushington.

19. Simpson, *Poets in Their Youth*, pp. 239–240; Simpson, *The Maze*, pp. 215, 110.

20. Quoted in Haffenden, *John Berryman*, p. 239; Berryman, "From the Middle and Senior Generations," *Freedom of the Poet*, pp. 310–311; W. D. Snodgrass, "Spring Verse Chronicle," *Hudson Review*, 12 (1959), 116; Kostelanetz, "Conversation with Berryman," *Massachusetts Review*, pp. 343–344.

21. Quoted in Haffenden, *John Berryman*, p. 331; quoted in Bowers, *Theodore Roethke*, p. 10.

22. Berryman, "From the Middle and Senior Generations," *Freedom of the Poet*, p. 310; Sisson, "My Whiskers Fly: An Interview with John Berryman," *Ivory Tower*, p. 35.

23. Roethke, "Sale," *Collected Poems*, p. 30; Lowell, "For Sale," *Life Studies*, p. 76.

24. Roethke, "Meditation in Hydrotherapy," *Collected Poems*, p. 248; Lowell, "Hydrotherapy," *Notebook*, p. 180.

25. Roethke, "Four for Sir John Davies," *Collected Poems*, p. 101; "An Interview with Stanley Kunitz," *Salmagundi*, 22–23 (1973), 79.

26. Seager, *The Glass House*, p. 106; James Breslin, *From Modern to Contemporary* (Chicago, 1984), pp. 121–122.

27. Heymann, *American Aristocracy*, p. 306. Hamilton, *Robert Lowell*, p. 334, incorrectly states that Lowell "first met him at Yaddo in 1947."

28. Quoted in Hamilton, *Robert Lowell*, p. 127; quoted in Seager, *The Glass House*, p. 56; Roethke, *Selected Letters*, p. 158.

29. Roethke, *Selected Letters*, p. 134; letter from J. F. Powers to Jeffrey Meyers, July 23, 1985.

30. The first letter is quoted in Hamilton, *Robert Lowell*, p. 334. The other letters are by courtesy of Professor Powers.

31. Quoted in Hamilton, *Robert Lowell*, p. 230; letter from Robert Lowell to J. F. Powers, November 13, 1957.

32. Quoted in Hamilton, *Robert Lowell*, p. 336; letter from Robert Lowell to Theodore Roethke, April 19, 1958, University of Washington. For A. E. Housman's comment on Meredith, see his *Letters*, ed. Henry Maas (Cambridge, Mass., 1971), p. 67.

33. Letter from Robert Lowell to Theodore Roethke, January 19, 1948, University of Washington; letter from Theodore Roethke to Robert Lowell, September 24, 1958, Harvard University.

34. Interview with Stanley Kunitz; Kunitz, "The Sense of a Life," *New York Times Book Review*, p. 3; Roethke, *Straw for the Fire*, p. 157.

35. Hamilton, *Robert Lowell*, p. 335; letters from Robert Lowell to Theodore Roethke, February 9, 1959 and January 7, 1960, University of Washington.

36. I heard Roethke read at Harvard and was struck by his trembling agitation as well as by his impressive performance.

37. Philip Booth, "Summers in Castine. Contact Prints: 1955–1965," *Salmagundi*, 37 (1977), 48; quoted in Hamilton, *Robert Lowell*, p. 336.

38. Roethke, "Some Remarks on Rhythm," *On the Poet and*

His Craft, p. 83; Lowell, "The Art of Poetry," *Writers at Work*, p. 362.

39. Roethke, *Selected Letters*, pp. 248, 258; quoted in Neal Bowers, "Theodore Roethke Speaks," *New Letters*, 49 (1982), 16.
40. Quoted in Seager, *The Glass House*, pp. 284–285.
41. Letter from Theodore Roethke to Robert Lowell [spring 1963], Harvard University.
42. Quoted in Hamilton, *Robert Lowell*, pp. 336–337.
43. Booth, "Summers in Castine," *Salmagundi*, p. 47; Hamilton, "Conversation with Robert Lowell," *The Review*, pp. 14–15.
44. Lowell, "For Theodore Roethke: 1908–1963," *Notebook*, pp. 202–203.

Chapter Six: Epilogue: Sylvia Plath

1. Joel Connoroe, *John Berryman: Introduction to the Poetry* (New York, 1977), p. 132.
2. Kostelanetz, "Conversation with Berryman," *Massachusetts Review*, pp. 344–345.
3. Ted Hughes, Notes to Sylvia Plath's *Collected Poems* (New York, 1981), p. 289 and Ted Hughes, "The Chronological Order of Sylvia Plath's Poems," *The Art of Sylvia Plath*, p. 192.
4. Sylvia Plath, *Journals*, ed. Ted Hughes and Frances McCullough (New York: Ballantine, 1983), pp. 322–323.
5. Roethke, "Some Remarks on Rhythm," *On the Poet and His Craft*, p. 83; Sylvia Plath, "Context," *London Magazine*, 1 (February 1962), 46.
6. Marjorie Perloff, "Sylvia Plath's 'Sivvy' Poems," *Sylvia Plath: New Views on the Poetry*, ed. Gary Lane (Baltimore, 1979), pp. 168–169; Margaret Uroff, *Sylvia Plath and Ted Hughes* (Urbana, Illinois, 1977), pp. 116, 120. Roethke's children's poems in *Words for the Wind* (1958) may also have influenced Plath's story in verse, *The Bed Book* (New York, 1976).

7. Plath, "Edge," *Collected Poems*, pp. 272–273.

8. Sexton, "The Barfly Ought to Sing," *The Art of Sylvia Plath*, p. 178; Robert Boyers, "W. D. Snodgrass: An Interview," *Salmagundi*, 22–23 (1973), 154.

9. Sylvia Plath, *Letters Home*, ed. Aurelia Plath (New York: Bantam, 1977), p. 476; Seager, *The Glass House*, p. 271.

10. Elizabeth Hardwick, "Sylvia Plath," *Seduction and Betrayal* (New York, 1975), pp. 112, 115; Plath, *Letters Home*, p. 396.

11. Plath, *Journals*, pp. 296–297, 299, 305; Sexton, "The Barfly Ought to Sing," *The Art of Sylvia Plath*, p. 177.

12. Plath, *Journals*, p. 222; "Sylvia Plath," *The Poet Speaks*, ed. Peter Orr (London, 1967), pp. 167–168; quoted in Edward Butscher, *Sylvia Plath: Method and Madness* (New York: Pocket, 1977), p. 400.

13. Quoted in Ekbert Faas, "Ted Hughes and *Gaudete*" (1977), in Ekbert Faas, *Ted Hughes: The Unaccommodated Universe* (Santa Barbara, 1980), p. 210, and Hughes, Notes to Plath's *Collected Poems*, p. 289.

14. Hamilton, *Robert Lowell*, p. 183; Katha Pollitt, "A Note of Triumph," *Ariel Ascending*, ed. Paul Alexander (New York, 1985), p. 98; Jerome Mazzaro, "Sylvia Plath and the Cycles of History," *Sylvia Plath: New Views on the Poetry*, p. 219.

15. Plath, "Kindness," *Collected Poems*, p. 270; Lowell, "The Severed Head," *For the Union Dead*, p. 53.

16. Quoted in M. L. Rosenthal, "Sylvia Plath and Confessional Poetry," *The Art of Sylvia Plath*, pp. 73–74; Robert Lowell, Foreword to *Ariel* (New York, 1966), pp. viii-ix.

17. Hamilton, "A Conversation with Robert Lowell," *The Review*, p. 27; Lowell, "For John Berryman," *New York Review of Books*, p. 3.

18. Lowell, "Sylvia Plath," *History*, p. 135; John Bayley, "The King as Commoner," *The Review*, 24 (December 1970), 3 (on Lowell's *Notebook*); John Carey, "Heroes and Villains," *New Review*, 1 (June 1974), 77; Robert Lowell,

"Not Me," *New Review*, 1 (July 1974), 64.

19. In California, in the summer of 1913, Otto began to study insect pests that kill young birds; and in the summer of 1919 he completed research under Professor W. W. Cort of the Zoology Department of the University of California, Berkeley, for his article "A Muscid [Fly] Larva of the San Francisco Bay Region which Sucks the Blood of Nestling Birds" (Berkeley: University of California Press, 1919), vol. 19, no. 5, pp. 191–200. The last part of the title foreshadows the themes of the *Ariel* poems.

20. Aurelia Plath, Introduction to Sylvia Plath's *Letters Home*, pp. 14–16, 20, 22.

21. Quoted in Butscher, *Sylvia Plath*, p. 135; Sylvia Plath, *The Bell Jar* (New York: Bantam, 1972), pp. 27, 32; Plath, *Journals*, pp. 129, 266–267, 278.

22. Plath, *Journals*, p. 298; Plath, *The Bell Jar*, pp. 135–137.

23. Plath, "Electra on Azalea Path," *Collected Poems*, pp. 116–117; quoted in Nancy Hunter Steiner, *A Closer Look at Ariel: A Memory of Sylvia Plath* (New York, 1973), pp. 62–63.

24. Aurelia Plath, Introduction to *Letters Home*, p. 27; Plath, *Letters Home*, p. 123; quoted in Butscher, *Sylvia Plath*, p. 120.

25. Plath, *Letters Home*, pp. 72–73, 345, 536.

26. *Ibid.*, p. 155; Steiner, *Closer Look at Ariel*, p. 59.

27. Plath, *Letters Home*, p. 60; Plath, *Journals*, p. 273.

28. Plath, *Letters Home*, pp. 67, 53, 103.

29. Plath, *Journals*, p. 63; Plath, *Letters Home*, p. 134.

30. Plath, *The Bell Jar*, pp. 117–118; Plath, *Letters Home*, p. 141.

31. Plath, *The Bell Jar*, p. 138; Butscher, *Sylvia Plath*, p. 130. Ruth Beuscher, born in France in 1923, earned her medical degree at Columbia in 1950, was assistant attending psychiatrist at McLean's from 1958 to 1979, and now practices in Washington, D. C.

32. Plath, *Journals*, p. 113; Plath, *Letters Home*, p. 263.

33. Ted Hughes, Note to Sylvia Plath's "Ten Poems,"

Encounter, 21 (October 1963), 45; Plath, "The Other Two," *Collected Poems*, p. 68; Plath, *Letters Home*, p. 288.

34. Plath, *Letters Home*, pp. 298, 307–308, 330.

35. Plath, *Journals*, pp. 156, 221, 326; Plath, *Letters Home*, p. 522.

36. Plath, *Letters Home*, pp. 537, 540; Hugh Kenner, Review of *Letters Home*, *National Review*, 28 (April 30, 1976), 460; Ted Hughes, "Lovesong," *Crow* (New York, 1971), pp. 76–77.

37. A. Alvarez, "Prologue: Sylvia Plath," *The Savage God* (New York, 1972), p. 18; quoted in Butscher, *Sylvia Plath*, p. 353.

38. Sylvia Plath, "Suffering Angel," *New Statesman*, 64 (December 7, 1962), 829; Plath, *Letters Home*, pp. 542, 551; Clarissa Roche, "Sylvia Plath: Vignettes from England," *Sylvia Plath: The Woman and the Work*, ed. Edward Butscher (New York, 1977), p. 85.

39. Plath, *Letters Home*, pp. 567, 549.

40. Ted Hughes, "Sylvia Plath and Her Journals," *Ariel Ascending*, p. 162; Ted Hughes, "Sylvia Plath," *Poetry Book Society Bulletin*, 44 (February 1965), 1.

41. Plath, *Letters Home*, p. 560; Plath, "Three Women," *Collected Poems*, p. 185.

42. Quoted in Elinor Klein, "A Friend Recalls Sylvia Plath," *Glamour*, November 1966, p. 168; Dorothea Krook, "Recollections of Sylvia Plath," *Sylvia Plath: The Woman and Her Work*, p. 49.

43. Plath, *The Bell Jar*, p. 118; Plath, *Collected Poems*, p. 293; Joyce Carol Oates, "The Death Throes of Romanticism: The Poetry of Sylvia Plath," *Sylvia Plath: The Woman and Her Work*, p. 209.

44. George Orwell, *Nineteen Eighty-Four* (New York, 1949), p. 271; Plath, *The Bell Jar*, p. 27; Plath, "Daddy," *Collected Poems*, pp. 222–224.

45. James Dickey, "The Art of Poetry," *Writers at Work: The "Paris Review" Interviews*, Fifth Series, ed. George Plimpton (New York, 1981), pp. 217–218; George Steiner, "Dying

is an Art," *The Art of Sylvia Plath*, p. 218.

46. Plath, *Journals*, p. 100; Friedrich Nietzsche, *Ecce Homo*, trans. Walter Kaufmann (New York, 1967), p. 303; Plath, "Lady Lazarus," *Collected Poems*, pp. 294, 245–247.

47. Plath, "Death & Co.," *Collected Poems*, pp. 294, 254–255; "Sylvia Plath," *The Poet Speaks*, p. 172.

48. The manic poets include Collins, Smart, Cowper, Chatterton, Clare, Beddoes, Hölderlin, Kleist, Nerval, Pound, Artaud, Roethke, Schwartz and Lowell; the suicidal modern writers are Trakl, Esenin, Mayakovsky, Lindsay, Hart Crane, Teasdale, Tsvetayeva, Woolf, Pavese, Weldon Kees, Hemingway and—after Plath—Jarrell, Berryman, Celan and Sexton.

49. Plath, *Letters Home*, p. 578; Alvarez, *The Savage God*, pp. 30–31.

50. Quoted in Butscher, *Sylvia Plath*, p. 316; Plath, *Letters Home*, p. 400; Plath, *Journals*, p. 247.

51. Alvarez, *The Savage God*, pp. 37–38; Ted Hughes, in *Times Literary Supplement*, November 19, 1971, p. 1448. Alvarez defended himself in a letter to *TLS*, November 26, 1971, p. 1478.

52. Ted Hughes, Foreword to *The Journals of Sylvia Plath* (New York: Ballantine, 1983), p. xv.

53. Hughes wrote the following works on Plath: Note to Sylvia Plath's "Ten Poems," *Encounter*, 21 (October 1963), 45; "Sylvia Plath," *Poetry Book Society Bulletin*, 44 (February 1965), 1–2, reprinted in Ekbert Faas, *Ted Hughes: The Unaccommodated Universe* (Santa Barbara, 1980), pp. 178–180; "The Chronological Order of Sylvia Plath's Poems," *Tri-Quarterly*, 7 (Fall 1966), 81–88, reprinted in *The Art of Sylvia Plath*, ed. Charles Newman (Bloomington, Indiana, 1970), pp. 187–195 and revised in Faas, pp. 180–182; Introduction to Sylvia Plath's *Fiesta Melons* (Exeter: Rougemont Press, 1971), n.p.; "Sylvia Plath's *Crossing the Water*: Some Reflections," *Critical Quarterly*, 13 (Summer 1971), 165–172; Letter on A. Alvarez's *The Savage God*, *Times Literary Supplement*,

November 19, 1971, p. 1448: "Sylvia Plath," *Observer*, November 21, 1971, p. 10 (another letter on *The Savage God*); "Winter Trees," *Poetry Book Society Bulletin*, 70 (Autumn 1971), reprinted as Note to Sylvia Plath's *Winter Trees* (London 1971), p. 7; Introduction to Sylvia Plath's *Pursuit* (London: Rainbow Press, 1973); "Ted Hughes and *Gaudete*" (1977) in Faas, p. 210; Introduction to Sylvia Plath's *Johnny Panic and the Bible of Dreams* (New York, 1979), pp. 1–9; Introduction and Notes to Sylvia Plath's *Collected Poems* (New York, 1981), pp. 13–17, 275–296; Foreword to *The Journals of Sylvia Plath* (New York, 1982), pp. xi-xiii; "Sylvia Plath and Her Journals," *Grand Street*, 1 (Spring 1982), 86-99, reprinted in *Ariel Ascending*, ed. Paul Alexander (New York, 1985), pp. 152-164.

54. Jarrell, "90 North," *Complete Poems*, p. 114.

Select Bibliography

Some of the basic scholarship on these poets has not yet been done. There is no bibliography, letters, collected poems or collected essays of Lowell; no letters of Berryman; no biography of Jarrell.

JOHN BERRYMAN

Berryman's Sonnets. New York, 1967.
Delusions, Etc. New York, 1972.
The Dream Songs. New York, 1969.
The Freedom of the Poet. New York, 1976.
Henry's Fate. New York, 1977.
Homage to Mistress Bradstreet and Other Poems. New York, 1959.
Love & Fame, 2nd edition, revised. New York, 1972.
Recovery. New York, 1973.
Short Poems. New York, 1967.
Arpin, Gary. *The Poetry of John Berryman.* Port Washington, New York, 1978.
Connoroe, Joel. *John Berryman: An Introduction to the Poetry.* New York, 1977.
Haffenden, John. *John Berryman: A Critical Commentary.* New York, 1980.
Haffenden, John. *The Life of John Berryman.* London, 1982.
Linebarger, J. M. *John Berryman.* Boston, 1974.

Meyers, Jeffrey. "Review of Eileen Simpson's *Poets in Their Youth*," *Boston Review*, 8 (February 1983), 37.
Simpson, Eileen. *The Maze*. New York, 1975.
Simpson, Eileen. *Poets in Their Youth*. New York, 1982.
Stefanik, Ernest, Jr. *John Berryman: A Descriptive Bibliography*. New York, 1982.

RANDALL JARRELL

The Complete Poems. New York, 1969.
Kipling, Auden & Co. New York, 1980.
Letters. Ed. Mary Jarrell. Boston, 1985.
Poetry and the Age. New York, 1953.
The Third Book of Criticism. New York, 1965.
Ferguson, Suzanne. *The Poetry of Randall Jarrell*. Baton Rouge, 1971.
Hagenbüchle, Helen. *The Black Goddess*. Berne, 1975.
Lowell, Robert, Peter Taylor and Robert Penn Warren, eds. *Randall Jarrell, 1914–1965*. New York, 1967.
Meyers, Jeffrey. "The Death of Randall Jarrell," *Virginia Quarterly Review*, 58 (Summer 1982), 450–467.
Meyers, Jeffrey. "Randall Jarrell: A Bibliography of Criticism, 1941–1981," *Bulletin of Bibliography*, 39 (December 1982), 227–234.
Meyers, Jeffrey. "Randall Jarrell and German Culture," *Salmagundi*, 61 (Fall 1983), 71–89.
Meyers, Jeffrey. "Randall Jarrell: The Paintings in the Poems," *Southern Review*, 20 (September 1984), 300–315.
Meyers, Jeffrey. "Review–essay of Delmore Schwartz's *Letters* and Randall Jarrell's *Letters*," *Virginia Quarterly Review*, 62 (Spring 1986), 348–355.
Meyers, Jeffrey. "Review of Stuart Wright's *Randall Jarrell: A Descriptive Bibliography*," *Bulletin of Bibliography* (1987).
Shapiro, Karl. *Randall Jarrell*. Washington, D. C., 1967.
Wright, Stuart. *Randall Jarrell: A Descriptive Bibliography, 1929–1983*. Charlottesville, Virginia, 1986.

ROBERT LOWELL

Day by Day. New York, 1977.

The Dolphin. New York, 1973.

For Lizzie and Harriet. New York, 1973.

For the Union Dead. New York, 1964.

History. New York, 1973.

Life Studies. New York, 1959.

Lord Weary's Castle. New York, 1946.

The Mills of the Kavanaughs. New York, 1951.

Near the Ocean. New York, 1967.

Notebook. Revised edition. New York, 1970.

Axelrod, Stephen. *Robert Lowell: Life and Art*. Princeton, 1978.

Bell, Vereen. *Robert Lowell: Nihilist as Hero*. Cambridge, Massachusetts, 1983.

Cooper, Philip. *The Autobiographical Myth of Robert Lowell*. Chapel Hill, North Carolina, 1970.

Hamilton, Ian. *Robert Lowell: A Biography*. New York, 1982.

Hecht, Anthony. *Robert Lowell*. Washington, D. C., 1983.

Heymann, David. *The American Aristocracy: The Life and Times of James Russell, Amy and Robert Lowell*. New York, 1980.

London, Michael and Robert Boyers, eds. *Robert Lowell: A Portrait of the Artist in His Time*. New York, 1970.

Meyers, Jeffrey. "Review–essay of Ian Hamilton's *Robert Lowell*," *Virginia Quarterly Review*, 59 (Summer 1983), 516–522.

Meyers, Jeffrey. "Lowell as Critic," *Journal of Modern Literature* (1987).

Meyers, Jeffrey. "Robert Lowell: The Paintings in the Poems," *Papers on Language and Literature* (1987) (forthcoming).

Ostroff, Anthony, ed. *The Contemporary Poet as Artist and Critic*. Boston, 1964.

Staples, Hugh. *Robert Lowell: The First Twenty Years*. New York, 1962.

Williamson, Alan. *Pity the Monsters: The Political Vision of Robert Lowell*. New Haven, 1974.

Yenser, Stephen. *Circle to Circle: The Poetry of Robert Lowell.* Berkeley, 1975.

SYLVIA PLATH

The Bell Jar. London, 1963.
Collected Poems. Ed. Ted Hughes. New York, 1981.
Journals. Ed. Ted Hughes and Frances McCullough. New York, 1982.
Letters Home. Ed. Aurelia Plath. New York, 1975.
Alexander, Paul, ed. *Ariel Ascending.* New York, 1985.
Alvarez, A. *The Savage God.* New York, 1972.
Butscher, Edward. *Sylvia Plath: Method and Madness.* New York, 1976.
Butscher, Edward, ed. *Sylvia Plath: The Woman and Her Work.* New York, 1977.
Lane, Gary and Maria Stevens. *Sylvia Plath: A Bibliography.* Metuchen, New Jersey, 1978.
Lane, Gary, ed. *Sylvia Plath: New Views on the Poetry.* Baltimore, 1979.
Newman, Charles, ed. *The Art of Sylvia Plath.* Bloomington, Indiana, 1970.
Steiner, Nancy Hunter. *A Closer Look at Ariel: A Memory of Sylvia Plath.* New York, 1973.

THEODORE ROETHKE

Collected Poems. Garden City, New York, 1966.
On the Poet and His Craft. Ed. Ralph Mills, Jr. Seattle, 1965.
Selected Letters. Ed. Ralph Mills, Jr. Seattle, 1968.
Straw for the Fire: Notebooks, 1943-63. Ed. David Wagoner. Garden City, New York, 1972.
Bowers, Neal. *Theodore Roethke: The Journey from I to Otherwise.* Columbia, Missouri, 1982.
La Belle, Jenijoy. *The Echoing Wood of Theodore Roethke.* Princeton, 1976.

Malkoff, Karl. *Theodore Roethke: An Introduction to the Poetry.* New York, 1966.

McLeod, James. *Theodore Roethke: A Bibliography.* Kent, Ohio, 1973.

Meyers, Jeffrey. "Review of Neal Bowers' *Theodore Roethke,*" *English Language Notes,* 21 (December 1983), 60–62.

Meyers, Jeffrey. "The Background of Theodore Roethke's 'Elegy for Jane,'" *Resources for American Literary Study* (1987).

Meyers, Jeffrey. "Poets and Tennis," *New York Times Book Review,* June 2, 1985, p. 5; and *London Magazine,* 25 (July 1985), 47–56.

Seager, Allan. *The Glass House: The Life of Theodore Roethke.* New York, 1968.

Stein, Arnold, ed. *Theodore Roethke: Essays on the Poetry.* Seattle, 1965.

Sullivan, Rosemary. *Theodore Roethke: The Garden Master.* Seattle, 1975.

Index